POWER BI

DATA MASTERY MADE EASY

4 BOOKS IN 1

BOOK 1
POWER BI ESSENTIALS: A BEGINNER'S GUIDE TO DATA VISUALIZATION MASTERY

BOOK 2
MASTERING POWER BI: ADVANCED TECHNIQUES AND BEST PRACTICES FOR ANALYSTS

BOOK 3
POWER BI DATA MODELING: BUILDING ROBUST DATASETS FOR EFFECTIVE ANALYSIS

BOOK 4
EXPERT POWER BI: ADVANCED ANALYTICS AND CUSTOM VISUALIZATIONS MASTERY

ROB BOTWRIGHT

Published by Rob Botwright
Library of Congress Cataloging-in-Publication Data
ISBN 978-1-83938-668-8
Cover design by Rizzo

Disclaimer

The contents of this book are based on extensive research and the best available historical sources. However, the author and publisher make no claims, promises, or guarantees about the accuracy, completeness, or adequacy of the information contained herein. The information in this book is provided on an "as is" basis, and the author and publisher disclaim any and all liability for any errors, omissions, or inaccuracies in the information or for any actions taken in reliance on such information. The opinions and views expressed in this book are those of the author and do not necessarily reflect the official policy or position of any organization or individual mentioned in this book. Any reference to specific people, places, or events is intended only to provide historical context and is not intended to defame or malign any group, individual, or entity. The information in this book is intended for educational and entertainment purposes only. It is not intended to be a substitute for professional advice or judgment. Readers are encouraged to conduct their own research and to seek professional advice where appropriate. Every effort has been made to obtain necessary permissions and acknowledgments for all images and other copyrighted material used in this book. Any errors or omissions in this regard are unintentional, and the author and publisher will correct them in future editions.

BOOK 1 - POWER BI ESSENTIALS: A BEGINNER'S GUIDE TO DATA VISUALIZATION MASTERY

Introduction 5
Chapter 1: Introduction to Power BI 8
Chapter 2: Getting Started with Data Sources 16
Chapter 3: Basic Data Transformation Techniques 24
Chapter 4: Creating Your First Visualizations 32
Chapter 5: Understanding Data Modeling in Power BI 41
Chapter 6: Building Dashboards and Reports 48
Chapter 7: Using Filters and Slicers Effectively 56
Chapter 8: Sharing and Collaborating with Power BI 62
Chapter 9: Tips for Designing Effective Visuals 71
Chapter 10: Troubleshooting and Best Practices 78

BOOK 2 - MASTERING POWER BI: ADVANCED TECHNIQUES AND BEST PRACTICES FOR ANALYSTS

Chapter 1: Advanced Data Transformation and Cleansing 87
Chapter 2: Advanced Data Modeling Strategies 96
Chapter 3: Leveraging DAX Functions for Complex Calculations 103
Chapter 4: Advanced Visualization Techniques 110
Chapter 5: Interactivity and Customization in Power BI 117
Chapter 6: Optimizing Performance and Data Refresh 123
Chapter 7: Power Query M Language for Advanced Users 132
Chapter 8: Managing Large and Complex Data Sets 147
Chapter 9: Advanced Data Security and Permissions 154
Chapter 10: Best Practices for Enterprise-Level Power BI Solutions 160

BOOK 3 - POWER BI DATA MODELING: BUILDING ROBUST DATASETS FOR EFFECTIVE ANALYSIS

Chapter 1: Foundations of Data Modeling in Power BI 168
Chapter 2: Importing and Transforming Data for Modeling 175
Chapter 3: Understanding Relationships in Power BI 183
Chapter 4: Advanced Techniques for DAX Modeling 191
Chapter 5: Hierarchies and Time Intelligence in Data Models 198
Chapter 6: Calculated Tables and Columns for Enhanced Insights 205
Chapter 7: Managing and Optimizing Data Models 211
Chapter 8: Aggregations and Summarization for Large Datasets 217
Chapter 9: Data Modeling for Complex Business Scenarios 223
Chapter 10: Data Model Documentation and Maintenance Strategies 230

BOOK 4 - EXPERT POWER BI: ADVANCED ANALYTICS AND CUSTOM VISUALIZATIONS MASTERY

Chapter 1: Advanced Analytics with Power BI 237
Chapter 2: Mastering Advanced DAX Formulas 243
Chapter 3: Advanced Data Mining and Forecasting 251
Chapter 4: Advanced Data Transformation Techniques 257
Chapter 5: Creating Custom Visualizations with Power BI 263
Chapter 6: Advanced Interactivity and Drill-Through Actions 269
Chapter 7: Geographic Mapping and Spatial Analysis 276
Chapter 8: Integrating R and Python for Advanced Analytics 283
Chapter 9: Machine Learning Integration in Power BI 286
Chapter 10: Real-world Case Studies in Advanced Power BI Applications 292
Conclusion 299

Introduction

Welcome to the "Power BI Data Mastery Made Easy" book bundle—a comprehensive collection of resources designed to empower individuals and organizations to harness the full potential of Power BI, Microsoft's leading business intelligence and data visualization tool. Whether you're a newcomer looking to embark on your data analytics journey or an experienced analyst seeking to elevate your skills, this bundle is your key to unlocking the true power of your data.

In a data-driven world, the ability to transform raw information into actionable insights is a game-changer. Power BI, with its user-friendly interface and powerful capabilities, has become the go-to solution for professionals in various industries. This book bundle is crafted to cater to a wide audience, from beginners who are just starting to explore the world of data visualization to experts seeking advanced techniques and custom visualization mastery.
Let's take a closer look at what each book in this bundle has to offer:

Book 1 - Power BI Essentials: A Beginner's Guide to Data Visualization Mastery This is where your journey begins. In "Power BI Essentials," we provide you with a solid foundation in data visualization and analysis. You'll learn how to import data from various sources, transform it into meaningful insights, and create stunning visualizations that tell a compelling data story. This book is the ideal starting point for those new to Power BI.

Book 2 - Mastering Power BI: Advanced Techniques and Best Practices for Analysts For those who have already dipped their toes into Power BI, "Mastering Power BI" takes you to the next level. Discover advanced techniques and best practices that will help you tackle complex analytical challenges. From mastering DAX formulas to optimizing data models, this book equips you with the skills needed to become an analytics expert.

Book 3 - Power BI Data Modeling: Building Robust Datasets for Effective Analysis Data modeling is at the core of Power BI's capabilities, and "Power BI Data Modeling" explores this critical aspect in detail. Learn how to design efficient and flexible data models, establish relationships between tables, and optimize your data for peak performance. Building robust datasets is the key to unlocking the full potential of Power BI.

Book 4 - Expert Power BI: Advanced Analytics and Custom Visualizations Mastery In the world of data analytics, custom visualizations and advanced analytics are the path to deeper insights. "Expert Power BI" delves into the realm of custom visuals, machine learning integration, and geographic analysis. Discover how to push the boundaries of data analysis and create custom solutions tailored to your unique needs.

Whether you're a business professional, data analyst, or IT specialist, the knowledge and skills gained from this book bundle will empower you to transform your data into a valuable asset. Power BI offers a dynamic and ever-evolving landscape, and these books will keep you on the cutting edge of data analytics.

Prepare to embark on a journey of discovery, learning, and mastery as we explore the vast world of Power BI together. Your ability to turn data into actionable insights is the key to informed decision-making and driving success in today's data-centric environment.

Let's begin this exciting adventure into the world of Power BI—a world where data mastery is within reach for everyone.

BOOK 1
POWER BI ESSENTIALS
A BEGINNER'S GUIDE TO DATA VISUALIZATION MASTERY

ROB BOTWRIGHT

Chapter 1: Introduction to Power BI

In exploring the Power BI ecosystem, it's crucial to understand that Power BI is a comprehensive suite of business analytics tools that enables you to analyze data, share insights, and make informed decisions. At its core, Power BI is designed to help you connect to various data sources, transform raw data into meaningful information, and create interactive visualizations that can convey insights effectively. This ecosystem encompasses multiple components and features, each serving a specific purpose in the data analytics and reporting process.

Power BI Desktop, the primary authoring tool, is where you create your reports, dashboards, and data models. It provides a user-friendly interface for building data visualizations using drag-and-drop functionality. Within Power BI Desktop, you can import data from various sources, clean and shape it using Power Query, and design custom visualizations with the help of the powerful DAX (Data Analysis Expressions) language.

As you delve deeper into the Power BI ecosystem, you'll encounter Power Query, a data transformation and preparation tool. Power Query enables you to connect to data from diverse sources, such as databases, spreadsheets, online services, and APIs. You can apply data transformations, merge and append tables, and remove inconsistencies to ensure that your data is clean and ready for analysis. To use Power Query effectively, you'll learn to write custom M language expressions, which allow for advanced data transformations beyond the built-in capabilities.

Power BI's data modeling capabilities are a pivotal aspect of the ecosystem. In this context, you'll explore the concept of creating relationships between tables, defining measures and calculated columns using DAX, and building data hierarchies. Data modeling is the foundation that enables you to perform advanced analytics, create complex calculations, and generate valuable insights from your datasets.

Once your data model is established, you can begin crafting interactive reports and dashboards using Power BI Desktop. The tool offers a wide range of visualizations, from basic bar charts to advanced custom visuals, allowing you to represent data in a way that suits your analysis goals. You'll also explore the formatting and customization options available to enhance the visual appeal and usability of your reports.

Power BI's cloud-based service, known as the Power BI Service, plays a crucial role in sharing and collaboration. With the Power BI Service, you can publish your reports and dashboards to the cloud, making them accessible to colleagues and stakeholders. Users can interact with your reports online, applying filters, exploring data, and gaining insights in real-time. Sharing options include secure embedding in websites and applications, ensuring broader access to your insights.

As you progress through your exploration of Power BI, you'll come across Power BI Mobile, a mobile application that enables you to access your reports and dashboards on the go. With Power BI Mobile, you can stay connected to your data and make informed decisions from anywhere, whether it's on your smartphone or tablet.

Power BI's integration capabilities are worth highlighting. You can seamlessly connect Power BI with other Microsoft products and services, such as Azure Data Services, SharePoint, and Teams. Additionally, you can integrate third-party services and applications through connectors and APIs. This integration expands the possibilities of data analysis and reporting by allowing you to pull in data from a variety of sources and create comprehensive solutions.

To ensure data security and compliance, the Power BI ecosystem offers robust features for managing access and permissions. You can implement role-based security to restrict data access based on user roles, and row-level security to filter data at the individual user level. Moreover, you can apply encryption and compliance features to meet regulatory requirements and protect sensitive information.

Performance optimization is a critical aspect of working with large datasets and complex reports. Power BI offers tools and techniques for optimizing data models and reports to ensure smooth and responsive user experiences. Techniques like data modeling best practices, indexing, and partitioning can significantly enhance performance.

Power BI's extensibility is another facet you'll explore. You can enhance your reports by incorporating custom visuals developed by the community or building your own using the Power BI Custom Visuals SDK. Additionally, Power BI offers APIs and PowerShell commands that allow you to automate tasks, manage resources, and perform administrative functions within the ecosystem.

In your journey through the Power BI ecosystem, you'll encounter a vibrant community of users, experts, and resources. Online forums, user groups, and documentation provide valuable support and insights. Engaging with this community can be instrumental in expanding your knowledge and tackling complex challenges.

Deploying the techniques and capabilities of the Power BI ecosystem effectively requires a combination of learning, practice, and exploration. Whether you're a beginner just starting to visualize data or an advanced user seeking to unlock the full potential of Power BI, continuous exploration and hands-on experience will be your greatest allies in mastering this powerful toolset.

In summary, the Power BI ecosystem is a dynamic and multifaceted platform that empowers users to transform data into actionable insights. By understanding its components, features, and integration options, you'll be well-equipped to harness the full potential of Power BI in your data analysis and reporting endeavors. Installation and setup are the initial steps in your journey to harness the power of Power BI for data analysis and reporting. To begin, you'll need to download the Power BI Desktop application, which is the primary authoring tool for creating reports, dashboards, and data models.

This application is available for free on the official Power BI website and can be installed on Windows-based computers.

Once the download is complete, run the installer and follow the on-screen instructions to install Power BI Desktop.

The installation process is straightforward and typically takes only a few minutes to complete.

After installation, launch Power BI Desktop to get started.

You'll be greeted by a welcoming interface that offers a variety of options for connecting to data and building visualizations.

Before you can create your first report or dashboard, you'll need to become familiar with the Power BI interface.

At the top of the window, you'll find the Ribbon, which contains tabs such as "Home," "Model," "View," and "Help."

These tabs house various commands and tools that you'll use throughout your Power BI journey.

The "Home" tab, for instance, provides access to data loading, transformation, and visualization features.

To the left of the interface, you'll find the "Fields" pane, which displays the tables and fields from your data source once you've connected it.

In the center of the interface is the canvas, where you'll design your reports and dashboards by adding visuals like charts, tables, and images.

As you navigate through Power BI Desktop, you'll notice that there are three primary views: "Data View," "Model View," and "Report View."

The "Data View" allows you to load data, transform it using Power Query, and create data relationships.

The "Model View" provides a visual representation of your data model, showing tables and their relationships.

The "Report View" is where you design your reports and create interactive visualizations.

Before diving into data visualization and analysis, you'll need to connect to your data source.

Power BI supports a wide range of data sources, including Excel spreadsheets, databases, web services, and cloud platforms like Azure and SharePoint.

To connect to your data source, go to the "Home" tab in Power BI Desktop and click on the "Get Data" button.

A dialog box will appear, offering various options for data sources. Choose the appropriate data source type and follow the prompts to establish the connection.

For some data sources, you may need to provide server addresses, credentials, and connection details.

Once connected, you can use Power Query, an integral part of Power BI, to transform and shape your data.

Power Query provides a user-friendly interface for performing tasks such as filtering, sorting, and merging data tables.

You can also create calculated columns and custom expressions to derive new insights from your data.

To access Power Query, go to the "Home" tab and click on the "Edit Queries" button.

This opens the Power Query Editor, where you can apply a wide range of data transformation operations.

In the Power Query Editor, you'll see a series of steps that represent the transformations you've applied to your data.

These steps can be modified, reordered, or removed to fine-tune your data preparation process.

Once you've transformed your data to your satisfaction, you can load it into the Power BI data model.

The data model is where you define relationships between tables, create calculated columns, and build measures using the DAX language.

To access the data model, click on the "Model" tab in Power BI Desktop.

Here, you'll see the tables and fields from your data source, and you can drag and drop them to create relationships.

Power BI automatically detects and suggests relationships based on column names, but you can also define them manually.

Building relationships between tables is crucial for accurate data analysis, as it enables you to combine data from different sources and create meaningful insights.

With your data model in place, you can now start designing your reports and visualizations in the "Report View."

This is where you'll create charts, tables, maps, and other visuals to convey your data's story.

To add a visualization, simply drag and drop a field from the "Fields" pane onto the canvas, and Power BI will generate an appropriate visual based on the data type.

You can then customize the visual's appearance, formatting, and interactions to meet your specific needs.

Power BI offers a wide range of visualization options, from basic bar charts and pie charts to advanced visuals like heatmaps and tree maps.

You can access these visuals by clicking on the "Visualizations" pane on the right-hand side of the screen.

In the "Visualizations" pane, you'll also find options for formatting, such as changing colors, fonts, and data labels.

To create more complex calculations and measures, you'll use the DAX language, which stands for Data Analysis Expressions.

DAX is a formula language specifically designed for Power BI and other Microsoft BI tools.

With DAX, you can create custom calculations, aggregations, and time-based functions to derive insights from your data.

To create a DAX measure, go to the "Model" tab and click on "New Measure."

A formula bar will appear, where you can enter your DAX expression.

DAX measures can perform calculations like summing, averaging, and counting, as well as more advanced operations.

For example, you can create a measure to calculate year-to-date (YTD) sales or compare current sales to the previous year.

As you design your reports and dashboards, you can add interactivity by using features like filters, slicers, and drill-through actions.

Filters allow users to narrow down the data they see in a visual, while slicers provide a more visual way to filter data across multiple visuals.

Drill-through actions enable users to explore details by clicking on specific data points in a visual.

To create filters and slicers, you can use the "Visualizations" pane and add these elements to your report canvas.

Customizing the behavior and appearance of filters and slicers is also possible through the "Format" and "Options" sections in the "Visualizations" pane.

Once you've designed your reports and dashboards to your satisfaction, you can save your work in Power BI Desktop.

It's advisable to save your report files with meaningful names and in a well-organized directory structure to facilitate future access and collaboration.

Power BI Desktop files have the ".pbix" extension, and they encapsulate all the data, transformations, and visualizations you've created.

Now that your report is ready, you can publish it to the Power BI Service, Microsoft's cloud-based platform for sharing and collaborating on Power BI content.

To publish your report, go to the "File" menu in Power BI Desktop and select "Publish" or "Publish to Power BI."

You'll be prompted to sign in to your Microsoft account or Power BI Service account if you haven't already.

Once signed in, choose the workspace where you want to publish the report.

Workspaces are containers for organizing and collaborating on Power BI content.

After publishing, your report will be available in the Power BI Service, accessible from any web browser.

You can share the report with colleagues and stakeholders by assigning them appropriate access permissions.

The Power BI Service offers various collaboration and sharing options, such as sharing a link, embedding the report in a website, or using Power BI apps for distribution.

To keep your data up-to-date and refreshed in the Power BI Service, you can configure automatic refresh schedules.

By setting up data source credentials and refresh intervals, you ensure that your reports always reflect the latest data.

To schedule data refresh, go to the "Datasets" section in the Power BI Service, select your dataset, and configure the refresh settings.

For advanced data source connections and automation, you can use Power BI Gateway, a tool that allows secure access to on-premises data sources from the cloud.

Power BI Gateway is especially useful when dealing with data stored within your organization's network.

To deploy Power BI Gateway, download and install it on a server within your network, and configure it to connect to your on-premises data sources.

Once configured, the gateway acts as a bridge between your on-premises data and the Power BI Service in the cloud.

This ensures that your cloud-based reports always have access to the most current data.

In addition to data refresh and gateway deployment, Power BI offers a range of administrative and security features for managing your organization's BI assets.

You can define user roles and permissions, set up row-level security, and enable Single Sign-On (SSO) integration with your organization's identity provider.

These features ensure that your data remains secure and accessible only to authorized users.

Moreover, you can monitor the performance and usage of your Power BI content through the Power BI Service's administrative and audit logs.

This allows you to gain insights into user engagement and optimize your reports and dashboards accordingly.

In summary, the installation and setup of Power BI are essential first steps in your journey toward effective data analysis and reporting.

Understanding the Power BI Desktop interface, connecting to data sources, transforming and modeling data, and creating interactive visuals are fundamental skills that will serve as the foundation for your Power BI expertise.

As you progress, you'll explore more advanced topics, such as DAX calculations, report interactivity, and cloud-based collaboration, enabling you to unlock the full potential of Power BI in your data-driven decision-making processes.

Chapter 2: Getting Started with Data Sources

Connecting to different data sources is a fundamental aspect of data analysis and reporting with Power BI, as it allows you to access and utilize a wide range of data to derive insights and make informed decisions.

Power BI offers versatile and powerful capabilities for data connectivity, enabling you to gather data from various sources, such as databases, files, online services, and even custom-built applications.

To connect to different data sources in Power BI, you can begin by launching the Power BI Desktop application, where you will build your reports and models.

Upon opening Power BI Desktop, you will find the "Get Data" option prominently displayed in the "Home" tab, which serves as the gateway to various data connectors.

Clicking on the "Get Data" option opens a dialog box that presents you with a list of available data sources and connectors.

These connectors are categorized by type, making it easier for you to find and select the most appropriate one for your data source.

For instance, you may want to connect to a relational database like Microsoft SQL Server or MySQL.

In this case, you would navigate to the "Database" category and select the relevant connector, which will initiate the connection process.

Power BI provides a variety of database connectors, each tailored to a specific database system, such as SQL Server Database, Oracle Database, or PostgreSQL.

Once you select the appropriate database connector, a configuration window will appear, prompting you to provide connection details.

These details typically include the server address, database name, and authentication credentials, which may vary depending on your specific database setup.

For instance, if you are connecting to a SQL Server database hosted on a local server, you may specify "localhost" as the server address and choose Windows or SQL Server authentication.

Alternatively, if your database is hosted in the cloud, you would provide the cloud-specific server address and credentials.

After entering the required information, you can test the connection to ensure that Power BI can successfully communicate with the database.

Once the connection test is successful, you can proceed to the next step, which is selecting the tables or views from the database that you wish to import into Power BI.

Power BI provides a visual interface that displays the available tables and views within the database, allowing you to choose the relevant ones.

You can select multiple tables and views if necessary, and Power BI will automatically generate a query to retrieve the data from these sources.

Furthermore, Power BI allows you to transform the imported data during the connection process, which is particularly useful when you need to clean, reshape, or aggregate the data before using it in your reports and visualizations.

To perform data transformation, you can click on the "Edit" button, which opens the Power Query Editor—an integral component of Power BI.

The Power Query Editor provides a user-friendly interface for data manipulation and transformation, enabling you to apply a wide range of operations to your data.

These operations include filtering rows, removing duplicates, merging tables, and creating custom columns using the M language.

The Power Query Editor also allows you to handle missing data, pivot and unpivot tables, and perform various mathematical and text transformations.

By leveraging the capabilities of Power Query, you can ensure that your data is clean, structured, and ready for analysis.

After completing the necessary data transformations, you can load the data into the Power BI data model.

The data model serves as the foundation for your reports and visualizations, enabling you to establish relationships between tables, define calculations, and build measures.

Power BI also offers connectors for connecting to various file-based data sources, such as Excel workbooks, CSV files, JSON files, and XML files.

To connect to these file-based sources, you can simply select the corresponding connector from the "Get Data" dialog and navigate to the location of the file on your computer or network.

Power BI provides options for importing data from a single file or combining data from multiple files located in a folder.

This feature is particularly valuable when dealing with data split across multiple files or when you have regular data updates in a designated folder.

In addition to relational databases and file-based sources, Power BI offers connectors for cloud-based data sources and online services.

For instance, you can connect to cloud storage services like Microsoft OneDrive, SharePoint Online, or Azure Data Lake Storage to access files and documents stored in the cloud.

Similarly, you can connect to online services like Salesforce, Google Analytics, or Facebook Ads to retrieve data directly from these platforms.

To connect to a cloud-based data source, you will typically need to provide authentication credentials and specify the data source's URL or API endpoint.

Power BI also supports web scraping by enabling you to connect to web pages and extract tabular data using the "Web" connector.

With this capability, you can gather data from publicly accessible websites or internal web applications by specifying the URL and defining the data extraction process.

Once you've established a connection to your desired data source and imported the data into Power BI, you can begin shaping the data model to suit your analytical needs.

This involves defining relationships between tables, creating calculated columns, and building measures using the Data Analysis Expressions (DAX) language.

By defining relationships, you enable Power BI to combine data from different tables seamlessly, allowing for comprehensive analysis and reporting.

Calculated columns and measures empower you to perform calculations, aggregations, and custom calculations on the data, generating valuable insights and metrics.

Connecting to different data sources is a critical skill in the realm of Power BI, as it grants you access to a wealth of information that can drive data-driven decision-making and reporting.

Whether you're connecting to databases, files, cloud services, or web pages, Power BI's versatile set of connectors and data transformation capabilities ensures that you can work with a wide array of data sources.

The ability to connect to and harness data from diverse sources is at the core of Power BI's data analysis and reporting capabilities, empowering you to derive meaningful insights and unlock the full potential of your data.

Importing and loading data is a pivotal step in the process of harnessing the full power of Power BI for data analysis and reporting.

Power BI offers a robust set of features and capabilities to help you seamlessly bring your data into the application, transforming it into a format that's conducive to meaningful insights.

To embark on this journey, launch the Power BI Desktop application, where you'll create and shape your data models and visualizations.

Once you're within Power BI Desktop, you'll find the "Get Data" button prominently displayed in the "Home" tab, serving as your gateway to various data connectors and import options.

Clicking on the "Get Data" button initiates the process of importing and loading data from a wide range of sources.

Your data sources can span diverse categories, including databases, files, online services, and custom data connectors.

To connect to a specific data source, you'll begin by selecting the appropriate data connector, tailored to the type of data source you're working with.

For instance, if your data resides in a relational database, you'll navigate to the "Database" category and choose the connector that corresponds to your database system, such as "SQL Server Database" or "MySQL Database."

Each connector is designed to accommodate the unique characteristics and requirements of its respective data source, ensuring a seamless connection.

Upon selecting the relevant connector, a configuration window will appear, prompting you to input essential details to establish the connection.

These details often include the server or database address, authentication credentials, and any additional settings specific to your data source setup.

For instance, if you're connecting to a SQL Server database hosted on a local server, you may input "localhost" as the server address and choose between Windows or SQL Server authentication, depending on your security and access preferences.

Conversely, if your database is hosted in the cloud, you'll provide the cloud-specific server address and credentials.

Once you've entered the requisite information, you can perform a connection test to verify that Power BI can successfully communicate with your data source.

This test ensures that the connection details are accurate and that there are no issues preventing the retrieval of data.

Successfully establishing a connection is an essential prerequisite for proceeding with data import and loading.

With the connection validated, you can advance to the next phase of the process, which involves selecting the specific tables or data entities from your data source that you wish to import into Power BI.

Power BI offers a user-friendly interface for this purpose, presenting a visual representation of the tables and data available within the data source.

This intuitive interface allows you to select one or multiple tables that you want to include in your Power BI project.

By choosing the relevant tables, you specify which data will be retrieved and incorporated into your analysis and reporting endeavors.

Moreover, Power BI facilitates the process of joining or merging multiple tables from the same or different data sources, enabling you to consolidate data from disparate places into a single cohesive dataset.

The ability to combine data from multiple tables can be invaluable when you're dealing with complex datasets and wish to create comprehensive reports and analyses.

Beyond selecting tables for import, Power BI grants you the power to define data transformations during the import process.

Data transformations are particularly significant when you need to refine, cleanse, or reshape your data to make it more conducive to analysis.

Power BI's data transformation capabilities are facilitated through Power Query, a versatile tool embedded within the application.

To embark on data transformation, you can click on the "Edit" button, which opens the Power Query Editor—a dedicated environment for shaping your data.

Within the Power Query Editor, you'll find an array of data transformation operations at your disposal.

These operations encompass filtering rows, removing duplicates, merging and appending tables, unpivoting and pivoting data, and creating custom columns using the M language.

The M language, a robust and expressive scripting language, allows for advanced data transformation operations that extend beyond the built-in capabilities of Power Query.

In addition to M language scripting, Power Query empowers you to handle missing data, split columns, aggregate data, and perform a myriad of mathematical and text transformations.

Your data transformation journey in Power Query is facilitated by a series of applied steps.

Each step represents a specific transformation operation you've performed on your data.

These steps can be easily viewed, modified, reordered, or removed within the Power Query Editor, affording you the flexibility to tailor your data preparation process to your precise requirements.

Upon completing your data transformations, you'll proceed to load the data into the Power BI data model.

The data model serves as the heart of your Power BI project, enabling you to establish relationships between tables, define calculated columns, and build measures using the Data Analysis Expressions (DAX) language.

Before data loading occurs, you have the option to choose between two modes: "Load" and "Transform Data."

Selecting "Load" instructs Power BI to load the data directly into the data model as-is, without performing any additional transformations.

Alternatively, choosing "Transform Data" directs Power BI to open the Power Query Editor once more, allowing you to make further adjustments to the data before it's loaded into the model.

The "Transform Data" option is particularly useful when you want to perform additional data cleaning or reshaping operations after the initial transformations.

After making your selection and confirming the data loading process, Power BI proceeds to load the data into the data model, making it available for analysis and visualization within the application.

The data model is where you can establish relationships between tables by defining primary and foreign keys, enabling you to link related data and perform more complex analyses.

Additionally, you can create calculated columns and measures using the DAX language to derive valuable insights from your data.

Calculated columns allow you to add new columns to your tables based on custom calculations, while measures enable you to perform calculations, aggregations, and advanced calculations that operate on your data model.

These calculated columns and measures serve as the building blocks for constructing reports and visualizations in Power BI.

In summary, the process of importing and loading data in Power BI is a foundational step that lays the groundwork for your data analysis and reporting endeavors.

By connecting to diverse data sources, configuring data connections, selecting tables, performing data transformations, and shaping the data model, you set the stage for generating meaningful insights and creating impactful visualizations.

The power of Power BI lies in its ability to seamlessly bring data from various sources into a unified platform, empowering you to explore, analyze, and communicate your findings effectively.

Chapter 3: Basic Data Transformation Techniques

Data cleaning and transformation are foundational processes in the realm of data analysis, serving as essential steps in the journey towards obtaining accurate and meaningful insights.

When working with real-world data, it's common to encounter imperfections, inconsistencies, and discrepancies that necessitate cleaning and refinement.

Data cleaning involves the identification and correction of errors, inaccuracies, and anomalies within a dataset, ensuring that the data is reliable and accurate for analysis.

One of the most common data cleaning tasks is handling missing values, which can arise from various reasons, such as data entry errors, sensor malfunctions, or simply the absence of data.

To address missing values, data analysts often employ techniques like imputation, where missing values are replaced with estimated or interpolated values based on surrounding data points.

Imputation can be performed using statistical methods or domain-specific knowledge, depending on the context of the data.

Another aspect of data cleaning involves dealing with outliers, which are data points that significantly deviate from the typical distribution of values within a dataset.

Outliers can skew statistical analyses and models, so identifying and either removing or transforming them is crucial.

Common methods for handling outliers include visual inspection, mathematical tests, and the use of robust statistical techniques.

In some cases, outliers may represent valid data points and should not be discarded without careful consideration of their significance.

Data consistency is another aspect of data cleaning, which entails ensuring that data values adhere to a consistent format, unit, or naming convention.

Inconsistent data can lead to confusion and errors in analysis, making it essential to standardize data where necessary.

For example, dates might need to be formatted uniformly, units of measurement converted, or categorical variables standardized for consistency.

Data transformation, on the other hand, involves altering the structure or content of the data to make it more suitable for analysis or modeling.

Data transformation can encompass various operations, including encoding categorical variables, aggregating data, or creating new features.

One common data transformation technique is one-hot encoding, which converts categorical variables into binary (0 or 1) values for use in machine learning models.

This technique ensures that machine learning algorithms can interpret categorical data correctly.

Data aggregation involves summarizing data at a higher level of granularity, often by grouping data points and applying aggregation functions like sum, average, or count.

Aggregation can simplify complex datasets and reveal patterns or trends that are not apparent in the raw data.

Feature engineering is a vital aspect of data transformation, involving the creation of new features or variables that capture relevant information from the existing data.

These new features can enhance the performance of machine learning models by providing additional insights or context.

For instance, in a retail dataset, feature engineering might involve creating variables such as "total sales per customer" or "average purchase amount."

Data cleaning and transformation can be performed using various tools and programming languages, depending on the complexity of the tasks and the preferences of the data analyst.

One widely used tool for data cleaning and transformation is Microsoft Excel, which offers a user-friendly interface for handling common data cleaning tasks, such as filtering, sorting, and removing duplicates.

Excel also provides basic functions for data transformation, making it accessible to users with varying levels of technical expertise.

For more advanced data cleaning and transformation tasks, programming languages like Python and R are popular choices among data analysts.

These languages offer extensive libraries and packages specifically designed for data manipulation, cleaning, and transformation.

In Python, libraries like Pandas provide versatile data structures and functions for tasks such as missing value imputation, outlier detection, and data aggregation.

The Pandas library enables data analysts to perform complex data cleaning and transformation operations efficiently.

In R, the dplyr package is widely used for data manipulation and transformation.

It offers a concise and expressive syntax for filtering, summarizing, and transforming data, making it a powerful tool for data cleaning tasks.

SQL (Structured Query Language) is another valuable tool for data cleaning and transformation, particularly when working with relational databases.

SQL allows data analysts to perform operations like filtering, grouping, and joining tables to clean and transform data directly within the database.

For example, to aggregate sales data by region, an SQL query might involve grouping the data by region and calculating the total sales for each group.

Data analysts often use a combination of tools and techniques to address specific data cleaning and transformation challenges.

Moreover, data cleaning and transformation are iterative processes that may require multiple iterations and adjustments to achieve the desired data quality and structure.

In addition to basic data cleaning and transformation, data analysts frequently encounter more advanced tasks when dealing with complex datasets.

Text data, for instance, may require preprocessing techniques such as tokenization, stemming, and sentiment analysis to extract meaningful insights.

Time series data often involves tasks like resampling, seasonality decomposition, and anomaly detection to uncover patterns and anomalies in temporal data.

Geospatial data may require geocoding, spatial joins, and spatial analysis to extract location-based insights.

Machine learning models may benefit from feature scaling, dimensionality reduction, and feature selection to improve predictive accuracy.

When performing data cleaning and transformation, data analysts must consider the implications of their decisions on the downstream analysis or modeling process.

Decisions made during data cleaning and transformation can have a significant impact on the validity and reliability of the results.

Therefore, it is essential to document and communicate data cleaning and transformation steps, ensuring transparency and reproducibility.

Furthermore, data cleaning and transformation should be conducted in accordance with data privacy and security regulations, especially when dealing with sensitive or personally identifiable information (PII).

This may involve anonymizing data, applying access controls, or encrypting sensitive data during the process.

In summary, data cleaning and transformation are fundamental processes in data analysis, serving as the bedrock upon which meaningful insights and accurate models are built.

These processes encompass tasks such as handling missing values, addressing outliers, standardizing data, and creating new features, all of which contribute to enhancing data quality and relevance.

Data analysts rely on various tools and programming languages to perform these tasks, ranging from user-friendly spreadsheet software to powerful data manipulation libraries in Python and R.

Data cleaning and transformation are iterative processes that require careful consideration of the specific challenges presented by the data at hand.

Through these processes, data analysts can uncover hidden insights, reveal patterns, and prepare data for further analysis or modeling, ultimately enabling data-driven decision-making and valuable discoveries.

Handling missing data is a critical aspect of data analysis and plays a pivotal role in ensuring the integrity and reliability of your findings.

In the real world, datasets are rarely perfect, and missing data can occur for various reasons, such as data entry errors, equipment failures, or simply the absence of information.

Failure to address missing data appropriately can lead to biased or inaccurate results and may compromise the validity of your analysis.

Therefore, understanding techniques for handling missing data is essential for any data analyst or scientist.

One common approach to handling missing data is to identify and quantify the extent of missingness within your dataset.

This step involves assessing how many data points are missing in each column or variable.

By understanding the scope of the problem, you can make informed decisions about how to address missing data effectively.

In Python, you can use the Pandas library to calculate the percentage of missing values in each column of a DataFrame:

pythonCopy code

```
import pandas as pd # Load your dataset into a DataFrame (replace 'data.csv' with your dataset's filename) df = pd.read_csv('data.csv') # Calculate the percentage of missing values in each column missing_percentage = df.isnull().mean() * 100
```

This code snippet calculates the percentage of missing values for each column and stores the results in the 'missing_percentage' variable.

Once you have assessed the extent of missing data, you can decide how to handle it based on the nature of the missingness and the goals of your analysis.

One straightforward approach is to remove rows or columns with missing data entirely.

This approach is known as listwise deletion or complete case analysis.

In Pandas, you can drop rows with missing values using the **dropna()** method:

pythonCopy code

```
# Remove rows with missing values df_cleaned = df.dropna()
```

However, this approach has limitations and may result in a significant loss of data, especially if many rows contain missing values.

Another option is to impute missing data by filling in the gaps with estimated or predicted values.

One common imputation technique is mean imputation, where missing values are replaced with the mean (average) value of the column.

In Pandas, you can perform mean imputation like this:

pythonCopy code

```
# Impute missing values with the mean of each column df_imputed = df.fillna(df.mean())
```

While mean imputation is a simple method, it may not be suitable for all types of data, especially when missing values are not missing completely at random (MCAR) or when imputing categorical variables.

For categorical data, you can use mode imputation, where missing values are replaced with the most frequent category in the column.

In Pandas, you can perform mode imputation like this:

pythonCopy code

```
# Impute missing values with the mode (most frequent value) of each column df_imputed = df.fillna(df.mode().iloc[0])
```

Alternatively, you can employ more advanced imputation techniques, such as regression imputation, k-nearest neighbors (KNN) imputation, or predictive modeling-based imputation.

Regression imputation involves using regression models to predict missing values based on the relationships between variables.

K-nearest neighbors imputation estimates missing values by averaging the values of the K-nearest data points with complete information.

Predictive modeling-based imputation entails training machine learning models to predict missing values based on other variables in the dataset.

Choosing the appropriate imputation method depends on the specific characteristics of your data and the assumptions you are willing to make.

When dealing with time series data, missing values may need to be handled differently.

In time series analysis, it's common to perform forward-fill or backward-fill imputation, where missing values are replaced with the nearest non-missing value that precedes or follows them in time.

In Pandas, you can use the **fillna()** method with the **method** parameter set to 'ffill' for forward-fill or 'bfill' for backward-fill:

pythonCopy code

```
# Forward-fill missing values in a time series df_filled_forward = df.fillna(method='ffill') # Backward-fill missing values in a time series df_filled_backward = df.fillna(method='bfill')
```

These techniques are especially useful when working with sequential data, such as financial time series or sensor readings.

Sometimes, missing data may contain valuable information or indicate a meaningful pattern.

In such cases, it may be inappropriate to impute the missing values, as doing so could distort the data's true nature.

Instead, you can create an indicator variable or flag to capture the presence of missing values.

This approach allows you to include the missingness information in your analysis, potentially uncovering insights related to why certain data points are missing.

In Python, you can create an indicator variable using Pandas like this:

pythonCopy code

```
# Create an indicator variable for missing values
df['column_with_missing_data_indicator'] = df['column_with_missing_data'].isnull().astype(int)
```

The 'column_with_missing_data_indicator' will have a value of 1 for rows with missing data and 0 for rows with complete data.

This approach ensures that the missingness information is preserved while still allowing you to use the rest of the data for analysis.

Additionally, missing data can be addressed through multiple imputation, a technique that generates multiple datasets with imputed values.

Multiple imputation involves creating several imputed datasets, each with different imputed values.

These datasets are then used to perform analyses, and the results are combined to provide more accurate estimates and account for the uncertainty introduced by imputation.

Tools like the 'mice' package in R and libraries such as 'sklearn' in Python offer implementations of multiple imputation techniques.

Handling missing data is a nuanced and context-dependent process that requires careful consideration of the data's characteristics and the goals of the analysis.

It's crucial to assess the extent of missingness, choose appropriate imputation methods, and document the decisions made during the data cleaning process.

Furthermore, transparency and communication are essential when reporting and interpreting results that involve missing data, ensuring that the potential impact of missingness on the findings is well-understood.

In summary, missing data is a common challenge in data analysis, but it can be managed effectively through techniques such as imputation, data removal, or the creation of indicator variables.

By understanding the nature of missingness and choosing the most suitable approach, data analysts can ensure that their analyses are robust and reliable, ultimately leading to more accurate and meaningful insights.

Chapter 4: Creating Your First Visualizations

Visualizing data with charts and graphs is a powerful way to communicate insights, patterns, and trends that may be hidden within raw data.

Charts and graphs transform complex datasets into accessible and comprehensible visuals, making it easier for decision-makers to understand and act upon the information presented.

The choice of the right type of chart or graph depends on the nature of the data and the message you want to convey.

One of the simplest and most common chart types is the bar chart, which uses rectangular bars to represent data values.

Bar charts are ideal for comparing discrete categories or groups of data, such as sales figures for different months or the performance of various products.

To create a bar chart in Excel, you can select your data, go to the "Insert" tab, and choose "Bar Chart" from the chart types.

Line charts, on the other hand, are suitable for displaying trends over time, making them a preferred choice for visualizing time-series data.

In Excel, you can create a line chart by selecting your data and choosing the "Line Chart" option from the "Insert" tab.

Pie charts are effective for illustrating the composition of a whole, showing how individual components contribute to the overall total.

However, it's essential to use pie charts sparingly, as they can become cluttered and challenging to interpret when there are too many categories.

To create a pie chart in Excel, select your data and choose the "Pie Chart" option from the "Insert" tab.

Scatter plots are useful for visualizing the relationships between two continuous variables, highlighting correlations, clusters, or outliers.

In Excel, you can create a scatter plot by selecting your data and choosing the "Scatter Plot" option from the "Insert" tab.

Histograms provide insights into the distribution of a single continuous variable, allowing you to see patterns such as normal distributions, skewness, or bimodality.

To create a histogram in Excel, you need to use the "Data Analysis" tool or create a frequency distribution table manually.

Box plots, also known as box-and-whisker plots, display the distribution of a dataset's values, including the median, quartiles, and potential outliers.

Box plots are valuable for identifying variations and comparing multiple datasets simultaneously.

In Excel, you can create box plots using specialized charting software or by manually calculating the necessary statistics.

Heatmaps are excellent for visualizing large datasets, particularly in the context of multidimensional data or correlation matrices.

Heatmaps use color intensity to represent the values of a matrix, making patterns and relationships more apparent.

Excel and various data visualization libraries in programming languages like Python (e.g., Seaborn) offer heatmap creation capabilities.

Treemaps are hierarchical visualizations that represent data as nested rectangles, where each branch represents a category and its subcategories.

Treemaps are effective for displaying hierarchical data structures, such as file directories or organizational structures.

Excel and specialized visualization software offer options for creating treemaps.

Radar charts, also known as spider charts or star plots, display multivariate data on a radial grid.

They are suitable for comparing the performance of multiple entities across various dimensions or attributes.

Excel and data visualization libraries in Python (e.g., Matplotlib) can be used to create radar charts.

Gantt charts are essential for project management, illustrating tasks or activities over time.

Gantt charts provide a visual timeline of project components, dependencies, and durations.

Specialized project management software like Microsoft Project or Gantt chart templates in Excel are commonly used for Gantt chart creation.

Bubble charts extend the capabilities of scatter plots by adding a third variable, represented by the size of the bubbles.

Bubble charts allow for the visualization of three dimensions of data in a two-dimensional space.

They are particularly useful for highlighting relationships between variables.

Creating bubble charts in Excel involves customizing a scatter plot with additional data series.

Choropleth maps use color variations to represent data values in geographical regions, making them ideal for visualizing regional or spatial patterns.

Mapping software, Geographic Information Systems (GIS) tools, and libraries like D3.js enable the creation of choropleth maps.

Word clouds provide a visually engaging way to highlight word frequency in text data.

The size of each word in the cloud corresponds to its frequency in the text.

Various online word cloud generators and Python libraries like WordCloud can be used to create word clouds.

Sankey diagrams display the flow of resources or quantities from one set of categories to another.

Sankey diagrams are commonly used in engineering, economics, and sustainability analysis.

Specialized visualization software or libraries like Plotly can be employed to create Sankey diagrams.

Interactive visualizations enable users to interact with data, explore details, and gain deeper insights by hovering, clicking, or filtering.

Tools like Tableau, Power BI, and Plotly offer interactive visualization capabilities, allowing users to engage with data dynamically.

Custom visualizations offer flexibility to create unique charts and graphics tailored to specific requirements.

Programmatic libraries like D3.js in JavaScript or custom code in Python enable the development of custom visualizations.

To create a custom visualization, you need a solid understanding of programming and data visualization principles.

Color choices in data visualization are crucial, as they can significantly impact the clarity and interpretation of the visualizations.

Effective use of color can enhance the distinction between data categories, emphasize key points, and improve overall readability.

However, it's essential to consider colorblind-friendliness, as certain color combinations may be challenging for individuals with color vision deficiencies.

In data visualization, the principle of simplicity is vital.

Avoid cluttering charts with excessive data points, labels, or decorations, as this can hinder comprehension.

Simplicity in design and presentation promotes clear communication of the intended message.

Labels and annotations play a vital role in data visualization, providing context and explanations for the audience.

Properly labeled axes, data points, and legends make it easier for viewers to understand the visualized data.

Annotations can also be used to highlight specific insights or interesting observations within a chart or graph.

The choice of chart or graph type should align with the objectives of your analysis and the characteristics of your data.

Consider whether your data is categorical or continuous, one-dimensional or multidimensional, and whether you aim to show trends, comparisons, distributions, or relationships.

Engage in exploratory data visualization to uncover patterns and trends in your data before proceeding with more formal analysis.

Exploratory visualization involves creating various charts and graphs to gain a deeper understanding of the data's structure and characteristics.

Iterative design is a valuable approach to data visualization, where you refine and revise your visualizations based on feedback, testing, and insights gained from initial versions.

Iterative design ensures that your visualizations effectively convey the intended message and insights.

Data visualization tools and software offer a range of customization options for designing charts and graphs to suit your needs.

These options include adjusting colors, fonts, labels, and layout, as well as adding titles, legends, and annotations.

By customizing your visualizations, you can make them more visually appealing and tailored to your audience.

In summary, data visualization is a potent tool for transforming data into meaningful insights.

Choosing the right chart or graph type, applying effective color choices, maintaining simplicity in design, and using labels and annotations wisely are essential principles in creating informative and impactful visualizations.

By following best practices and considering the characteristics of your data and your audience's needs, you can harness the power of data visualization to communicate and explore data effectively.

Formatting and customizing visualizations is a crucial step in creating effective and aesthetically pleasing data presentations.

Visualizations need to convey information clearly, and proper formatting enhances their readability and impact.

Customization allows you to tailor visual elements to align with your intended message and audience.

One fundamental aspect of formatting is the choice of colors in your visualizations, as colors play a significant role in conveying meaning and highlighting key data points.

When selecting colors, consider color theory principles, such as complementary colors or color schemes, to create visually harmonious and meaningful visuals.

In many data visualization tools, including Excel and Python libraries like Matplotlib, you can specify custom colors for data points, lines, bars, or areas within your charts.

For example, in Matplotlib, you can set custom colors using hexadecimal color codes:

pythonCopy code

import matplotlib.pyplot as plt # Create a bar chart with custom colors plt.bar(['A', 'B', 'C'], [10, 20, 15], color=['#FF5733', '#33FF57', '#5733FF']) plt.show()

Typography and text formatting are essential for labeling and annotating visualizations effectively.

Choose fonts that are legible and appropriate for your audience, and adjust text size, weight, and style to emphasize titles, labels, and annotations.

In data visualization tools like Tableau, you can customize fonts, text color, and alignment for various elements within your visualization.

Titles and labels should be clear and concise, providing context and aiding interpretation.

Consider using a title that summarizes the main message of your visualization, while axis labels should be descriptive and include units of measurement when applicable.

Annotations can provide additional insights or highlight specific data points within your visualization.

Customizing annotations involves placing text or shapes at strategic positions on your chart or graph.

In Python libraries like Matplotlib, you can add annotations using functions like **annotate()**:

pythonCopy code

import matplotlib.pyplot as plt # Create a scatter plot with annotations plt.scatter([1, 2, 3], [4, 5, 6]) plt.annotate('Point A', xy=(1, 4), xytext=(1.2, 4.5), arrowprops=dict(facecolor='black', shrink=0.05)) plt.show()

Gridlines and tick marks assist in interpreting the scale and values within your visualization.

Customize gridlines by specifying their appearance, such as color, style, and thickness.

In Excel, you can adjust gridlines by right-clicking on the chart and selecting "Format Gridlines."

Tick marks on axes should be appropriately spaced and labeled to aid in reading data values accurately.

In data visualization tools like Tableau, you can control the position and labeling of tick marks on axes.

The use of white space or padding around your visualizations can significantly impact their overall appearance.

Adequate white space can enhance readability and focus viewers' attention on the data.

When customizing visualizations in tools like Tableau or Matplotlib, consider adjusting the margins, spacing, and padding to achieve the desired balance of white space.

Legends are essential for interpreting visualizations that involve multiple data series or categories.

Customize legends by choosing their location, orientation, font size, and background color to ensure they are easily readable and do not clutter the visualization.

In Python libraries like Matplotlib, you can customize legends using the **legend()** function:

pythonCopy code

```
import matplotlib.pyplot as plt # Create a line chart with a customized legend plt.plot([1, 2, 3], label='Series A') plt.plot([4, 5, 6], label='Series B') plt.legend(loc='upper left', fontsize='medium') plt.show()
```

When working with bar charts, you can customize bar widths, gaps, and orientation to achieve the desired visual effect.

In Excel, for instance, you can right-click on the bars and choose "Format Data Series" to adjust the gap width and overlap.

Data markers, such as dots or shapes, can be customized to improve their visibility and differentiation.

Customize data markers in scatter plots, line charts, or bubble charts by specifying their size, color, and shape.

In Python libraries like Matplotlib, you can adjust data marker properties using the **marker** parameter:

pythonCopy code

```
import matplotlib.pyplot as plt # Create a scatter plot with customized data markers plt.scatter([1, 2, 3], [4, 5, 6], s=100, c='red', marker='o') plt.show()
```

38

Background colors and borders can be customized for chart areas, plot areas, or specific elements within your visualization.

In Excel, for instance, you can format chart elements by right-clicking on them and selecting "Format."

Customizing borders and backgrounds can help draw attention to specific areas or highlight key insights.

Gradients and shading can be applied to various chart elements to create depth and visual interest.

Customize gradients by specifying colors, direction, and intensity to create a three-dimensional effect.

In tools like Tableau, you can apply gradients to various elements, including background colors and shapes.

Transparency or opacity settings can be adjusted to make certain elements more or less prominent within your visualization.

Customize transparency to create layered effects or emphasize specific data points.

In Python libraries like Matplotlib, you can set transparency using the **alpha** parameter:

pythonCopy code

```
import matplotlib.pyplot as plt # Create a scatter plot with customized transparency plt.scatter([1, 2, 3], [4, 5, 6], alpha=0.5) plt.show()
```

Custom backgrounds or images can be added to your visualizations to enhance their visual appeal or convey a specific theme or message.

In tools like Tableau, you can import custom images or background templates to create unique visualizations.

Interactive elements, such as tooltips, hover effects, or clickable actions, can enhance user engagement and interactivity within your visualizations. Customize interactive elements in data visualization tools like Tableau or JavaScript libraries like D3.js to provide dynamic insights and exploration capabilities.

When exporting or sharing your visualizations, consider customization options that allow you to save them in various formats, such as images (PNG, JPEG), PDFs, or interactive web-based formats (HTML, SVG).

Customize the resolution, size, and aspect ratio to ensure your visualizations are suitable for different viewing platforms and purposes.

Testing and feedback are essential during the formatting and customization process.

Review your visualizations on different devices and screen sizes to ensure they remain legible and visually appealing.

Seek feedback from colleagues or stakeholders to gather insights and make improvements.

Customization in data visualization is a creative process that requires a balance between aesthetics and effective communication.

By customizing colors, typography, annotations, and visual elements, you can create compelling and informative visualizations that convey your data's story effectively.

Remember to consider your audience and the context in which your visualizations will be used to make informed customization decisions.

In summary, formatting and customization are integral parts of the data visualization process, allowing you to create visually engaging and informative representations of your data.

Chapter 5: Understanding Data Modeling in Power BI

Data modeling is a fundamental concept in the field of data management and analysis, serving as a framework for organizing and representing data in a structured manner.

It plays a crucial role in various domains, including database design, business intelligence, machine learning, and more.

At its core, data modeling involves creating a conceptual representation of data and its relationships, which enables better understanding, analysis, and decision-making.

A well-designed data model serves as a blueprint for structuring and storing data efficiently, ensuring data accuracy and supporting various analytical processes.

Data modeling encompasses several key concepts, each of which plays a specific role in the modeling process.

One fundamental concept is entities, which represent objects or concepts in the real world that are of interest to the organization or analysis.

Entities can range from tangible objects like products or customers to abstract concepts like orders or transactions.

In data modeling, entities are typically represented as tables or classes, with each instance of the entity corresponding to a row or object in the table or class.

Attributes are another essential concept in data modeling, as they describe the properties or characteristics of entities.

Attributes provide detailed information about the data within an entity and can be thought of as columns in a table or properties of a class.

For example, in a customer entity, attributes may include name, address, phone number, and email.

Relationships between entities are a critical aspect of data modeling, as they define how different entities are connected or related to each other.

Relationships help establish the structure and constraints of the data model, facilitating data retrieval and analysis.

Common types of relationships include one-to-one, one-to-many, and many-to-many, each describing the cardinality of the connection between entities.

Cardinality represents the number of instances of one entity that can be related to the number of instances of another entity.

For instance, a one-to-many relationship between customers and orders means that each customer can have multiple orders, while each order is associated with a single customer.

Normalization is a key concept in database design, aiming to reduce data redundancy and improve data integrity.

It involves organizing data into separate tables to eliminate duplicate information and ensure that each piece of data is stored in only one place.

Normalization is achieved through a series of rules, known as normal forms, which guide the decomposition of complex tables into simpler, related tables.

The goal of normalization is to reduce data anomalies, such as update anomalies (inconsistent data) and insertion anomalies (difficulty in adding new data).

In data modeling, a schema is a logical blueprint that defines the structure, organization, and relationships of data within a database or dataset.

Schemas help ensure consistency and clarity in data representation, making it easier for users and applications to understand and interact with the data.

There are different types of schemas, including conceptual, logical, and physical schemas, each serving a distinct purpose in the data modeling process.

The conceptual schema represents the high-level view of the data model, focusing on entities, their attributes, and their relationships without considering implementation details.

The logical schema provides a more detailed representation of the data model, specifying data types, keys, and constraints, often using a data modeling language like Entity-Relationship Diagrams (ERD) or Unified Modeling Language (UML).

The physical schema describes how the data model is implemented in a specific database management system (DBMS) or storage technology.

It includes details such as table structures, indexes, and storage mechanisms.

Normalization, as mentioned earlier, is a critical aspect of the logical schema design.

Data modeling also involves making decisions about data types, which determine the kind of data that can be stored in an attribute.

Common data types include integers, strings, dates, and floating-point numbers, each suitable for different types of data.

Choosing the appropriate data type ensures data accuracy and storage efficiency.

In the context of database systems, data modeling helps in defining the structure of the database, including the creation of tables, specifying primary keys, and establishing relationships between tables.

For example, in a relational database, the data model defines the tables for customers, orders, and products, as well as the relationships between them.

Database management systems like MySQL, Oracle, or PostgreSQL use SQL (Structured Query Language) to create and manipulate tables based on the data model.

In business intelligence and data warehousing, data modeling is essential for designing multidimensional data models known as star schemas or snowflake schemas.

These models organize data into fact tables (containing measures or metrics) and dimension tables (containing descriptive attributes), enabling efficient querying and reporting.

Tools like Microsoft SQL Server Analysis Services (SSAS) or IBM Cognos are used to create and deploy these data models.

Data modeling also plays a critical role in machine learning and predictive analytics.

In this context, data scientists and analysts use data modeling techniques to prepare and structure data for training machine learning models.

Feature engineering, which involves selecting and transforming relevant attributes, is a common data modeling task in machine learning.

Tools like Python's Pandas library or scikit-learn provide functions and libraries to perform these tasks.

When developing data models for machine learning, it's essential to consider the impact of the model on real-world decision-making and ensure that the data model aligns with the goals of the analysis.

In summary, data modeling is a fundamental concept in data management, analysis, and decision-making.

It involves defining entities, attributes, relationships, and schemas to structure and represent data effectively.

Data modeling plays a crucial role in database design, business intelligence, machine learning, and other data-related disciplines.

Understanding data modeling concepts and applying them appropriately can lead to more accurate and meaningful insights from data. Building relationships between tables is a fundamental aspect of database design and data modeling.

In relational databases, data is typically stored in multiple tables, and establishing relationships between these tables is crucial for maintaining data integrity and enabling efficient queries.

These relationships define how data in one table relates to data in another, allowing for complex and meaningful data retrieval.

One common type of relationship in relational databases is the foreign key relationship.

A foreign key is a column or a set of columns in one table that refers to the primary key of another table, creating a link between the two tables.

This relationship is often used to represent associations or dependencies between data entities.

For example, consider a database for an e-commerce website.

You might have a "Customers" table with a primary key "CustomerID" and an "Orders" table with a primary key "OrderID."

To establish a relationship between them, the "Orders" table can include a foreign key column "CustomerID" that references the "CustomerID" column in the "Customers" table.

This foreign key relationship allows you to associate each order with a specific customer.

In database management systems like MySQL, PostgreSQL, or Microsoft SQL Server, you can create foreign key relationships using SQL commands when defining table structures.

Here's an example SQL command to create a foreign key relationship between the "Orders" and "Customers" tables:

sqlCopy code

```
CREATE TABLE Customers ( CustomerID INT PRIMARY KEY,
FirstName VARCHAR(50), LastName VARCHAR(50) ); CREATE
TABLE Orders ( OrderID INT PRIMARY KEY, CustomerID INT,
OrderDate DATE, FOREIGN KEY (CustomerID) REFERENCES
Customers(CustomerID) );
```

In this SQL code, the "CustomerID" column in the "Orders" table is declared as a foreign key that references the "CustomerID" column in the "Customers" table.

This establishes the relationship between the two tables.

Another type of relationship is the one-to-many relationship, where one record in the primary table can be associated with multiple records in the related table.

In our e-commerce example, each customer can have multiple orders, creating a one-to-many relationship between the "Customers" and "Orders" tables.

In a one-to-many relationship, the foreign key is typically located in the table on the "many" side of the relationship.

A one-to-one relationship exists when one record in the primary table is associated with only one record in the related table.

For example, in a healthcare database, each patient may have only one medical history record, creating a one-to-one relationship between the "Patients" and "MedicalHistory" tables.

In a one-to-one relationship, the foreign key is often located in either of the two tables.

A many-to-many relationship occurs when multiple records in one table can be associated with multiple records in another table.

For example, in a music library database, each song can be associated with multiple genres, and each genre can be associated with multiple songs, creating a many-to-many relationship between the "Songs" and "Genres" tables.

To represent many-to-many relationships, an intermediate table, often called a junction table or a linking table, is used.

This table contains foreign keys to both tables involved in the relationship.

In our music library example, the "SongGenres" table could serve as the junction table, with foreign keys referencing both the "Songs" and "Genres" tables.

Establishing many-to-many relationships typically involves the use of three tables: two primary tables and one junction table.

The junction table's foreign keys reference the primary keys of both primary tables, facilitating the association between them.

Data modeling tools like ERwin, Toad Data Modeler, or even database management systems themselves often provide visual interfaces for designing and managing relationships between tables.

These tools allow you to define relationships, specify cardinality (such as one-to-one, one-to-many, or many-to-many), and enforce referential integrity constraints.

Referential integrity constraints ensure that data in the related tables remains consistent and accurate.

One important constraint is the cascading delete, which specifies what happens when a record in the primary table is deleted.

For example, if a customer record is deleted, you may want to cascade the deletion to all related orders to maintain data consistency.

In SQL, you can define cascading delete using the **ON DELETE CASCADE** option when creating a foreign key constraint.

Here's an example:

sqlCopy code

```
CREATE TABLE Customers ( CustomerID INT PRIMARY KEY,
FirstName VARCHAR(50), LastName VARCHAR(50) ); CREATE
TABLE Orders ( OrderID INT PRIMARY KEY, CustomerID INT,
OrderDate DATE, FOREIGN KEY (CustomerID) REFERENCES
Customers(CustomerID) ON DELETE CASCADE );
```

In this SQL code, the **ON DELETE CASCADE** option ensures that when a customer record is deleted, all related order records will also be deleted automatically.

This helps maintain data integrity and prevents orphaned records.

Another important constraint is the cascading update, which specifies what happens when a value in the primary key of the primary table is updated.

For instance, if a customer's ID is changed, you may want to update the corresponding customer ID in all related orders.

You can define cascading updates using the **ON UPDATE CASCADE** option when creating a foreign key constraint.

Here's an example:

sqlCopy code

```
CREATE TABLE Customers ( CustomerID INT PRIMARY KEY,
FirstName VARCHAR(50), LastName VARCHAR(50) ); CREATE
TABLE Orders ( OrderID INT PRIMARY KEY, CustomerID INT,
OrderDate DATE, FOREIGN KEY (CustomerID) REFERENCES
Customers(CustomerID) ON UPDATE CASCADE );
```

In this SQL code, the **ON UPDATE CASCADE** option ensures that when a customer's ID is updated, the corresponding customer ID in all related order records will also be updated automatically.

This helps maintain consistency in the data.

In summary, building relationships between tables is a crucial aspect of database design and data modeling.

It enables the representation of complex data structures and associations, allowing for efficient data retrieval and maintaining data integrity.

Understanding different types of relationships, using foreign keys, and enforcing referential integrity constraints are essential skills in the world of database management and design.

Chapter 6: Building Dashboards and Reports

Creating interactive dashboards is an essential aspect of data visualization, enabling users to explore data, gain insights, and make informed decisions.

Interactive dashboards go beyond static charts and graphs by allowing users to interact with the data, apply filters, and customize their view.

These dashboards are widely used in business intelligence, reporting, and analytics to provide a dynamic and engaging user experience.

To create interactive dashboards, you can leverage various tools and technologies, such as Tableau, Power BI, or custom web development.

Next, we'll explore the principles and techniques behind creating interactive dashboards.

One fundamental concept in interactive dashboards is interactivity, which refers to the ability of users to interact with the data and the dashboard elements.

Interactivity allows users to explore specific data points, drill down into details, or change the visualization parameters to suit their needs.

A common example of interactivity is the use of filters, which enable users to select specific criteria or time periods to focus on in the dashboard.

For example, in a sales dashboard, users can apply filters to view sales data for a particular region or product category.

Interactivity enhances user engagement and helps uncover valuable insights.

Filters are essential components of interactive dashboards, allowing users to control the data displayed in the visualization.

Filters can be based on various criteria, such as date ranges, categories, or numerical values.

In tools like Tableau or Power BI, you can create filters by adding filter controls to your dashboard and specifying the filtering criteria.

For instance, in Tableau, you can create a filter by selecting a field (e.g., "Region") and dragging it to the "Filters" shelf.

Users can then interact with the filter to select specific regions and dynamically update the dashboard's content.

Another interactive element in dashboards is the use of actions, which are triggered by user interactions and can affect other dashboard components.

Actions allow you to create dynamic relationships between visualizations and enhance the user's ability to explore data.

For example, you can set up a dashboard action that, when a user clicks on a particular data point in a chart, highlights related data points in other charts or updates additional information.

In Tableau, you can create actions through the "Dashboard" menu and specify the source and target sheets, as well as the triggering event (e.g., selection, hover).

Dashboard actions make it easier for users to discover correlations and patterns within the data.

To provide a seamless and responsive user experience, it's important to optimize the performance of interactive dashboards.

Performance optimization involves designing dashboards that load quickly and respond to user interactions without delays.

One way to achieve this is through data aggregation, where you precompute and summarize data before visualizing it.

Aggregated data reduces the amount of information that needs to be processed in real-time, resulting in faster dashboard performance.

In tools like Tableau, you can create calculated fields or summary tables to store aggregated data, which can then be used in your visualizations.

Another performance optimization technique is data source optimization, which involves structuring your data source for efficiency.

This includes using appropriate data types, indexing columns, and optimizing database queries.

In addition, consider using caching mechanisms to store frequently accessed data, reducing the need for repeated data retrieval.

In Tableau, you can configure data source settings to optimize query performance and refresh schedules.

Responsive design is another aspect of interactive dashboard creation, ensuring that dashboards adapt to different screen sizes and devices.

Responsive design techniques include using flexible layouts, responsive grid systems, and dynamic sizing for dashboard components.

This ensures that users can access and interact with the dashboard on desktops, tablets, or mobile devices without loss of functionality or readability.

In dashboard design, usability and user experience are paramount.

Consider the needs and preferences of your target audience when designing the layout, color schemes, and visualizations within the dashboard.

Effective use of visual cues, such as color, tooltips, and legends, can guide users and enhance their understanding of the data.

Testing with actual users and collecting feedback is essential to refine and improve the dashboard's usability and user experience.

In addition to filters, actions, and performance optimization, you can enhance the interactivity of your dashboard with parameters.

Parameters allow users to change certain aspects of the visualization dynamically.

For example, you can create a parameter that lets users switch between different dimensions or measures in a chart without modifying the underlying data source.

In Tableau, parameters are created by defining a list of allowable values and then using the parameter in calculated fields, filters, or actions.

Parameters provide users with more control and flexibility over the dashboard's visualizations.

Annotations are another interactive feature that can add value to dashboards by providing context and insights.

Annotations allow users to add comments, notes, or highlights to specific data points or visualizations.

In Tableau, users can add annotations by selecting data points and choosing the "Annotate" option.

Annotations can help users collaborate, share insights, and document important findings within the dashboard.

Integration with external data sources or APIs can further enhance the interactivity of dashboards.

You can incorporate real-time data updates or external data feeds to provide users with the most current information.

For example, a financial dashboard can fetch stock market data from an external API and display real-time stock prices.

To implement this, you may need to use scripting languages like Python or JavaScript to fetch and update data in the dashboard.

In summary, creating interactive dashboards involves designing engaging and responsive data visualizations that empower users to explore data, gain insights, and make informed decisions.

Key elements of interactive dashboards include interactivity, filters, actions, performance optimization, responsive design, usability, parameters, annotations, and integration with external data sources.

By applying these principles and techniques, you can create interactive dashboards that provide a valuable and dynamic user experience.

Designing effective reports is a critical skill in the world of data analysis and business intelligence, as reports serve as a primary means of communicating data-driven insights to stakeholders.

A well-designed report can provide clarity, highlight important findings, and support informed decision-making.

Next, we will explore the principles and best practices for designing effective reports that convey information efficiently and effectively.

The first step in designing an effective report is to define its purpose and audience.

Understanding why you are creating the report and who will be using it is essential in determining what information to include and how to present it.

Consider the specific questions the report needs to answer or the decisions it should support.

For example, a sales report may aim to provide insights into monthly revenue trends for sales managers, while a financial report may be intended for executives to assess the company's financial health.

Once you have a clear purpose and audience in mind, it's important to structure the report logically.

Start by organizing the content into sections or chapters, with each section addressing a specific aspect of the report's purpose.

Provide clear headings and subheadings to guide readers and help them navigate the report.

In digital reports, you can include a table of contents or interactive navigation elements to facilitate easy access to different sections.

In printed reports, ensure that page numbers and section headings are clearly visible.

Effective report design also involves choosing the appropriate format and layout.

Consider whether the report will be delivered in print, as a PDF, or as an interactive web page.

The format may influence the layout, design elements, and interactivity options available.

For example, an online dashboard report may allow users to explore data interactively, while a printed annual report may focus on visual appeal and readability.

In digital reports, responsive design principles can ensure that the report looks and functions well on different devices, such as desktops, tablets, and smartphones.

When selecting fonts and typography, prioritize readability and consistency.

Choose legible fonts for both headings and body text, and maintain a consistent font style and size throughout the report.

Avoid using too many font styles or sizes, as this can make the report appear cluttered and less cohesive.

For reports with large datasets, consider using data visualization techniques to convey information efficiently.

Charts, graphs, and tables can help readers quickly grasp trends, comparisons, and patterns in the data.

Choose the most appropriate visualization type for the data you are presenting.

For example, use bar charts for comparisons, line charts for trends over time, and pie charts for showing part-to-whole relationships.

In data visualization tools like Tableau or Power BI, you can create interactive charts and dashboards that allow users to explore data in-depth.

Consider the use of color in your report design, but do so thoughtfully.

Color can be a powerful tool for highlighting important information or creating visual interest.

However, excessive or inconsistent use of color can lead to confusion and distract from the message.

Maintain a consistent color scheme and reserve vibrant colors for emphasizing key points or highlighting data outliers.

In digital reports, take advantage of interactive features to enhance user engagement.

Interactive elements can include tooltips, clickable links, drill-down capabilities, and filters that allow users to explore data dynamically.

For example, an interactive map in a report can enable users to click on regions to access more detailed information.

Ensure that interactive elements are intuitive and user-friendly, with clear instructions or guidance provided as needed.

Accessibility is an important consideration in report design.

Make sure that your report is accessible to individuals with disabilities, including those using screen readers or assistive technologies.

Provide alternative text for images and charts, use proper heading structures for screen readers, and ensure that interactive elements are navigable using keyboard controls.

Testing the report with a variety of users, including those with disabilities, can help identify and address accessibility issues.

When designing reports, pay attention to the use of whitespace and layout.

Whitespace, or the empty space around text and visuals, plays a crucial role in visual clarity and readability.

Proper use of whitespace can help separate content, reduce clutter, and draw attention to key information.

In digital reports, consider responsive design principles to ensure that content adjusts gracefully to different screen sizes.

For example, use responsive grids and flexible layouts to maintain readability on both large monitors and small screens.

Another important aspect of effective report design is the use of storytelling.

Tell a compelling narrative through your report, guiding readers through the data and helping them understand the insights and implications.

Use introductory sections to set the context and objectives, and provide clear explanations for charts and graphs.

Use concise and engaging language to communicate findings, and consider incorporating real-world examples or case studies to illustrate key points.

In addition to the main content, include a summary or executive summary that provides a concise overview of the most important findings and recommendations.

The summary should be clear and actionable, allowing readers to quickly grasp the report's key takeaways.

In longer reports, consider adding an index or glossary to help readers navigate and understand technical terms or acronyms.

Lastly, consider the distribution and delivery of your report.

Determine the best method for sharing the report with your audience.

For printed reports, ensure high-quality printing and binding for a professional appearance.

In digital reports, consider the use of secure file-sharing platforms or online report publishing tools that provide controlled access and tracking.

Regularly update and maintain the report to keep the information current and relevant.

Collect feedback from readers and stakeholders to identify areas for improvement in both content and design.

In summary, designing effective reports involves careful consideration of purpose, audience, structure, format, typography, visual elements, interactivity, accessibility, layout, storytelling, and distribution.

By applying these principles and best practices, you can create reports that convey information clearly, engage readers, and support data-driven decision-making.

Chapter 7: Using Filters and Slicers Effectively

Applying filters for data analysis is a fundamental technique used to extract specific subsets of data from a larger dataset, allowing for focused and targeted analysis.

Filters enable data analysts and scientists to refine their exploration and gain deeper insights into the data.

Whether you are working with spreadsheets, databases, or data visualization tools, understanding how to apply filters effectively is a valuable skill in the world of data analysis.

To apply filters, you need to have a clear objective in mind.

Consider the questions you want to answer or the patterns you want to discover within the dataset.

For example, if you have a sales dataset, you may want to analyze sales data for a specific time period or for a particular product category.

Once you have a well-defined objective, you can choose the appropriate filtering criteria to narrow down the data.

In data analysis tools like Microsoft Excel, Google Sheets, or database management systems like SQL, you can use SQL queries or functions to apply filters.

For example, to filter sales data for a specific time period, you can use the SQL WHERE clause:

```sql
Copy code
SELECT * FROM SalesData WHERE Date BETWEEN '2023-01-01' AND '2023-12-31';
```

In this SQL query, the WHERE clause filters the data to include only records where the date falls within the specified range.

Similarly, you can apply filters in spreadsheet software by selecting the data range and using the filter or sort functions to narrow down the data based on specific conditions.

Filters can be applied to both numerical and categorical data.

For numerical data, you can filter based on ranges, minimum or maximum values, or specific values.

For example, you can filter a dataset of customer ages to include only customers aged between 25 and 40.

In database systems, you can use comparison operators like >, <, >=, and <= to filter numerical data.

For categorical data, filters can be applied based on specific categories or values.

For instance, you can filter a dataset of products to include only products in the "Electronics" category.

In SQL, you can use the IN clause to filter data based on a list of specified values:

sqlCopy code

```
SELECT * FROM Products WHERE Category IN ('Electronics', 'Appliances', 'Computers');
```

Filtering can be applied to single variables or multiple variables simultaneously, allowing for more complex data analysis.

In many data analysis tools, you can create compound filters by combining multiple conditions using logical operators such as AND and OR.

For example, you can filter a dataset of customer reviews to include only reviews that are both positive (rating >= 4) and related to a specific product category (category = 'Electronics').

In SQL, you can use logical operators to create compound filters:

sqlCopy code

```
SELECT * FROM CustomerReviews WHERE Rating >= 4 AND Category = 'Electronics';
```

Applying filters not only helps you isolate specific subsets of data but also supports data exploration by allowing you to view the impact of different filtering criteria on your analysis.

You can compare multiple filter conditions to understand how they affect the dataset and your insights.

For instance, you can compare sales data for different product categories by applying filters for each category separately and observing the differences in sales performance.

In data visualization tools like Tableau or Power BI, filters can be applied interactively to dashboards and visualizations, enabling dynamic exploration of data.

Users can click on data points or use filter controls to adjust the view, making it easier to identify trends and patterns.

When applying filters, it's crucial to consider the impact on your analysis and the validity of your conclusions.

Be aware that filtering can lead to data loss, as it removes or hides certain data points.

Ensure that your filtering criteria align with your research question or analysis goals and that you are not inadvertently excluding relevant data.

To mitigate the risk of bias or oversimplification, document your filtering choices and the rationale behind them.

For example, if you exclude certain outliers from your analysis, provide a clear explanation for doing so and justify how it affects the interpretation of your results.

Regularly revisiting and adjusting your filters as your analysis progresses can help you refine your insights and ensure that you are not missing valuable information.

In summary, applying filters for data analysis is a fundamental technique that allows you to extract specific subsets of data based on predefined criteria.

Filters help you focus your analysis, explore data in-depth, and answer specific research questions.

Whether you are working with spreadsheets, databases, or data visualization tools, understanding how to apply filters effectively is essential for gaining deeper insights into your data and making informed decisions.

Advanced slicer techniques are a valuable asset for data analysts and Power BI users looking to enhance their data exploration and visualization capabilities.

Slicers, in the context of Power BI, are interactive filtering controls that allow users to manipulate and filter data visualizations dynamically.

While basic slicers are essential for simple filtering tasks, advanced slicer techniques unlock a world of possibilities for more intricate data analysis and reporting.

One of the advanced slicer techniques involves the use of hierarchy slicers.

Hierarchies are used to organize data into multiple levels of granularity, such as year, quarter, month, and day for a date hierarchy.

With hierarchy slicers, users can drill down or roll up through different levels of data, enabling deeper exploration and analysis.

To create a hierarchy slicer in Power BI, you need to define a hierarchy in your data model.

For instance, you can create a date hierarchy by selecting the "Date" field, right-clicking, and choosing the "New Hierarchy" option.

Once the hierarchy is defined, you can add it to the slicer visualization, allowing users to expand or collapse levels as needed.

Another advanced slicer technique is the integration of relative date slicers.

Relative date slicers enable users to select dynamic date ranges, such as "Last 7 days" or "Next month," without the need to manually specify fixed date ranges.

To create a relative date slicer in Power BI, you can utilize the built-in relative date filtering options.

By selecting the date field and choosing the relative date filter type, you can enable users to interact with the slicer and choose from predefined date ranges.

This dynamic feature simplifies the process of exploring time-based data and is particularly useful for trend analysis and forecasting.

Additionally, advanced slicer techniques can involve the use of advanced filter types beyond simple list or dropdown options.

Power BI allows for the creation of custom slicers using DAX expressions.

This advanced technique enables you to build slicers that filter data based on complex logic or calculations.

For example, you can create a custom slicer that filters data based on specific aggregation thresholds, outliers, or calculated measures.

To implement custom slicers, you would typically define a DAX measure that returns a table of filter values and use that measure in the slicer visualization.

By doing so, you empower users with more sophisticated filtering options tailored to the specific needs of your analysis.

Cross-filtering is another advanced slicer technique that extends the filtering capabilities beyond individual visualizations.

With cross-filtering, slicers can influence not only the visualizations they are directly associated with but also other unrelated visualizations on the same report page.

This means that selecting a value in one slicer can dynamically update data in multiple visualizations, creating powerful interactive insights.

Cross-filtering can be enabled in Power BI by configuring relationships between tables in the data model.

By defining the appropriate relationships, you establish the flow of filtering interactions between tables and visualizations.

This advanced slicer technique enhances the overall user experience and fosters a more interconnected analysis environment.

Advanced slicer techniques also encompass the concept of synchronized slicers.

Synchronized slicers allow you to link multiple slicers together, ensuring that they filter data consistently across different report pages or even within the same page.

This is particularly useful when you want to maintain a synchronized view of data across various aspects or dimensions.

To create synchronized slicers in Power BI, you can use the "Sync Slicers" feature, which allows you to connect slicers from different visualizations or pages and maintain their synchronization settings.

By applying synchronized slicers, you provide users with a seamless and coordinated filtering experience, improving their ability to explore data comprehensively.

Advanced slicer techniques extend to the realm of custom visuals and custom slicer controls.

Power BI's custom visuals feature enables you to create custom slicer controls with unique designs, functionalities, and behaviors.

You can build custom slicers that cater to specific user preferences or business requirements.

Developing custom slicer visuals often involves using custom JavaScript or TypeScript code to design and implement the desired slicer control.

This advanced technique allows for highly tailored slicers that can enhance the visual appeal and usability of your reports.

To incorporate custom slicers into your Power BI reports, you can import custom visuals from the Power BI marketplace or create your own using the Power BI developer tools.

Advanced slicer techniques also encompass the use of bookmarking and advanced actions.

With bookmarks and advanced actions, you can create guided data exploration experiences for users.

Bookmarks allow you to capture the current state of the report, including slicer selections, visualizations, and page navigation.

You can then create buttons or interactive elements that trigger specific bookmarks, enabling users to follow predefined analytical paths or scenarios.

By combining bookmarks with advanced actions, you can design more interactive and engaging reports that guide users through complex analyses.

To implement bookmarks and advanced actions in Power BI, you can use the Power BI desktop's bookmark pane and the "Selection" option for buttons or shapes.

In summary, advanced slicer techniques in Power BI open up a wide range of possibilities for data analysts and report creators.

These techniques include hierarchy slicers, relative date slicers, custom slicers, cross-filtering, synchronized slicers, custom visuals, bookmarking, and advanced actions.

By mastering these advanced slicer techniques, you can create more interactive, dynamic, and insightful reports that empower users to explore data in depth and make data-driven decisions effectively.

Chapter 8: Sharing and Collaborating with Power BI

Publishing and sharing reports is the final and crucial step in the data analysis and reporting process, as it involves making your insights and findings accessible to a wider audience.

In today's data-driven world, effective communication of data-driven insights is essential for informed decision-making, collaboration, and driving business outcomes.

Next, we will explore the various methods, platforms, and best practices for publishing and sharing reports.

Before diving into the specifics, it's important to consider the audience and the purpose of the report.

Understanding who will be consuming the report and why they need it will guide your decisions on how, where, and in what format to publish and share the report.

Your audience may include executives, stakeholders, colleagues, or the general public, each with different needs and expectations.

Once you have a clear understanding of your audience and objectives, you can choose the appropriate platform for publishing and sharing your report.

There are several options available, ranging from traditional print and email distribution to modern online reporting and collaboration platforms.

Printed reports are a classic choice when a physical document is required for presentations, meetings, or documentation purposes.

To publish a printed report, you can use word processing software or desktop publishing tools to design and format the document.

Ensure that the report is well-structured, visually appealing, and optimized for print quality.

Consider using professional printing services for high-quality results.

Email distribution is another common method for sharing reports, especially for smaller audiences or one-time communication.

You can attach the report as a PDF or other document format to an email and send it directly to the recipients.

Be mindful of file size limitations and compatibility with various email clients.

Online reporting platforms have become increasingly popular for sharing reports with broader audiences and facilitating collaboration.

Tools like Google Data Studio, Microsoft Power BI Service, Tableau Server, and online spreadsheet applications allow you to publish reports online and share them as web links.

This method provides several advantages, including real-time access to updated data, interactive visualizations, and collaborative commenting features.

To publish a report online, you typically need to upload it to the chosen platform, configure sharing settings, and generate a shareable link.

Ensure that your online report is well-designed, user-friendly, and optimized for web viewing.

Cloud storage and file-sharing services, such as Google Drive, Dropbox, or Microsoft OneDrive, offer a convenient way to share reports and collaborate on documents.

You can upload your report files to these services and share them with specific individuals or groups by granting access permissions.

This method is suitable for sharing large files or collaborating on reports with colleagues.

Additionally, data analysis and visualization tools often provide built-in options for publishing and sharing reports.

For example, in Power BI, you can publish reports to the Power BI Service and share them with authorized users or embed them in websites and applications.

Similarly, Tableau provides options for publishing and sharing reports through Tableau Server or Tableau Online.

When publishing reports, it's essential to consider data security and privacy.

Ensure that sensitive or confidential information is appropriately redacted or anonymized before sharing the report.

Implement access controls, user authentication, and encryption measures to protect sensitive data from unauthorized access.

Compliance with data protection regulations, such as GDPR or HIPAA, is crucial when dealing with personal or sensitive data.

Once you have chosen the platform and prepared your report for publishing, you need to determine the sharing and distribution methods.

Consider whether the report will be shared with a specific list of recipients, a broader audience, or the public.

Tailor the sharing settings and access controls accordingly to limit or grant access as needed.

For reports with a limited audience, you can share them directly with individuals or groups by providing email addresses or usernames.

In cases where wider distribution is desired, you can generate shareable links or embed the report in a website or portal.

Email distribution lists, mailing lists, or distribution groups can streamline the process of sharing reports with predefined groups of recipients.

Automate email distribution if necessary by scheduling reports to be sent at specific intervals or triggered by events.

For online reports hosted on platforms like Google Data Studio or Power BI Service, sharing options typically involve generating shareable links with various access levels.

You can choose whether to allow anyone with the link to view the report, restrict access to specific individuals, or require user authentication.

Embedding reports in websites or applications provides a seamless and integrated experience for report consumers.

To embed a report, you usually need to generate an embed code or integrate it with the hosting platform's API.

Embedding is commonly used for sharing interactive dashboards, data visualizations, or reports within corporate portals or customer-facing websites.

Version control is a critical consideration when publishing and sharing reports, particularly in collaborative environments.

Maintain a clear versioning system to track changes, updates, and revisions to the report.

Document the changes made in each version, and communicate them to stakeholders as necessary.

Use version control tools or features provided by collaboration platforms to manage and track report versions effectively.

Regularly updating and maintaining reports is essential to ensure that the information remains accurate, relevant, and up-to-date.

Consider setting up scheduled data refreshes for reports that rely on live data sources to keep the content current.

Implement a process for reviewing and validating data before publishing updates to avoid inaccuracies or errors.

Feedback and collaboration play a crucial role in improving the quality and relevance of reports.

Encourage recipients and users to provide feedback, comments, and suggestions for improvements.

Create a feedback loop to capture insights from the audience and iterate on the report's design and content accordingly.

Data usage and performance analytics can provide valuable insights into how reports are being consumed and whether they meet their objectives.

Use analytics tools or reporting features to track user engagement, access patterns, and popular report sections.

This data can inform decisions about report optimization, content prioritization, and future enhancements.

Accessibility is an essential aspect of publishing and sharing reports, as it ensures that the information is available to all users, including those with disabilities.

Ensure that your reports are designed and formatted to be accessible to individuals using screen readers or assistive technologies.

Provide alternative text for images, use semantic headings, and follow accessibility guidelines such as WCAG (Web Content Accessibility Guidelines).

When sharing reports with a wider audience or the public, consider branding and customization to align the report's appearance with your organization's identity.

Add logos, colors, and style elements that reinforce your branding and create a consistent visual identity.

Customization options may vary depending on the platform or tools used for report publishing.

In summary, publishing and sharing reports involve selecting the appropriate platform, configuring access controls, determining distribution methods, ensuring data security and privacy, version control, regular updates, feedback collection, performance analytics, accessibility, and customization.

By following best practices and considering the needs of your audience, you can effectively communicate data-driven insights, drive informed decision-making, and foster collaboration within your organization or with external stakeholders.

Collaborating with workspaces and apps is an integral part of sharing and disseminating data-driven insights within organizations, teams, and across departments.

Next, we will delve into the concepts and best practices of utilizing workspaces and apps to enhance collaboration in data analysis and reporting.

Workspaces in data analysis and visualization tools like Power BI, Tableau, and Google Data Studio serve as dedicated areas where teams or groups of users can collaborate on data projects, reports, and dashboards.

These workspaces provide a structured and organized environment for managing and sharing data assets.

The first step in collaborating effectively with workspaces is to create and configure them to align with your team's goals and objectives.

Naming conventions, access permissions, and content organization within workspaces are essential factors to consider during the setup phase.

For example, you can create a workspace for the marketing department, giving marketing analysts and managers access to relevant data and reports.

Configuring access permissions allows you to define who can view, edit, or publish content within the workspace.

In Power BI, for instance, you can designate members as "contributors" or "viewers" with varying levels of access and editing privileges.

Moreover, it's important to implement clear content organization within workspaces to ensure that users can easily locate and collaborate on specific reports, dashboards, or datasets.

Organizing content into folders or categories can facilitate efficient collaboration and content management.

Once your workspace is configured, the next step is to invite team members or collaborators to join.

Invitations can be sent by email or through collaboration tools within the data analysis platform.

Upon acceptance, team members gain access to the workspace and can begin collaborating on shared projects.

In Power BI, for instance, you can invite collaborators to a workspace by specifying their email addresses, granting them access, and assigning roles.

Collaboration within workspaces typically involves co-authoring reports, sharing insights, and reviewing data visualizations.

Team members can collaborate in real-time, making updates, adding comments, and discussing findings within the workspace environment.

This collaborative approach fosters teamwork and streamlines the process of data analysis and reporting.

Moreover, collaboration features often extend to version control and content history tracking.

Users can track changes, revisions, and modifications made to reports or dashboards, helping to maintain data integrity and transparency.

When multiple users are working on the same report or dashboard simultaneously, version control ensures that changes are documented, and conflicts are resolved seamlessly.

Version history logs provide visibility into who made specific changes and when, making it easier to track the evolution of a report.

In Power BI workspaces, you can access version history to view and restore previous versions of reports and datasets.

Another essential aspect of collaborating with workspaces is data governance and security.

Workspaces should adhere to data governance policies and security measures to protect sensitive information and maintain compliance with regulatory requirements.

Implement access controls, encryption, and data protection measures to safeguard confidential data.

Consider data sensitivity levels and classify data accordingly, ensuring that only authorized users can access and edit sensitive reports or datasets.

Collaboration extends beyond individual workspaces through the sharing of apps and content packs.

Apps are a convenient way to package and distribute a collection of reports, dashboards, and datasets to a broader audience.

They enable organizations to share insights and analytics with specific user groups or external stakeholders.

In Power BI, for example, you can create apps that include reports, dashboards, and custom branding.

These apps can be published to the Power BI service and shared with users who need access to the data and insights.

Content packs, on the other hand, are predefined collections of reports and dashboards that can be shared with specific groups or individuals.

Content packs simplify the process of sharing data assets and insights by packaging them into reusable templates.

Users can install content packs to access pre-built reports and dashboards tailored to their needs.

In addition to sharing apps and content packs, collaboration with workspaces also involves integrating data analysis platforms with external tools and services.

For example, you can connect data visualization tools to collaboration platforms like Microsoft Teams, Slack, or email services to streamline communication and notifications.

This integration allows team members to receive updates, alerts, and notifications related to workspace activities, ensuring that they stay informed and engaged.

Collaboration tools often provide chat, discussion, or commenting features that facilitate communication and feedback within workspaces.

Users can leave comments on reports, datasets, or dashboards, enabling discussions, clarifications, and suggestions related to the data.

These comments can serve as a valuable record of collaboration and decision-making throughout the data analysis process.

Furthermore, collaboration features within workspaces can support data storytelling and narrative building.

Team members can work together to craft data-driven narratives, explanations, and annotations that enhance the understanding of data insights.

Narrative storytelling helps stakeholders interpret data effectively and derive actionable insights.

Collaborating with workspaces also extends to the review and approval processes.

For example, you can implement workflows that involve data validation, quality assurance, and approvals before publishing reports or dashboards to wider audiences.

Designate individuals or teams responsible for reviewing and verifying the accuracy and relevance of data assets.

Use workflow management tools or built-in approval processes within the data analysis platform to streamline these tasks.

Finally, it's crucial to establish a culture of collaboration within your organization.

Encourage a collaborative mindset among team members, emphasizing the importance of sharing knowledge, insights, and best practices.

Foster a culture of continuous learning and improvement by facilitating training and knowledge-sharing sessions related to data analysis and reporting tools.

In summary, collaborating with workspaces and apps is essential for effective data analysis and reporting within organizations.

Key considerations include workspace configuration, access permissions, content organization, co-authoring, version control, data governance, security, app and content pack sharing, integration with collaboration tools, communication features, data storytelling, review processes, and fostering a culture of collaboration.

By implementing these best practices and leveraging collaboration features within data analysis platforms, organizations can maximize the value of their data assets and drive data-driven decision-making.

Chapter 9: Tips for Designing Effective Visuals

Design principles for effective data visualization are crucial for conveying complex information clearly and compellingly.

Next, we will explore the fundamental principles that guide the creation of visually impactful and informative data visualizations.

The first design principle to consider is clarity.

Clarity involves ensuring that the message of the visualization is readily understandable to the audience.

To achieve clarity, start by defining a clear objective for your visualization.

Ask yourself what message you want to convey and what insights you want the audience to gain.

Once you have a clear objective, select the most appropriate visualization type to convey your message.

For example, if you want to show trends over time, a line chart may be more effective than a pie chart.

The choice of colors in your visualization also plays a critical role in clarity.

Use a limited color palette that enhances the readability of the data.

Avoid using too many colors, as this can lead to confusion and distract from the main message.

Consider colorblind-friendly palettes to ensure that your visualization is accessible to all users.

Another important design principle is simplicity.

Simplicity involves reducing complexity and focusing on the essential information.

Avoid cluttering your visualization with unnecessary elements or decorations.

Each element in your visualization should serve a clear purpose and contribute to the overall message.

Remove chartjunk, which includes embellishments, excessive gridlines, or 3D effects that do not add value to the visualization.

Instead, keep the visualization clean and uncluttered, allowing the data to take center stage.

In data visualization, accuracy is paramount.

Ensure that your data is accurately represented in the visualization, and avoid distorting or misrepresenting the information.

Double-check the accuracy of your data sources, calculations, and labels.

When using numerical values in the visualization, use appropriate scales and units to prevent misinterpretation.

For example, if you are visualizing currency values, clearly indicate the currency symbol and decimal places.

Labels and annotations are essential for providing context and enhancing the understanding of the data.

Use descriptive labels for axes, data points, and legends to clarify what each element represents.

Consider adding annotations or callouts to highlight specific data points or trends that are particularly relevant.

Annotations can draw the audience's attention to key insights within the visualization.

Consistency in design is another crucial principle.

Maintain consistency in the use of colors, fonts, and formatting throughout your visualization.

Consistency creates a cohesive and visually pleasing experience for the audience.

Establish a consistent visual language for your data visualizations within your organization to ensure that reports and dashboards have a unified look and feel.

When designing a data visualization, consider the context in which it will be viewed.

Think about the medium, platform, and device that the audience will use to access the visualization.

Ensure that the visualization is responsive and optimized for various screen sizes and orientations.

For example, a mobile-friendly design may require a different layout and font size compared to a desktop view.

Interactivity can enhance the engagement and usability of data visualizations.

Consider adding interactive elements that allow users to explore the data further.

Interactive features such as tooltips, filters, and drill-down options can provide users with more control and insights.

For instance, users can hover over data points to see additional information or filter the data to focus on specific aspects.

Testing and feedback are crucial steps in the design process.

Test your visualization with a sample audience or colleagues to gather feedback on its effectiveness and clarity.

Listen to user feedback and make adjustments as needed to improve the visualization.

Iterate on the design to refine it further, taking into account the insights gained from testing.

Accessibility is an essential consideration in data visualization design.

Ensure that your visualization is accessible to individuals with disabilities, including those using screen readers.

Provide alternative text for images and charts, use semantic headings, and follow accessibility guidelines such as WCAG.

Accessibility ensures that your visualization can be used and understood by a broader audience.

Engage in continuous learning and stay updated with the latest trends and best practices in data visualization.

Attend workshops, webinars, or conferences related to data visualization to expand your knowledge and skills.

Explore new tools and technologies that can aid in creating more effective visualizations.

Keep up with emerging design trends and apply them judiciously to enhance your visualizations.

In summary, design principles for effective data visualization include clarity, simplicity, accuracy, consistency, context, interactivity, testing, accessibility, and continuous learning.

By applying these principles, you can create data visualizations that not only convey information clearly but also engage and inform your audience effectively.

Remember that data visualization is both an art and a science, and mastering these principles will help you become a more proficient and impactful data communicator.

Choosing the right visualizations for your data is a critical decision that significantly impacts how effectively you communicate insights and information to your audience.
Next, we will explore the key factors and considerations that guide the selection of appropriate visualizations for various types of data.
The first step in choosing the right visualization is to understand your data and the story it tells.
Begin by examining the nature of your data, including its structure, dimensions, and relationships.
Identify the key variables, trends, and patterns that you want to convey through the visualization.
Consider the data's context and the questions you aim to answer with the visualization.
For example, if you are working with time-series data, you may want to visualize trends, seasonality, or anomalies.
Once you have a clear understanding of your data and objectives, you can match them with suitable visualization types.
One of the most common visualization types is the bar chart, which is effective for comparing discrete categories or showing distributions.
Bar charts come in various forms, such as vertical bars (column charts) or horizontal bars (bar charts), and can be clustered or stacked.
Use bar charts when you need to compare values across categories or show ranking.
Line charts, on the other hand, are ideal for visualizing trends over time or displaying continuous data points.
Line charts connect data points with lines, making it easy to observe patterns, fluctuations, and changes.
Line charts are particularly useful for time-series data, stock prices, and scientific experiments.

Pie charts are suitable for displaying parts of a whole and showing the distribution of categories as proportions of a circle.

Use pie charts when you want to emphasize the composition of a dataset or highlight the relationship between individual components and the total.

Scatter plots are valuable for visualizing the relationship between two continuous variables.

Scatter plots use points or markers to represent data points, allowing you to assess correlations, clusters, or outliers.

Heatmaps are excellent for displaying large datasets with a grid of colored cells.

Heatmaps represent data values with color intensity, making it easy to identify patterns, clusters, or variations.

Heatmaps are frequently used in data analysis, genetics, and geographical data.

Histograms are essential for showing the distribution of a single continuous variable.

Histograms group data into bins or intervals and display the frequency or count of data points within each bin.

Use histograms to understand the shape, central tendency, and spread of data distributions.

Area charts, similar to line charts, are suitable for showing trends over time but emphasize the area under the line.

Area charts are effective for illustrating accumulated values or comparing multiple datasets with a shared baseline.

Box plots, also known as box-and-whisker plots, provide insights into the distribution and spread of data.

Box plots display the median, quartiles, and potential outliers in a dataset, helping to identify skewness or variation.

Choosing the right visualization also involves considering the audience and their familiarity with different chart types.

Select visualizations that are intuitive and easily understandable to your target audience.

For example, bar charts and line charts are widely recognized and familiar to most people, making them suitable choices for general audiences.

However, if your audience has expertise in a specific field, you may opt for more specialized visualization types that cater to their domain knowledge.

Consider the platform or medium through which the visualization will be presented.

Different platforms may have limitations on the types of visualizations they support or the space available.

Ensure that your chosen visualization type is compatible with the platform and can be easily viewed and interacted with by the audience.

For example, if you are creating a web-based dashboard, choose visualizations that can be embedded and viewed in web browsers effectively.

Interactivity is another factor to consider when choosing visualizations.

Some data visualization tools allow for interactive features such as tooltips, zooming, filtering, and drill-down.

Evaluate whether interactivity enhances the user's ability to explore and gain insights from the data.

For instance, a map with interactive zooming and filtering capabilities can provide a more engaging experience for users exploring geographic data.

Color selection is a crucial aspect of visualization design.

Choose colors that are not only aesthetically pleasing but also enhance the clarity and interpretation of the data.

Use color effectively to highlight important data points or categories, create visual hierarchy, and convey meaning.

Consider using color schemes that are colorblind-friendly to ensure accessibility.

Avoid using overly bright or saturated colors that can strain the viewer's eyes or distract from the data.

Accessibility is a fundamental consideration in visualization design.

Ensure that your visualization is accessible to individuals with disabilities, including those with visual impairments.

Provide alternative text for images, use high contrast between text and background, and follow accessibility guidelines such as WCAG.

Accessibility ensures that your visualization can be used and understood by a broader audience.

When choosing visualizations, be mindful of the data's scale and distribution.

Select visualization types that effectively represent the data's scale, whether it is nominal, ordinal, interval, or ratio.

For instance, nominal data can be represented using bar charts, while interval data may be better suited for line charts or scatter plots.

Consider the data's distribution, such as whether it follows a normal distribution, is skewed, or has outliers.

Choose visualizations that reveal the distribution characteristics accurately.

Storytelling is a powerful aspect of data visualization.

Consider how your chosen visualization type fits into the narrative you want to convey.

Use the visualization to tell a story, guiding the audience through key insights, findings, and conclusions.

Provide context, annotations, and explanations that help the audience interpret the visualization and understand its implications. Testing and feedback are essential in the process of choosing the right visualization.

Test your chosen visualization with a sample audience or colleagues to gather feedback on its effectiveness and clarity.

Listen to user feedback and make adjustments as needed to improve the visualization.

Iterate on the design to refine it further, taking into account the insights gained from testing.

In summary, choosing the right visualizations for your data involves understanding your data, setting clear objectives, considering the audience and context, evaluating interactivity, selecting appropriate colors, ensuring accessibility, matching data scale and distribution, storytelling, and gathering feedback.

By carefully considering these factors and principles, you can create data visualizations that effectively communicate insights, engage the audience, and support data-driven decision-making.

Chapter 10: Troubleshooting and Best Practices

In the world of data analysis and visualization, encountering common issues is a natural part of the process, but knowing how to identify and resolve these challenges is essential for producing accurate and effective insights.

One common issue that data analysts often face is data quality problems, which can manifest in various forms, such as missing data, duplicates, or outliers.

To address these issues, data cleaning and preprocessing steps are necessary.

Data cleaning involves identifying and removing or correcting inaccurate or incomplete data points.

In Python, for example, you can use the Pandas library to drop rows with missing data using the **dropna()** function.

Duplicates can be detected and removed using the **drop_duplicates()** function.

Outliers, on the other hand, may require more advanced statistical techniques, such as the Z-score or the Interquartile Range (IQR) method.

Another common issue is data inconsistency, where data from different sources or time periods do not align.

To tackle this problem, data integration and standardization techniques can be employed.

Data integration involves combining data from multiple sources into a unified dataset, ensuring that variables and data formats are consistent.

Standardization involves converting data into a common format or unit, making it easier to compare and analyze.

In SQL, for instance, you can use the **JOIN** statement to integrate data from different tables, and the **CAST** function to standardize data types.

Data visualization issues often arise when choosing the wrong type of visualization for the data or the message.

A common solution is to carefully evaluate the data and the message's objectives before selecting the visualization type.

For example, if you want to compare data across categories, a bar chart may be more suitable than a pie chart.

If your data has a temporal aspect, a line chart might be the better choice.

Furthermore, overcrowded or cluttered visualizations can impede understanding.

Solutions to this issue include simplifying the visualization, reducing unnecessary elements, and using whitespace effectively to improve readability.

In Python's Matplotlib library, you can customize the layout and spacing of subplots to reduce overcrowding.

Data interpretation challenges often occur when the audience lacks domain knowledge or context.

A potential solution is to provide clear and concise explanations alongside the visualizations.

Adding annotations, captions, or tooltips that clarify the meaning of data points or trends can improve understanding.

In Python's Matplotlib, you can use the **annotate()** function to add annotations to specific data points on a chart.

Data security and privacy concerns have become increasingly important in data analysis and visualization.

To address these issues, organizations should implement data protection measures, access controls, and comply with relevant regulations.

Using encryption, user authentication, and role-based access controls can help safeguard sensitive data.

In SQL Server, for example, you can use the **GRANT** statement to assign specific permissions to users or roles.

Performance issues can arise when dealing with large datasets or complex calculations.

Optimizing data processing and visualization can mitigate these challenges.

Techniques such as indexing, caching, and using summary tables can improve query performance.

In SQL, creating indexes on frequently queried columns can significantly speed up database queries.

Compatibility issues can occur when trying to integrate data or visualizations from different tools or platforms.

To address this, organizations should ensure compatibility by using standardized data formats or implementing data connectors and APIs.

For example, using the JSON format for data exchange can facilitate compatibility between various applications and platforms.

Version control is crucial for managing changes and revisions in data analysis and visualization projects.

Version control systems like Git help track changes, collaborate with team members, and maintain a history of project updates.

In Git, the **git commit** command is used to save changes to a repository, and the **git push** command uploads those changes to a remote repository.

Collaboration challenges often arise when multiple team members are working on the same data analysis project.

To overcome these issues, organizations can implement collaborative tools, communication channels, and project management methodologies.

Using project management tools like Jira or Trello can help teams coordinate tasks and track progress.

Data governance is essential for maintaining data quality, security, and compliance.

Implementing data governance policies and practices ensures that data is well-managed throughout its lifecycle.

Incorporate data governance into your organization's data strategy, including data stewardship, data lineage tracking, and metadata management.

In SQL, documenting data definitions and relationships can support data governance efforts.

Ethical considerations in data analysis and visualization are becoming increasingly important.

Organizations should establish ethical guidelines and principles for handling data, especially when dealing with sensitive or personal information.

Ensure that data analysis and visualization practices align with ethical standards and respect user privacy.

Incorporate ethical considerations into data policies and training programs.

In summary, common issues in data analysis and visualization encompass data quality, consistency, visualization selection, data interpretation, security, privacy, performance, compatibility, version control, collaboration, data governance, and ethics.

Addressing these issues requires a combination of technical skills, tools, and best practices.

By recognizing and proactively addressing these challenges, data analysts and organizations can improve the accuracy, effectiveness, and ethical integrity of their data-driven insights.

Best practices for Power BI development are essential for creating effective and efficient data models, reports, and dashboards that empower users with meaningful insights.

One of the foundational principles of Power BI development is the importance of data modeling.

Effective data modeling involves designing a well-structured and optimized data model that serves as the foundation for your reports and dashboards.

In Power BI, data modeling starts with importing and transforming data using Power Query, a tool integrated into Power BI Desktop.

Using Power Query, you can clean, reshape, and combine data from various sources to create a unified dataset that aligns with your reporting objectives.

For example, you can use the Power Query editor to remove duplicates, filter rows, and create calculated columns.

Once your data is prepared, the next step in data modeling is defining relationships between tables.

In Power BI, relationships establish connections between tables based on common columns, enabling you to create relationships similar to those in a relational database.

You can create relationships in Power BI Desktop by specifying the related fields between tables.

For example, if you have a "Sales" table and a "Customers" table, you can create a relationship between them using the "CustomerID" field.

The use of relationships is a fundamental best practice in Power BI development, as it allows you to combine data from multiple tables seamlessly and create meaningful visualizations.

Another critical aspect of data modeling is creating calculated columns and measures using the Data Analysis Expressions (DAX) language.

DAX is a powerful formula language in Power BI that enables you to perform calculations, aggregations, and complex calculations on your data.

For instance, you can create calculated columns to derive new data based on existing columns or measures to perform calculations like sums, averages, or ratios.

Effective use of DAX is crucial for enhancing the analytical capabilities of your reports and dashboards.

Power BI Desktop provides a DAX formula bar where you can write and test your DAX expressions.

When developing calculated columns and measures, it's essential to follow best practices such as using meaningful names, writing efficient code, and commenting on complex calculations.

Naming conventions should be consistent and descriptive to ensure that your DAX objects are easily understandable by yourself and other users.

To create efficient DAX calculations, avoid using expensive functions that require heavy computational resources whenever possible.

Optimize DAX code by using filter context and row context efficiently.

Commenting on complex DAX calculations is essential for documentation and collaboration with team members.

Documentation within the DAX code helps others understand the logic behind your calculations and facilitates troubleshooting.

Data modeling best practices also include managing the size and performance of your data models.

Large datasets can impact report performance and responsiveness.

To address this, you can implement strategies such as data compression, using summarized tables, and filtering data at the source.

In Power BI, data compression techniques are applied automatically to reduce the size of the data model.

However, you can further optimize by using techniques like creating summary tables or aggregating data before importing it into Power BI.

Applying filters at the source, such as using SQL queries to limit the data extracted, can help reduce the volume of data brought into your data model.

Managing data refresh schedules is another critical aspect of Power BI development.

Regularly updating your data ensures that your reports and dashboards reflect the most current information.

In Power BI, you can set up data refresh schedules for datasets published to the Power BI service.

Consider the frequency of data updates and the performance impact on your data source when configuring refresh schedules.

Monitoring and troubleshooting refresh errors is also an important part of data management.

Power BI provides tools and logs to track and diagnose issues related to data refresh.

Effective data modeling and management contribute to improved report and dashboard performance.

However, it's equally crucial to design visually appealing and user-friendly reports.

Power BI offers a wide range of visualization options, including charts, tables, maps, and custom visuals.

When designing reports, consider the principles of data visualization, such as choosing the right type of visualization for your data and ensuring clarity and simplicity.

Use appropriate visualizations that effectively convey the insights you want to communicate.

For example, bar charts are suitable for comparing categories, while line charts are ideal for displaying trends over time.

Custom visuals and custom themes can be used to tailor your reports to your organization's branding and specific requirements.

In Power BI Desktop, you can customize themes and apply them to your reports consistently.

Consistency in design, including color schemes, fonts, and layout, is essential for creating a cohesive and professional look.

Accessibility is a crucial aspect of report development, ensuring that reports are usable by individuals with disabilities.

Follow accessibility guidelines such as WCAG (Web Content Accessibility Guidelines) when designing reports.

Incorporate alternative text for images, ensure readable text contrast, and provide accessible navigation.

Testing reports with screen readers and keyboard navigation is essential to ensure accessibility.

Effective report development also involves organizing and structuring your reports logically.

Use bookmarks and page navigation to create interactive and user-friendly reports.

Bookmarks allow you to capture the current state of a report, including filters, slicer selections, and visuals, and then apply those settings with a single click.

Page navigation can be used to create a guided experience for users, leading them through the report's content.

Consider the user's journey through the report and create a flow that guides them from one section to another.

Additionally, report tooltips and drill-through actions can enhance interactivity and provide additional context for specific data points.

When publishing reports to the Power BI service, consider how users will access and consume the reports.

The Power BI service offers various features for sharing and collaboration, such as workspaces, sharing with specific individuals or groups, and embedding reports in websites or applications.

Choose the appropriate sharing and distribution methods based on your organization's needs and user requirements.

Collaboration in Power BI is facilitated through workspaces, where team members can co-author, review, and collaborate on reports and dashboards.

Use workspaces to organize content and manage permissions effectively.

Furthermore, consider implementing role-level security (RLS) to restrict access to specific data based on user roles.

RLS allows you to define rules that determine which data users can see, ensuring data privacy and security.

When sharing reports externally or embedding them in applications, you can use the Power BI Embedded service or the Power BI API to integrate reports seamlessly.

Power BI offers extensive customization options for embedding reports, including setting up authentication, filtering data, and configuring visual settings.

Lastly, maintaining and managing your Power BI assets is an ongoing best practice.

Regularly review and update your reports and dashboards to reflect changes in data or business requirements.

Use version control systems like Git to track changes and collaborate with team members on report development.

Create documentation and user guides to help users understand how to interact with and interpret the reports.

Monitoring report usage and performance in the Power BI service allows you to identify issues and optimize your reports continually.

In summary, best practices for Power BI development encompass data modeling, DAX calculations, data management, report design, accessibility, interactivity, sharing and collaboration, and ongoing maintenance.

By following these best practices, you can create impactful and user-friendly reports and dashboards that empower users with actionable insights.

BOOK 2
MASTERING POWER BI
ADVANCED TECHNIQUES AND BEST PRACTICES FOR ANALYSTS

ROB BOTWRIGHT

Chapter 1: Advanced Data Transformation and Cleansing

Data profiling and quality assessment are critical steps in the data preparation process that ensure the data used for analysis and reporting is accurate, complete, and reliable.

To begin, data profiling involves the systematic examination of a dataset to gain an understanding of its structure, content, and quality.

In Power BI, you can use the Power Query editor to perform data profiling tasks.

The first step in data profiling is to assess the basic statistics of the dataset, including measures of central tendency and dispersion for numeric columns, and counts of unique values for categorical columns.

You can easily calculate these statistics using the Group By and Aggregate functions in Power Query.

For example, to calculate the average and standard deviation of a numeric column named "Sales," you can use the following CLI command:

mathematicaCopy code

```
= Table.Group(Source, {"Sales"}, {{"Average", each List.Average([Sales]), type number}, {"StdDev", each List.StandardDeviation([Sales]), type number}})
```

Next, data profiling involves identifying missing values within the dataset.

Missing data can significantly impact the accuracy of analysis and reporting.

Power Query provides functions like Table.RowCount and Table.ColumnCount to count the number of missing values in each column.

For instance, to count missing values in a column named "Product Name," you can use the following CLI command:

mathematicaCopy code

```
=       Table.AddColumn(Source,      "MissingValues",      each
Table.RowCount(Table.SelectRows(Source,     each     [Product
Name] = null)))
```

Additionally, data profiling includes identifying duplicates within the dataset.

Duplicate records can lead to inaccuracies in analysis and reporting.

You can use the Table.Distinct function in Power Query to identify and remove duplicates based on one or more columns.

For example, to remove duplicates based on the "Customer ID" column, you can use the following CLI command:

mathematicaCopy code

```
= Table.Distinct(Source, {"Customer ID"})
```

Another critical aspect of data profiling is identifying outlier values within numeric columns.

Outliers can skew statistical measures and affect the robustness of analysis.

Power Query provides functions like Table.Outliers and Table.Quartiles to identify and address outliers.

For instance, to flag values in a numeric column named "Price" that are considered outliers, you can use the following CLI command:

cssCopy code

```
=        Table.AddColumn (Source,        "IsOutlier",        each
List .Contains ( Table.Outliers (Source [Price] ), [Price] ))
```

Data profiling also involves assessing the distribution of values within categorical columns.

Understanding the distribution helps in selecting appropriate visualizations and analyzing the significance of categories.

You can use the Table.Group function in Power Query to calculate counts or percentages of values within categorical columns.

For example, to calculate the count of each unique value in a column named "Category," you can use the following CLI command:

mathematicaCopy code

```
= Table.Group(Source, {"Category"}, {{"Count", each
Table.RowCount(_), type number}})
```
After completing data profiling, the next step is data quality assessment.

Data quality assessment involves evaluating the accuracy, completeness, consistency, and reliability of the dataset.

One common data quality issue is data entry errors, such as typos or inconsistencies in naming conventions.

To address data entry errors, consider using functions like Text.Clean or Text.Replace in Power Query to standardize and clean text data.

For instance, to remove extra spaces and convert text in a column named "City" to uppercase, you can use the following CLI command:

mathematicaCopy code
```
= Table.TransformColumns(Source, {{"City", each
Text.Upper(Text.Trim(_))}})
```
Another data quality issue is data consistency across related columns.

In Power Query, you can use the Table.Join function to combine data from multiple tables and ensure consistency.

For example, if you have a "Products" table and a "Categories" table, you can join them based on the "CategoryID" column to ensure that product category information is consistent.

mathematicaCopy code
```
= Table.Join(Products, "CategoryID", Categories, "CategoryID",
JoinKind.LeftOuter)
```
Handling missing data is crucial for data quality.

One approach is to impute missing values using techniques like mean imputation or regression imputation.

In Power Query, you can use functions like Table.ReplaceValue to replace missing values with calculated values.

For example, to replace missing values in a numeric column named "Revenue" with the mean of the column, you can use the following CLI command:

mathematicaCopy code

```
=                     Table.ReplaceValue(Source,                     null,
List.Average(Source[Revenue]),              Replacer.ReplaceValue,
{"Revenue"})
```

Data validation is an essential component of data quality assessment.

Validating data involves ensuring that values fall within acceptable ranges or adhere to specific rules.

You can use conditional statements in Power Query to create custom validation rules.

For instance, to validate that values in a column named "Age" are between 18 and 100, you can use the following CLI command:

cssCopy code

```
= Table.AddColumn(Source, "IsValidAge", each [Age] >= 18 and
[Age] <= 100)
```

Data profiling and quality assessment also include checking for data consistency with external sources or benchmarks.

You can use Power Query to connect to external data sources and compare your dataset with reference data.

For example, you can use the Web.Contents function to fetch external data, and then use functions like Table.Join to compare it with your dataset.

mathematicaCopy code

```
externalData                                                       =
Web.Contents("https://example.com/reference_data.csv"),
referenceTable  =  Csv.Document(externalData,  [Delimiter=",",
Encoding=65001,   QuoteStyle=QuoteStyle.None]),   mergedTable
=        Table.Join(Source,        {"KeyColumn"},        referenceTable,
{"KeyColumn"}, JoinKind.LeftAnti)
```

In addition to assessing data quality, it's essential to document the data profiling and quality assessment processes.

Documenting these processes helps in maintaining transparency and ensuring that data quality efforts are reproducible.

You can use Power Query to create documentation tables or reports summarizing the results of data profiling and quality assessment.

For instance, you can create a summary table that lists the number of missing values, duplicates, and outliers for each column in your dataset.

Effective data profiling and quality assessment are ongoing processes that require continuous monitoring and improvement.

Regularly update and refine your data profiling and quality assessment techniques to adapt to changing data sources and business needs.

By integrating data profiling and quality assessment into your data preparation workflow, you can enhance the reliability and accuracy of your data-driven decisions and insights.

Combining and transforming data sources is a fundamental aspect of data analysis and reporting, allowing you to create comprehensive datasets that provide deeper insights.

Power BI offers a versatile set of tools and techniques to facilitate the combination and transformation of data from various sources.

One common scenario in data analysis is the need to merge or join data from multiple tables or sources.

Power BI provides an intuitive interface for combining data, making it accessible to both beginners and experienced data professionals.

The Merge Queries feature in Power Query allows you to perform joins between tables using familiar SQL-like operations.

For instance, you can use the Merge Queries option to join a "Sales" table with a "Customers" table based on a common column, such as "Customer ID."

This operation can be accomplished using the following CLI command:

mathematicaCopy code

```
= Table.NestedJoin(Sales, {"Customer ID"}, Customers, {"Customer ID"}, "CustomerDetails", JoinKind.Inner)
```

Once you've merged the data, you can further refine it by applying transformations to columns.

Power Query offers a wide range of transformation functions, including data type conversion, text extraction, and mathematical operations.

For instance, if you need to convert a column from text to a date data type, you can use the Date.FromText function:

mathematicaCopy code

```
=    Table.TransformColumns(MergedTable,    {{"DateColumn",
Date.FromText}})
```

In addition to merging and transforming data, another essential aspect of data preparation is handling missing values.

Missing data can lead to inaccurate analyses and visualizations, so it's crucial to address this issue.

Power BI provides several tools for managing missing data, including the Fill Down and Replace Values functions.

For example, to replace missing values in a column with the previous non-missing value, you can use the Fill Down function:

mathematicaCopy code

```
= Table.FillDown(Source, {"ColumnWithMissingValues"})
```

Power Query also allows you to filter and sort data, which can be valuable for organizing and focusing on relevant information.

You can use the Table.SelectRows function to filter data based on specific criteria.

To sort data in ascending order, you can use the Table.Sort function:

mathematicaCopy code

```
= Table.Sort(FilteredTable,{{"ColumnToSort", Order.Ascending}})
```

In cases where data transformation requires more complex logic, you can use custom functions and expressions.

Power Query supports the creation of custom functions using the M language, which provides flexibility in handling unique data requirements.

Custom functions can be defined using the let statement, allowing you to reuse them across your data transformation process.

For example, you can create a custom function that calculates the average of a column:

javascriptCopy code

```
AverageColumn = (table as table, columnName as text) => let
columnData = Table.Column(table, columnName), average =
List.Average(columnData) in average
```

Once defined, you can use this custom function in your data transformation steps:

scssCopy code

```
= AverageColumn (Source, "NumericColumn")
```

Another powerful feature in Power Query is the ability to pivot and unpivot data.

Pivoting allows you to transform column values into rows, while unpivoting does the opposite.

This capability is especially useful when dealing with datasets where information is stored in a wide format.

To pivot data in Power Query, you can use the Table.Pivot function:

lessCopy code

```
= Table.Pivot (Source, List. Distinct (Source[Category]), "Category", "Value")
```

To unpivot data, you can use the Table.Unpivot function:

mathematicaCopy code

```
= Table.Unpivot(Source, {"Year", "Quarter1", "Quarter2", "Quarter3", "Quarter4"}, "Quarter", "Value")
```

Data transformation often involves creating calculated columns and measures to derive new insights or perform calculations on the data.

Power BI's DAX (Data Analysis Expressions) language provides a powerful set of functions for creating calculated columns and measures.

For instance, you can create a calculated column that calculates the profit margin for each row:

cssCopy code

```
ProfitMargin = [Profit] / [Revenue]
```

Measures are particularly useful for performing aggregations and calculations across multiple rows or tables.

You can create measures to calculate sums, averages, or ratios, and they can be used in visualizations to provide dynamic calculations.

For example, you can create a measure to calculate the total sales:

scssCopy code

TotalSales = SUM (Sales[SalesAmount])

Combining data sources may also involve consolidating data from various files or folders.

Power BI allows you to connect to data stored in folders and automatically combine data from multiple files.

The Folder connector in Power Query simplifies the process by providing options to combine files with similar structures.

You can use the Folder.Files function to connect to a folder and merge the data from all files within that folder:

arduinoCopy code

```
= Folder. Files ("C:\MyFolder")
```

Power BI's ability to connect to a wide range of data sources, including databases, web services, and cloud platforms, makes it a versatile tool for data integration.

For instance, you can connect to a SQL database using the SQL.Database function:

graphqlCopy code

```
= Sql.Database ("ServerName", "DatabaseName", [Query="SELECT * FROM Sales"])
```

Furthermore, Power BI's support for APIs allows you to fetch real-time data from various web services and incorporate it into your analysis.

You can use the Web.Contents function to access web APIs and retrieve JSON or XML data:

arduinoCopy code

```
= Web. Contents ("https://api.example.com/data")
```

Combining and transforming data sources in Power BI is not limited to a single step; it often involves a series of iterative actions to clean, reshape, and enrich the data.

Power Query's query editor provides a visual interface that allows you to see and adjust each transformation step, making it easier to refine your data preparation process.

Additionally, you can create a query dependency chain by referencing other queries, ensuring that changes to one query are automatically reflected in subsequent steps.

In summary, combining and transforming data sources in Power BI is a crucial aspect of data preparation that enables you to create cohesive and insightful datasets for analysis and reporting.

By leveraging Power Query's rich set of functions and features, you can efficiently handle diverse data integration challenges and produce accurate and actionable insights.

Chapter 2: Advanced Data Modeling Strategies

Advanced dimensional modeling is a technique used in data warehousing to create robust and efficient data models that support complex analytical queries.

Dimensional modeling is a data modeling approach that organizes data into facts and dimensions, making it easier for users to retrieve meaningful insights.

In advanced dimensional modeling, the focus is on designing models that can handle intricate business scenarios and evolving data requirements.

One key aspect of advanced dimensional modeling is the design of fact tables and dimension tables.

Fact tables contain measures or metrics, such as sales revenue or quantity sold, and are associated with one or more dimension tables.

Dimension tables store descriptive attributes, such as product names, customer names, or dates, which provide context to the measures in the fact table.

Advanced dimensional modeling involves creating hierarchies within dimension tables to enable more granular or summarized analysis.

Hierarchies allow users to drill down into data or roll it up to different levels of aggregation.

For example, a time dimension table might have hierarchies for year, quarter, month, and day, allowing users to view data at various time granularities.

In advanced dimensional modeling, bridge tables are often used to handle complex relationships between dimensions.

Bridge tables are used when a dimension has a many-to-many relationship with a fact table.

They help resolve these relationships and ensure that queries return accurate results.

Consider a scenario where customers can belong to multiple customer segments.

A bridge table would be used to link customers to segments and capture the relationships accurately.

To create bridge tables, you can use SQL commands to define the relationships and populate the tables.

For example, to create a bridge table linking customers and segments, you can use SQL's CREATE TABLE and INSERT INTO commands.

sqlCopy code

```
CREATE TABLE CustomerSegmentBridge ( CustomerID INT, SegmentID INT ); INSERT INTO CustomerSegmentBridge (CustomerID, SegmentID) VALUES ( 1, 101 ), ( 2, 102 ), ( 3, 101 );
```

In advanced dimensional modeling, slowly changing dimensions (SCDs) are a critical consideration.

SCDs are used to manage changes in dimension attributes over time.

There are different types of SCDs, with Type 1 (overwrite) and Type 2 (add a new row) being the most common.

Type 1 SCDs overwrite existing dimension attributes with new values when changes occur, while Type 2 SCDs add a new row to capture historical changes.

Implementing SCDs requires creating additional columns in dimension tables to track changes and managing the logic for updating or inserting records.

For example, in a Type 2 SCD, you might add columns like "EffectiveDate" and "EndDate" to capture the time period during which a dimension row is valid.

Advanced dimensional modeling also involves considering data lineage and versioning.

Data lineage tracks the source and transformation history of data, helping users understand how data has been processed and derived.

Versioning ensures that historical versions of data are preserved, allowing for auditing and analysis of changes over time.

To implement data lineage, you can create metadata tables that record information about the source, transformations, and outputs of data pipelines.

For versioning, you can use version control systems or implement versioning within your data warehouse.

For instance, you might add a "Version" column to fact tables to track the version of data.

Advanced dimensional modeling often requires dealing with slowly changing facts (SCFs).

SCFs occur when facts change over time, but the changes need to be tracked and analyzed.

An example of SCFs is when historical financial data is restated due to accounting adjustments.

To handle SCFs, you can create additional fact tables to capture historical changes, similar to how Type 2 SCDs are used for dimensions.

These historical fact tables can then be joined with dimension tables to analyze changes over time accurately.

Another advanced dimensional modeling technique is the use of degenerate dimensions.

Degenerate dimensions are attributes that don't belong to a separate dimension table but are stored directly in the fact table.

For example, an invoice number or a transaction ID can be a degenerate dimension.

These attributes provide additional context to facts without the need for a separate dimension table.

In advanced dimensional modeling, it's crucial to consider performance optimization.

Optimizing query performance is essential for handling complex analytical workloads.

You can use techniques like indexing, partitioning, and materialized views to improve query response times.

Indexes can be added to columns that are frequently used in WHERE clauses or join conditions, speeding up data retrieval.

Partitioning involves splitting large fact and dimension tables into smaller, manageable partitions, which can enhance query performance.

Materialized views store precomputed results of common queries, reducing the need for complex calculations during query execution.

To create a materialized view, you can use SQL commands like CREATE MATERIALIZED VIEW.

sqlCopy code

```
CREATE MATERIALIZED VIEW SalesSummary AS SELECT Date,
SUM(SalesAmount) AS TotalSales FROM Sales GROUP BY Date;
```

Furthermore, advanced dimensional modeling often involves the use of advanced data modeling techniques such as star schemas and snowflake schemas.

Star schemas are a denormalized design where fact tables are directly connected to dimension tables.

Snowflake schemas are a normalized design where dimension tables are normalized into sub-dimensions.

The choice between star and snowflake schemas depends on factors like query performance and data maintenance requirements.

Advanced dimensional modeling also extends to data modeling tools and platforms.

Many data modeling tools, including those integrated with data warehouses like Snowflake, offer features for designing and managing advanced dimensional models.

These tools provide graphical interfaces and automation for generating SQL scripts to create and manage tables, relationships, and other aspects of the model.

In summary, advanced dimensional modeling is a complex but essential technique in data warehousing and business intelligence.

It involves designing intricate data models that can handle complex business scenarios, evolving data requirements, and optimize query performance.

By considering hierarchies, bridge tables, slowly changing dimensions, data lineage, versioning, slowly changing facts, degenerate dimensions, and performance optimization techniques, you can create data models that empower users to gain valuable insights from their data.

Handling Slowly Changing Dimensions (SCDs) is a critical aspect of data modeling in data warehousing and business intelligence.

SCDs refer to dimension tables where attributes change over time, and it's essential to manage these changes to maintain data accuracy and historical context.

There are several techniques for handling SCDs, each suited to different scenarios and requirements.

One common approach is to use Type 1 SCDs, where the old value is simply overwritten with the new value when a change occurs.

This method is straightforward and can work well when historical data is not needed.

To implement a Type 1 SCD, you can use SQL commands to update the dimension table with the new values.

For example, to update the "Product" dimension with a new product name for a specific product ID, you can use the following SQL command:

sqlCopy code

```
UPDATE ProductDimension SET ProductName = 'New Product Name' WHERE ProductID = 123;
```

While Type 1 SCDs are simple to implement, they do not preserve historical data, which can be a significant limitation in many scenarios.

When historical data is crucial, Type 2 SCDs are often preferred.

In Type 2 SCDs, a new row is added to the dimension table when an attribute changes, allowing you to track historical values over time.

To implement a Type 2 SCD, you can create a new row in the dimension table with the updated attribute values and assign a new surrogate key to differentiate it from the previous version.

For example, if the "Customer" dimension undergoes a change in the customer's name, you can insert a new row with the updated name and a new surrogate key.

sqlCopy code

```
INSERT INTO CustomerDimension (CustomerID, CustomerName, EffectiveStartDate, EffectiveEndDate) VALUES (456, 'New Customer Name', '2024-01-15', '9999-12-31');
```

To query data using Type 2 SCDs, you typically use the Effective Start Date and Effective End Date columns to filter the most relevant version of a dimension.

Another common technique for handling SCDs is to use Type 3 SCDs.

In Type 3 SCDs, a limited history of changes is maintained by adding columns to the dimension table to store a few historical values.

For example, you can add columns like "Previous Customer Name" and "Previous Customer Address" to the "Customer" dimension to capture the previous values when changes occur.

sqlCopy code

```
UPDATE CustomerDimension SET PreviousCustomerName = CustomerName, CustomerName = 'New Customer Name', PreviousCustomerAddress = CustomerAddress, CustomerAddress = 'New Customer Address' WHERE CustomerID = 789;
```

Type 3 SCDs are suitable when you need to keep a concise history of changes without creating an extensive historical record.

A more complex approach to handling SCDs is Type 4, also known as a "mini-dimension" or "snapshot" dimension.

In Type 4 SCDs, a separate table is created to store historical changes, while the primary dimension table remains relatively static.

The historical table contains a foreign key reference to the primary dimension table and captures the changes over time.

This method allows for efficient storage of historical data while keeping the primary dimension table relatively small.

Implementing Type 4 SCDs involves creating and maintaining the historical table and defining relationships between the tables.

Another technique is Type 6 SCDs, which combine elements of both Type 1 and Type 2 SCDs.

In Type 6 SCDs, you maintain the current value of an attribute in the dimension table (Type 1), but you also add a Type 2 history table to capture changes.

This approach provides flexibility in querying current and historical data, but it can be more complex to implement and maintain.

Handling SCDs often involves not only updating the dimension tables but also ensuring that the foreign key references in fact tables are correctly linked to the changing dimensions.

For example, if a customer's name changes in the "Customer" dimension, the corresponding foreign key references in fact tables must be updated to point to the correct version of the customer.

This updating process ensures that historical data in fact tables aligns with the changes in dimension tables.

To update foreign key references, you can use SQL commands to match the surrogate keys of dimensions with the corresponding foreign keys in fact tables.

In some cases, automated ETL (Extract, Transform, Load) processes or data integration tools are used to manage the updating of foreign key references.

Managing SCDs requires careful planning and consideration of the specific business requirements.

You should decide which SCD type best suits your needs, taking into account factors like data volume, query performance, and historical data retention.

Additionally, it's essential to establish data governance practices to maintain the integrity and accuracy of SCD handling.

This includes documenting SCD policies, managing versioning, and defining ownership and responsibilities for SCD maintenance.

Handling SCDs effectively can significantly enhance the quality and historical context of your data, providing valuable insights for analysis and reporting.

It's crucial to regularly review and update your SCD handling strategies to adapt to changing business needs and evolving data requirements.

By implementing the appropriate SCD techniques and maintaining data quality, you can ensure that your data remains a reliable foundation for decision-making in your organization.

Chapter 3: Leveraging DAX Functions for Complex Calculations

Mastering Time Intelligence Functions is essential for leveraging the full power of data analysis and reporting, especially when dealing with temporal data.

Time intelligence functions in SQL and BI tools like Power BI allow you to perform dynamic calculations and comparisons based on date and time attributes.

One fundamental aspect of time intelligence functions is the ability to create time-based calculations that adapt to the context of your data.

For instance, you can calculate year-to-date, month-to-date, or quarter-to-date values dynamically, regardless of the specific date range selected in your reports.

To create year-to-date calculations in Power BI, you can use the DATESYTD function, which calculates the sum of a measure up to the current year's end.

javascriptCopy code

```
YearToDateSales         =         DATESYTD ( 'Date' [ Date ],
'Sales' [ SalesAmount ])
```

Another crucial concept in mastering time intelligence functions is understanding the importance of a date table.

A date table is a dedicated dimension table that stores a continuous sequence of dates, allowing you to establish relationships with other fact and dimension tables.

Date tables are essential for time intelligence functions to work effectively, as they provide the necessary context for date-based calculations.

You can create a date table in Power BI by using the "Enter Data" or "Import" options and populating it with a range of dates.

Once you have a date table, you can create relationships between it and other tables in your data model.

This relationship enables you to perform time-based calculations that align with the date selections made in your reports.

Time intelligence functions also allow you to calculate moving averages, cumulative totals, and running totals over time.

For example, to calculate a 3-month moving average of sales, you can use the AVERAGEX function with the DATESINPERIOD function:

sqlCopy code

```
3MonthMovingAverage = AVERAGEX(
DATESINPERIOD('Date'[Date], LASTDATE('Date'[Date]), -3,
MONTH), 'Sales'[SalesAmount] )
```

This calculation considers the context of the last 3 months, adapting to the selected date range in your report.

Time intelligence functions are particularly valuable when analyzing data trends and patterns over time.

They enable you to compare data from different periods easily and identify seasonality, growth, or decline in your metrics.

Moreover, mastering time intelligence functions allows you to perform advanced calculations like year-over-year comparisons.

For instance, to calculate year-over-year sales growth, you can use the SAMEPERIODLASTYEAR function:

lessCopy code

```
YearOverYearGrowth = DIVIDE( SUM('Sales'[SalesAmount]),
CALCULATE( SUM('Sales'[SalesAmount]),
SAMEPERIODLASTYEAR('Date'[Date]) ) - 1 )
```

This calculation compares the current period's sales to the corresponding period in the previous year, adjusting for seasonality.

Time intelligence functions also enable you to perform complex time-based filtering and grouping.

You can use functions like TOTALYTD to calculate year-to-date totals, and TOTALQTD to calculate quarter-to-date totals.

sqlCopy code

```
YearToDateTotal = TOTALYTD(SUM('Sales'[SalesAmount]),
'Date'[Date]) QuarterToDateTotal =
TOTALQTD(SUM('Sales'[SalesAmount]), 'Date'[Date])
```

These functions consider the date context and provide accurate totals for the specified time periods.

Furthermore, time intelligence functions can be used for advanced forecasting and predictive modeling.

You can leverage functions like PERCENTILEX.INC and QUARTILE.INC to calculate percentiles for time series data.

For example, to calculate the 75th percentile of monthly sales, you can use the following formula:

```sql
sqlCopy code
75thPercentileSales                =                PERCENTILEX.INC(
VALUES('Date'[Month]), SUM('Sales'[SalesAmount]), 0.75 )
```

This calculation helps you identify outliers and distribution patterns in your data.

In addition to Power BI, time intelligence functions are available in various SQL-based BI tools and database management systems.

For instance, in SQL Server Analysis Services (SSAS), you can use MDX (Multidimensional Expressions) for time-based calculations.

To create a time-based calculation in SSAS, you can define a calculated member or measure using MDX syntax.

For example, to calculate the year-to-date total of a measure in SSAS, you can use the YTD function:

```css
cssCopy code
CREATE MEMBER CURRENTCUBE.[Measures].[YearToDateSales]
AS    YTD([Measures].[Sales    Amount]),    FORMAT_STRING    =
"#,##0.00";
```

This MDX calculation mirrors the DATESYTD function in Power BI.

In summary, mastering time intelligence functions is crucial for performing dynamic and insightful data analysis and reporting.

These functions empower you to create flexible time-based calculations, perform trend analysis, and make informed decisions based on temporal data.

Whether you're using Power BI, SQL Server Analysis Services, or other BI tools, understanding and applying time intelligence functions will enhance your ability to extract valuable insights from your data.

Advanced measures and aggregations are essential components of data analysis and reporting, enabling you to extract deeper insights from your data.

Measures in BI tools like Power BI and SQL-based systems are calculations that perform various operations on your data, such as summing, averaging, or counting.

While basic measures are useful, advanced measures take your data analysis to the next level by incorporating complex calculations and logic.

To create advanced measures, you can use DAX (Data Analysis Expressions) in Power BI, MDX (Multidimensional Expressions) in SQL Server Analysis Services (SSAS), or SQL commands in database management systems.

One common use case for advanced measures is calculating growth rates and percentages.

For instance, you can create a measure that calculates the month-over-month growth of sales:

mathematicaCopy code

```
MoM Sales Growth = DIVIDE( [Total Sales] - CALCULATE([Total Sales], PREVIOUSMONTH('Date'[Date])), CALCULATE([Total Sales], PREVIOUSMONTH('Date'[Date])) )
```

This measure subtracts the previous month's sales from the current month's sales and divides it by the previous month's sales to calculate the growth rate.

Advanced measures also enable you to perform advanced statistical calculations.

You can create measures to calculate standard deviations, variance, or correlation coefficients to analyze the variability and relationships in your data.

For example, to calculate the standard deviation of sales amounts, you can use the STDEV.P function in DAX:

javaCopy code

```
Standard Deviation Sales = STDEV.P('Sales'[Sales Amount])
```

This measure provides insights into the spread or dispersion of your sales data.

Another valuable application of advanced measures is calculating cumulative and running totals.

You can create measures to calculate cumulative sums, averages, or other aggregations over time or across categories.

For example, to calculate the cumulative sum of sales amounts, you can use the SUMX function with the FILTER function in DAX:

sqlCopy code

Cumulative Sales = SUMX(FILTER (ALL('Date'), 'Date'[Date] <= MAX('Date'[Date])), 'Sales'[Sales Amount])

This measure calculates the cumulative sum of sales amounts up to the maximum date selected in your report.

Advanced measures also play a crucial role in calculating complex financial metrics.

You can create measures to calculate metrics like Net Present Value (NPV), Internal Rate of Return (IRR), or Return on Investment (ROI).

For example, to calculate NPV, you can use the NPV function in DAX:

cssCopy code

Net Present Value = NPV(0.1, 'Cash Flow'[Cash Amount])

This measure calculates the present value of future cash flows with a discount rate of 10%.

Furthermore, advanced measures enable you to implement dynamic ranking and top N analysis.

You can create measures to rank items based on a measure's value or calculate the top N items in a category.

For example, to rank products by sales amount, you can use the RANKX function in DAX:

mathematicaCopy code

Product Sales Rank = RANKX(ALL('Product'), [Total Sales], , DESC, DENSE)

This measure ranks products by total sales in descending order with dense ranking.

Advanced measures are also valuable for implementing advanced time-based calculations.

You can create measures to calculate moving averages, rolling sums, and other time-dependent metrics.

For example, to calculate a 3-month rolling average of sales, you can use the AVERAGEX function with the DATESINPERIOD function in DAX:

sqlCopy code

3-Month Rolling Average = AVERAGEX(DATESINPERIOD('Date'[Date], MAX('Date'[Date]), -3, MONTH), [Total Sales])

This measure calculates the average sales amount over the last 3 months dynamically based on the selected date context.

In addition to advanced measures, aggregations are essential for optimizing query performance in large datasets.

Aggregations allow you to pre-calculate and store summarized data at different levels of granularity.

For instance, you can create aggregations for daily, monthly, and yearly data to improve query response times.

To define aggregations in Power BI, you can use the Power BI Desktop or the Power BI Service.

First, you need to create a dataset in Power BI Desktop and then configure aggregations in the Power BI Service.

You can choose which tables and columns to aggregate and specify aggregation functions like sum, average, or count.

Once aggregations are defined, Power BI will automatically use them to accelerate query execution when appropriate.

For example, if you have a large sales dataset and defined aggregations for monthly totals, queries requesting monthly sales will use the pre-calculated monthly aggregations, improving performance.

In SQL-based systems like SQL Server Analysis Services (SSAS), you can define aggregations in multidimensional models.

You can use SSAS Management Studio or define aggregations programmatically using XMLA scripts.

Aggregations in SSAS involve specifying measures, attributes, and levels for aggregation design.

Optimizing aggregations requires balancing query performance gains with storage space requirements.

Aggregations can significantly reduce query response times, especially for complex queries and large datasets.

However, they require additional storage space to store pre-computed aggregations, and maintaining aggregations involves processing and refreshing them when underlying data changes.

In summary, advanced measures and aggregations are powerful tools for data analysis and reporting.

They allow you to perform complex calculations, analyze trends, and optimize query performance.

Whether you're using BI tools like Power BI or SQL-based systems like SSAS, mastering advanced measures and aggregations will enhance your ability to extract valuable insights from your data and deliver faster query performance to end-users.

Chapter 4: Advanced Visualization Techniques

Customizing visual themes and styles is a crucial aspect of data visualization and reporting, as it allows you to tailor the look and feel of your visuals to match your organization's branding and convey information effectively.

Themes and styles encompass various elements such as colors, fonts, backgrounds, and layouts that collectively define the visual identity of your reports.

In BI tools like Power BI, customizing themes and styles can be achieved through a combination of built-in features, custom CSS (Cascading Style Sheets), and custom themes.

One of the fundamental aspects of visual customization is selecting an appropriate color scheme.

Colors play a significant role in conveying meaning and highlighting key data points, and choosing the right colors can enhance the overall readability of your reports.

Power BI provides a range of built-in color themes, and you can also create custom color palettes to match your organization's branding.

To apply a color theme in Power BI, you can navigate to the "View" tab, select "Themes," and choose from the available themes or import a custom theme file.

Custom themes are JSON files that define colors, fonts, and other styling elements, allowing you to achieve precise control over the visual appearance of your reports.

You can use tools like the Power BI Theme Generator to create custom themes or manually edit the JSON file to define your theme.

Customizing fonts is another essential aspect of visual styling.

Fonts affect readability and the overall look of your reports, and you can choose fonts that align with your organization's design guidelines.

In Power BI, you can set the default font for your report by going to "File" > "Options and settings" > "Options" > "Report settings" and specifying the font under "Default text box font family."

Moreover, you can use custom themes to define font families and sizes for various report elements, such as titles, axis labels, and data labels.

Backgrounds and layouts are elements that influence the overall visual appeal and organization of your reports.

You can customize backgrounds by setting colors, images, or patterns for report pages, visuals, and individual elements like cards and buttons.

Power BI allows you to set background colors for visuals and report pages by selecting the desired color from the formatting options.

For more advanced background customization, you can use custom themes to define background colors and images for different report elements.

Layout customization involves arranging visuals, text boxes, and other elements in a way that effectively communicates the information.

You can control the layout by resizing and positioning visuals, adjusting margins, and using gridlines and snap-to-grid options for precise alignment.

Power BI's built-in layout tools and gridlines make it easier to create consistent and visually appealing reports.

Furthermore, you can use custom themes to define layout-related properties, such as padding and spacing, to ensure a cohesive look and feel throughout your reports.

Customizing styles extends beyond individual visuals and elements to encompass the overall report design.

You can create a cohesive and professional look by defining consistent styles for titles, headers, footers, and other report components.

Power BI's formatting options allow you to customize font styles, text sizes, colors, and alignments for these components.

To create a custom report style, you can format a text box or shape as desired and then use the "Format Painter" tool to apply the style to other report elements.

Additionally, custom themes can include style definitions to ensure uniformity in report components and streamline the styling process.

It's important to consider accessibility when customizing visual themes and styles.

Accessibility ensures that your reports are usable by individuals with disabilities, and it's a fundamental aspect of creating inclusive and compliant reports.

Power BI provides features and guidelines for creating accessible reports, including support for high contrast mode and alt text for visuals.

When customizing themes and styles, it's essential to test your reports for accessibility and make adjustments as needed to ensure they meet accessibility standards.

Moreover, responsive design is a critical consideration in today's multi-device and multi-screen environment.

Customizing visual themes and styles should include optimizing your reports for different screen sizes and orientations.

Power BI's responsive layout options allow you to design reports that adapt to various devices, ensuring a consistent user experience.

You can use the "Phone layout" and "Tablet layout" views to customize the report layout for specific devices.

When it comes to customizing visuals themselves, you have a wide range of options to fine-tune their appearance.

In Power BI, each visual offers numerous formatting options, such as colors, fonts, labels, legends, and data labels.

You can access these formatting options by selecting a visual and navigating to the "Format" pane.

Additionally, you can use custom themes to define default formatting settings for visuals, ensuring a consistent look and feel across your reports.

When customizing visuals, it's essential to maintain a balance between aesthetics and readability.

While it's tempting to apply flashy styles and effects, they should not compromise the clarity and comprehensibility of the data.

Avoid clutter and excessive ornamentation, as they can distract from the message you intend to convey.

Instead, focus on using visuals that effectively communicate the data and support the narrative of your reports.

Moreover, customizing visual themes and styles should align with the principles of data visualization best practices.

Consider factors like color theory, gestalt principles, and information hierarchy when designing your reports.

Color choices should facilitate data interpretation, and the layout should guide the viewer's attention to the most critical information.

Furthermore, customizing visual themes and styles should evolve with your reporting needs and feedback from your audience.

Regularly review and update your themes and styles to ensure they remain relevant and effective.

Solicit feedback from report users to identify areas where customization can enhance their experience and comprehension.

In summary, customizing visual themes and styles is a critical aspect of data visualization and reporting.

It allows you to create visually appealing, accessible, and effective reports that align with your organization's branding and communication goals.

Whether you're using BI tools like Power BI or other reporting platforms, mastering the art of customization will empower you to convey data-driven insights in a compelling and engaging manner.

Advanced drill-through and cross-filtering techniques are pivotal for exploring data at a deeper level and gaining more precise insights from your reports.

Drill-through actions in BI tools such as Power BI allow you to create interactions that enable users to navigate from a summary view to detailed information, providing a richer context for their analysis.

Cross-filtering, on the other hand, lets you control how filters applied to one visual affect other visuals on the same report page, ensuring that data remains synchronized and relevant.

One essential aspect of advanced drill-through is customizing drill-through pages to display specific details.

To implement this in Power BI, you can create drill-through pages by right-clicking on a visual and selecting "Create drill-through." Then, you can design the drill-through page to show the desired details and link it to the summary visual.

For instance, you can create a drill-through page that displays a detailed table when users drill through a summary chart displaying sales data.

cssCopy code

1. Right-click on the chart visual. 2. Select "Create drill-through." 3. Design the drill-through page to include a table with detailed sales data. 4. Link the drill-through page to the summary chart.

Customizing drill-through pages empowers you to tailor the information presented to users when they explore data in more depth.

Moreover, advanced drill-through actions can be parameterized, allowing you to pass context-aware values from the summary to the drill-through page.

This feature is invaluable for dynamically filtering the details displayed on the drill-through page based on the user's selection.

To parameterize a drill-through action in Power BI, you can use the "Edit interactions" feature and specify which visual interactions pass filters to the drill-through page.

For instance, you can pass the selected product category from a summary visual to a drill-through page displaying details for that specific category.

cssCopy code

1. Create a drill-through page that filters data based on the selected product category. 2. Use the "Edit interactions" feature to specify that the summary visual filters the drill-through page by the product category. 3. When users drill through a category

in the summary visual, the drill-through page displays details only for that category.

Parameterized drill-through actions enhance the user experience by providing contextually relevant information and reducing the need for manual filtering.

In addition to custom drill-through actions, advanced cross-filtering techniques allow you to control how filters propagate between visuals on a report page.

You can use cross-filtering to establish specific filter directions and filter types, ensuring that data interactions behave as intended.

In Power BI, you can adjust cross-filtering settings by selecting a visual, navigating to the "Format" pane, and accessing the "Filter options" section.

For example, you can configure a visual to cross-filter other visuals in both directions, ensuring that selections made in one visual affect the others and vice versa.

vbnetCopy code

1. Select the visual for which you want to configure cross-filtering. 2. Go to the "Format" pane. 3. In the "Filter options" section, adjust the filter direction to "Both." 4. This setting allows filters to propagate in both directions between the selected visual and others on the report page.

Moreover, advanced cross-filtering techniques include setting up custom filter interactions between visuals.

This involves defining which visuals should filter others and which should not, providing granular control over data interactions.

For example, you can configure a slicer visual to filter specific visuals while leaving others unaffected.

vbnetCopy code

1. Select the slicer visual you want to customize. 2. In the "Format" pane, access the "Filter options" section. 3. Choose "Selected visuals" and specify which visuals the slicer should filter. 4. This allows you to create custom filter interactions tailored to your reporting needs.

Furthermore, cross-filtering can be combined with drill-through actions to create comprehensive data exploration experiences.

Users can drill through a summary visual to a detailed page while maintaining synchronized filters across visuals, ensuring that the drill-through page displays contextually relevant information.

To implement this in Power BI, you can design your summary visual with drill-through actions and configure cross-filtering settings as needed.

cssCopy code

1. Create a summary visual with drill-through actions. 2. Configure cross-filtering settings for the summary visual and other visuals on the same report page. 3. Users can drill through the summary visual to the detailed page while preserving synchronized filters for a seamless data exploration experience.

It's important to consider performance implications when working with advanced drill-through and cross-filtering techniques, especially in large datasets.

Excessive cross-filtering and complex interactions can impact query performance and user experience.

To mitigate performance issues, you can optimize data models, use aggregations, and leverage features like query folding in Power BI.

Additionally, monitoring and performance tuning are essential to ensure that reports remain responsive and provide a smooth user experience.

In summary, advanced drill-through and cross-filtering techniques are powerful tools for data exploration and analysis in BI reporting.

Customizing drill-through pages, parameterizing actions, and configuring cross-filtering settings enhance the depth and precision of insights that can be derived from your reports.

By mastering these techniques, you can create interactive and context-aware reports that empower users to uncover valuable information within their data.

Chapter 5: Interactivity and Customization in Power BI

Advanced interaction between visuals is a crucial aspect of creating dynamic and informative reports that empower users to explore data comprehensively.

In BI tools like Power BI, you can implement various techniques to enable interactions among visuals, allowing users to gain deeper insights and uncover patterns within their data.

One fundamental method for enhancing interaction between visuals is through cross-highlighting and cross-filtering.

Cross-highlighting involves selecting data points in one visual to highlight relevant data in other visuals, helping users focus on specific aspects of their analysis.

To enable cross-highlighting in Power BI, you can select a data point in one visual, and other visuals on the same report page will automatically highlight the corresponding data points.

This provides users with a dynamic and interactive way to explore data relationships.

Another interaction technique is cross-filtering, which allows users to filter data in one visual and have that filter applied to other visuals on the report page.

For example, if you have a scatter plot displaying sales data by region, users can select a specific region, and other visuals, such as a bar chart or table, will display data only for that selected region.

To implement cross-filtering in Power BI, you can configure filter interactions between visuals, ensuring that filters applied to one visual affect others.

These techniques significantly enhance users' ability to dissect data and derive insights by interactively exploring relationships and dependencies.

Moreover, advanced interactions between visuals can involve complex scenarios like drill-through actions.

Drill-through actions allow users to navigate from a summary view to a detailed view of data, providing a more comprehensive context for analysis.

In Power BI, you can create drill-through actions by defining which fields and visuals are used for drilling through to detailed pages.

For instance, if you have a summary visual displaying sales data by product category, users can drill through to a detailed page showing sales by product name within the selected category.

Creating drill-through actions adds depth to your reports, enabling users to explore data hierarchies and gain granular insights.

Custom interactions between visuals can also be implemented through custom visuals and extensions.

Power BI allows developers to create custom visuals or use third-party custom visuals that offer unique interaction capabilities.

For example, you can integrate custom visuals that provide interactive features like filtering, zooming, or highlighting specific data points based on user interactions.

To use custom visuals, you can import them into your Power BI report and configure their behavior to meet your specific interaction requirements.

Additionally, advanced interactions can leverage features like bookmarks and buttons in Power BI.

Bookmarks enable you to capture and save the current state of a report, including filter selections and visual interactions.

Users can then navigate between different report states using buttons or links, allowing for guided exploration and storytelling.

By combining bookmarks with buttons, you can create interactive narratives within your reports, helping users follow a predefined path or sequence of analysis.

Furthermore, advanced interactions extend to the use of external tools and applications.

Power BI supports embedding reports and visuals into other applications, websites, or portals, enabling users to interact with data outside of the Power BI environment.

To embed Power BI reports, you can use the Power BI Embedded service or Power BI APIs to integrate reports into your custom applications.

This allows users to access and interact with your reports seamlessly within the context of their workflows.

Moreover, Power BI supports integration with tools like Microsoft Teams, SharePoint, and Azure services, expanding the range of interactive possibilities and collaboration.

When implementing advanced interactions between visuals, it's essential to consider performance and usability.

Complex interactions and extensive use of visuals can impact report performance, especially with large datasets.

To optimize performance, you can use techniques such as aggregations, query optimizations, and data modeling best practices.

Additionally, it's crucial to ensure that interactions remain intuitive and user-friendly.

Testing and user feedback play a vital role in refining interactions to meet users' needs and expectations.

In summary, advanced interaction between visuals is a fundamental aspect of creating dynamic and insightful reports in BI tools like Power BI.

Cross-highlighting, cross-filtering, drill-through actions, custom visuals, bookmarks, and external integrations all contribute to a richer and more interactive user experience.

By leveraging these techniques and considering performance and usability, you can empower users to explore data, uncover patterns, and make informed decisions within their reports.

Creating custom interactivity with bookmarks is an advanced technique that allows you to enhance user experiences within your Power BI reports.

Bookmarks in Power BI are a feature that enables you to capture and save specific report states, including filter selections, visuals, and interactions.

By leveraging bookmarks creatively, you can build custom interactions that guide users through your reports, provide storytelling narratives, and facilitate data exploration.

One way to use bookmarks for custom interactivity is by creating interactive narratives within your reports.

This involves capturing different report states as bookmarks and using buttons or links to navigate between those states.

For example, you can create a series of bookmarks that represent different chapters or sections of your report, each with its own set of visuals and filter selections.

Then, by adding buttons or links, users can click through these bookmarks, effectively following a predefined path of analysis.

To create a bookmark in Power BI, you can go to the "View" tab, select "Bookmarks," and click on "Add." This allows you to capture the current state of the report.

Furthermore, you can specify which visuals and filters are included in the bookmark, giving you control over the content and focus of each narrative section.

Once you've created bookmarks, you can add buttons or links to your report by using shapes or images. By configuring these buttons to go to specific bookmarks, you enable users to interactively navigate the report.

For instance, you can add a "Next" button that takes users to the next bookmarked section, creating a seamless storytelling experience.

In addition to interactive narratives, bookmarks can be used to build guided tours or tutorials within your reports.

You can create a series of bookmarks that highlight specific features, showcase best practices, or explain complex concepts to users.

By providing a step-by-step tour, you can ensure that users fully leverage the capabilities of your report and gain a deeper understanding of the data.

To implement this, you can add buttons or links labeled with instructions like "Start Tour" or "Learn More." When users click on these elements, they are taken to the corresponding bookmarks, where they receive guided information.

Moreover, bookmarks can be employed to simulate the behavior of custom visuals and user-driven interactions.

If you have specific requirements that cannot be met with built-in Power BI visuals, you can use bookmarks to create the illusion of custom interactivity.

For instance, you can capture multiple report states with bookmarks, each representing a variation of a custom visual or interaction.

By toggling between these bookmarks using buttons or links, users can experience the desired interactivity within the report.

This approach allows you to tailor the report's behavior to your specific needs without extensive development efforts.

Another way to leverage bookmarks for custom interactivity is by combining them with the "Selection Pane."

The Selection Pane in Power BI allows you to control the visibility and order of visuals on a report page.

By associating bookmarks with specific Selection Pane settings, you can create dynamic content that appears or disappears based on user interactions.

For instance, you can have a bookmark that hides certain visuals and another bookmark that shows them. By triggering these bookmarks with buttons or links, users can toggle between different views of the report.

To adjust the Selection Pane settings, you can go to the "View" tab, select "Selection Pane," and organize the visibility and order of visuals as needed.

Additionally, bookmarks can be utilized to build drill-through actions that go beyond standard functionality.

While Power BI offers native drill-through actions, bookmarks allow you to create more customized and context-aware drill-through experiences.

You can use bookmarks to capture the drill-through state, including filter selections and visual contexts, and then trigger these bookmarks using buttons or links.

This approach enables you to control the drill-through behavior and provide users with more specific and tailored information.

To implement this, you can create a bookmark for each drill-through scenario you want to offer and configure buttons or links to activate the corresponding bookmarks.

Furthermore, bookmarks can be employed to create custom tooltips with additional information.

Tooltips in Power BI are typically associated with visuals and display details when users hover over data points.

However, by using bookmarks, you can design custom tooltips that appear when users click on specific visuals or elements within the report.

This allows you to provide in-depth explanations, related insights, or additional context for specific data points.

To create custom tooltips, you can design a separate report page with the desired information and then capture it as a bookmark. When users click on the visuals or elements you want to trigger the tooltip, you can use buttons or links to take them to the bookmarked page.

In summary, creating custom interactivity with bookmarks in Power BI offers endless possibilities for enhancing user experiences and storytelling within your reports.

Whether you're building interactive narratives, guided tours, custom visual simulations, dynamic content toggles, or context-aware drill-through actions, bookmarks provide the flexibility and control to implement these advanced techniques.

By mastering the use of bookmarks creatively, you can engage users more effectively, guide their exploration of data, and deliver compelling insights through your Power BI reports.

Chapter 6: Optimizing Performance and Data Refresh

Performance tuning and optimization techniques are critical for ensuring that your Power BI reports and dashboards deliver fast and responsive experiences to users.

Next, we will explore various strategies and best practices to optimize the performance of your Power BI solutions.

One fundamental aspect of performance tuning is data modeling.

Efficient data modeling involves designing your data structures in a way that minimizes query complexity and optimizes data retrieval.

To start, you should carefully consider your data sources and their structures.

Choose data sources that are well-suited for your reporting needs, and where possible, pre-process or transform the data before importing it into Power BI.

For example, you can use SQL Server Integration Services (SSIS) or Azure Data Factory to perform data transformations before loading data into Power BI.

Once the data is in Power BI, you should create a robust data model.

This includes defining relationships between tables, setting appropriate data types, and specifying data formatting.

Properly defining relationships is crucial, as it impacts how tables are joined and how efficiently data is retrieved.

You can use Power BI's diagram view to visualize and manage relationships between tables.

Furthermore, data modeling involves creating calculated columns and measures.

Calculated columns are useful for pre-computing values that are frequently used in calculations, reducing the need for complex real-time calculations.

Measures, on the other hand, are calculated on the fly and can be used for aggregations and calculations in visuals.

Optimizing your DAX (Data Analysis Expressions) measures is essential for performance.

Avoid using complex DAX expressions that involve heavy calculations or multiple iterations over large datasets.

Instead, strive for simplicity and efficiency in your DAX measures.

For example, use the SUMX or AVERAGEX functions sparingly, and consider using simpler aggregation functions like SUM, AVERAGE, or COUNT where appropriate.

Additionally, you can improve query performance by implementing query folding.

Query folding is a technique where Power BI pushes some of the data transformation operations back to the data source rather than performing them within Power BI.

This reduces the amount of data transferred from the source to Power BI and can significantly improve query performance.

To enable query folding, you should use Power Query (M language) in Power BI to perform data transformations.

When you design your data transformation steps in Power Query, Power BI will attempt to fold those steps back to the data source when executing queries.

To check if query folding is happening, you can use the Power Query Query Diagnostics feature to analyze query execution.

Furthermore, performance optimization can be achieved by using data summarization techniques.

Aggregating data and creating summary tables can significantly speed up query performance, especially when dealing with large datasets.

Consider creating summary tables that store pre-aggregated data for common reporting scenarios.

For instance, if you have a fact table with detailed sales data, you can create a summary table that stores total sales by product, region, and time period.

By using summary tables in your reports, you can avoid complex real-time aggregations and reduce query times.

To create summary tables, you can use Power Query to perform data summarization and then load the summarized data into Power BI.

In addition to data modeling and summarization, optimizing visuals is another crucial aspect of performance tuning.

Efficient visuals are essential for responsive report rendering and interactive user experiences.

One key practice is limiting the number of visuals on a single report page.

Each visual on a page consumes computational resources, and having too many visuals can slow down report rendering and responsiveness.

Consider using tabs or bookmarks to organize content if you have a large number of visuals to display.

Additionally, you should be mindful of the data volume displayed in visuals.

Avoid displaying excessively large datasets in visuals, as this can lead to slower rendering and reduced interactivity.

Use filtering, slicing, or summary visuals to present relevant subsets of data to users.

For example, you can use slicers to allow users to filter data interactively and focus on specific aspects of the report.

Furthermore, pay attention to visual design and formatting.

Complex visual designs with multiple layers, custom backgrounds, and intricate formatting can impact rendering performance.

Simplify visual designs where possible to ensure faster rendering times.

Optimizing visuals also involves using native Power BI visuals whenever suitable.

While custom visuals offer flexibility, they may not always perform as efficiently as native visuals.

Evaluate whether your reporting requirements can be met with built-in visuals before opting for custom visuals.

Another important consideration is the use of calculated tables and columns for enhanced insights.

Calculated tables and columns can be powerful for improving report performance by pre-computing and storing data.

You can use calculated tables to create summary tables or perform data transformations.

For instance, you can create a calculated table that stores unique values or hierarchies to speed up filter operations.

Calculated columns, on the other hand, can be used to store pre-computed values that reduce the need for complex calculations during query execution.

Be strategic in defining calculated tables and columns to address specific performance bottlenecks in your reports.

Furthermore, optimizing the data refresh process is crucial for maintaining report performance.

Scheduled data refresh in Power BI can be resource-intensive, especially for reports with large datasets.

To optimize data refresh, consider the following practices:

Incremental data loading: Whenever possible, load only new or changed data to reduce the amount of data refreshed.

Use query folding: As mentioned earlier, use Power Query to perform data transformations and enable query folding to reduce data transfer.

Data source optimizations: Tune your data source for efficient data extraction, and utilize database indexing and partitioning where applicable.

Compression and storage: Optimize data storage by using compression techniques to reduce data size.

Scheduled refresh timing: Schedule data refresh during periods of lower usage to minimize the impact on report performance.

Additionally, you can monitor and analyze data refresh performance using Power BI's built-in tools and logs to identify areas for improvement.

Another technique for performance optimization is data reduction through filtering and aggregation.

Consider applying filters to visuals and using aggregation functions to reduce the volume of data retrieved from the data source.

Filtering and aggregation can significantly improve query performance, especially when dealing with large datasets.

Furthermore, parameterization of queries can be a valuable optimization technique.

Parameters allow you to make your queries dynamic by enabling users to select filter criteria or input values when refreshing data or running reports.

By parameterizing queries, you can reuse query logic for different scenarios and improve report performance by eliminating the need for redundant queries.

To implement parameterization, you can define query parameters in Power Query and use them in your query expressions.

Additionally, parameterization can be combined with dynamic security to control data access based on user roles and filters.

Dynamic security allows you to restrict access to data at the row or column level, ensuring that users only see the data relevant to their roles and permissions.

By implementing dynamic security, you can enhance both data security and report performance.

To apply dynamic security, you can create role-based security rules in Power BI Desktop and define row-level filters based on user roles.

Furthermore, performance optimization should include considerations for data caching and data reduction techniques.

Caching involves storing query results or aggregated data in memory to reduce query execution times.

Power BI provides options for query caching, summary table caching, and calculated table caching, which can be configured based on your specific performance requirements.

Data reduction techniques, such as using drill-through or drill-down interactions, enable users to access detailed data only when necessary.

By providing the option to drill into data, you can strike a balance between performance and detailed data exploration.

Additionally, evaluating and optimizing visuals that heavily rely on custom visuals or complex DAX expressions is essential.

These visuals may require more processing power and can slow down report rendering.

Consider simplifying these visuals or using native visuals to improve report responsiveness.

Moreover, performance optimization should include considerations for report distribution and sharing.

When distributing reports, choose appropriate distribution methods to minimize data transfer and maximize user access.

Options such as Power BI Premium, Power BI Publish to Web, and Power BI Embedded offer different approaches for sharing reports with various user groups and scenarios.

For large-scale deployments or when dealing with large datasets, Power BI Premium offers dedicated capacity and better performance options.

Alternatively, Power BI Embedded allows embedding reports within custom applications, offering scalability and customization.

Additionally, leveraging Power BI REST APIs and embedding reports into custom applications can enhance report distribution and performance for specific use cases.

To sum it up, performance tuning and optimization in Power BI encompass various strategies and best practices, including efficient data modeling, DAX optimization, data summarization, query folding, visual design, and data refresh optimization.

By applying these techniques and continually monitoring and fine-tuning your Power BI solutions, you can ensure that your reports and dashboards deliver fast, responsive, and efficient experiences to users, enabling them to make data-driven decisions effectively.

Scheduling and monitoring data refresh is a critical aspect of maintaining the accuracy and reliability of your Power BI reports and dashboards.

Regular data refresh ensures that your reports reflect the most up-to-date information from your data sources.

Next, we will explore the techniques and best practices for scheduling and monitoring data refresh in Power BI.

To schedule data refresh in Power BI, you can use the Power BI Service, where you publish your reports for online consumption.

One of the fundamental steps is publishing your Power BI Desktop report to the Power BI Service.

This process involves uploading your report file (.pbix) to the Power BI Service through the Power BI web portal.

To publish a report, follow these steps:

Open your report in Power BI Desktop.

Click on the "Publish" button in the Home tab.

Sign in to your Power BI account if prompted.

Choose the workspace where you want to publish the report.

Click "Publish."

Once your report is published, it's accessible through the Power BI Service, and you can configure data refresh settings.

To schedule data refresh, you can follow these steps:

Open your report in the Power BI Service.

Click on the report's "More options" menu (represented by three dots) in the workspace.

Select "Settings."

In the "Data source credentials" section, provide the necessary credentials to access your data source(s).

In the "Scheduled refresh" section, toggle the switch to enable scheduled refresh.

Configure the frequency and time zone for the refresh schedule.

Click "Apply."

You can choose to refresh your data daily, multiple times a day, or on specific days of the week.

Select a refresh time that aligns with your data source update schedule and user usage patterns.

Additionally, consider the time zone to ensure that data refresh occurs when it's most convenient for your intended audience.

Monitoring data refresh is equally crucial to detect any issues or failures promptly.

Power BI provides several tools and mechanisms to monitor and troubleshoot data refresh:

Refresh history: In the Power BI Service, you can view the refresh history of your dataset.

To access refresh history, go to the dataset settings, and click on "Scheduled refresh" in the left sidebar.

Here, you can see the status of recent refreshes, including successful refreshes, partial failures, and complete failures.

Email notifications: You can set up email notifications to receive alerts when a data refresh fails.

To enable email notifications, go to the dataset settings, and click on "Scheduled refresh" in the left sidebar.

Enter the email addresses of recipients who should receive notifications.

Power BI will send an email notification whenever a refresh failure occurs.

Dataflow and dataset diagnostics: Power BI provides diagnostic tools to help you identify and troubleshoot issues related to data refresh.

You can access diagnostics from the dataset settings in the Power BI Service.

Diagnostics provide insights into query performance, dataflow execution, and data refresh.

Power BI Proactive Monitoring: Power BI offers a proactive monitoring feature that allows you to set up custom alerts and triggers for your datasets.

With proactive monitoring, you can define conditions that, when met, trigger specific actions or notifications.

This feature helps you stay ahead of potential refresh issues by addressing them proactively.

Power BI REST APIs: Advanced users and developers can leverage Power BI REST APIs to monitor and manage data refresh programmatically.

APIs provide programmatic access to refresh status, history, and diagnostic information.

To access the Power BI REST APIs, you need to use authentication methods like Azure Active Directory (Azure AD) tokens or service principals.

Monitoring your data refresh process is not only about identifying failures but also about optimizing performance and reliability.

Here are some best practices for ensuring smooth data refresh:

Review data source credentials: Ensure that the credentials provided for data sources are up to date and valid.

Check data source connectivity: Test the connection to your data source to ensure it's accessible from the Power BI Service.

Query optimization: Optimize your queries to minimize the time and resources required for data retrieval.

Data transformation: Use Power Query in Power BI Desktop to perform necessary data transformations before data refresh.

Incremental refresh: Consider implementing incremental refresh strategies to refresh only new or changed data, reducing data transfer and processing time.

Data source optimizations: Optimize your data source for efficient data extraction and ensure that data source performance meets the requirements.

Compression and storage: Implement data compression techniques to reduce data size, especially for large datasets.

Scheduled refresh timing: Schedule data refresh during periods of lower usage to minimize the impact on report performance.

Regular testing: Continuously test and monitor data refresh to identify and address issues promptly.

Documentation: Document your data refresh processes, schedules, and troubleshooting procedures to maintain transparency and knowledge sharing within your organization.

By following these best practices and actively monitoring your data refresh process, you can ensure that your Power BI reports and dashboards remain reliable and up to date, providing users with accurate insights for informed decision-making.

Chapter 7: Power Query M Language for Advanced Users

Mastering M Language for custom transformations in Power BI is a valuable skill that empowers you to manipulate and shape data precisely to meet your reporting needs.

M Language is the query language used by Power Query, the data transformation engine in Power BI, Excel, and other Microsoft products.

Next, we'll delve into the intricacies of M Language, exploring its syntax, functions, and techniques for creating custom transformations.

M Language operates within the Power Query Editor, an interface available in Power BI Desktop that allows you to perform data transformations.

To access the Power Query Editor, load your data into Power BI Desktop, select a query, and click the "Edit Queries" button.

Once inside the Power Query Editor, you can see the applied steps on the right, which represent the series of transformations applied to your data.

M Language is responsible for defining these transformations, and each step in the query corresponds to a function or expression in M Language.

M Language is case-sensitive, so be mindful of capitalization when writing M code.

The basic structure of an M function consists of the function name followed by a set of parentheses containing one or more arguments.

For example, the "Table.SelectColumns" function is used to select specific columns from a table, and it requires two arguments: the table to be filtered and a list of column names to keep.

Here's an example of how to use this function in M Language:
mathematicaCopy code

```
Table.SelectColumns(Source, {"Column1", "Column2"})
```

In this example, "Source" is the table to filter, and the list {"Column1", "Column2"} specifies the columns to keep.

M Language provides a wide range of built-in functions that you can leverage for data transformations.

These functions cover a spectrum of tasks, from filtering and sorting data to aggregating and reshaping it.

For instance, you can use the "Table.AddColumn" function to add calculated columns to a table, or "Table.Group" to perform group-based aggregations.

Here's an example of adding a calculated column using M Language:

cssCopy code

```
Table.AddColumn(Source, "NewColumn", each [Column1] + [Column2])
```

In this code, "Source" is the table, "NewColumn" is the name of the new calculated column, and the expression "each [Column1] + [Column2]" specifies the calculation.

To become proficient in M Language, it's essential to understand its functions and their syntax.

The Power Query M function documentation provided by Microsoft is a valuable resource for learning about M functions and their usage.

Custom transformations often require more than just basic functions.

M Language allows you to create custom functions and expressions tailored to your specific data transformation needs.

To create a custom function, you can use the "let" expression in M Language.

The "let" expression allows you to define variables and reusable expressions within your M code.

Here's an example of creating a custom function to calculate the average of a column:

mathematicaCopy code

```
let Source = Table.FromRecords({[Value: 10], [Value: 20],
[Value: 30]}), CalculateAverage = (table as table,
columnName as text) => let Total =
List.Sum(Table.Column(table, columnName)), Count =
Table.RowCount(table), Average = if Count <> 0 then Total /
```

Count else null in Average in CalculateAverage(Source, "Value")

In this example, we define a custom function "CalculateAverage" that takes a table and a column name as arguments and calculates the average of the specified column.

By using the "let" expression, we encapsulate the calculation logic, making it reusable within our M code.

To invoke the custom function, we call it at the end of the code with the "CalculateAverage(Source, "Value")" line, where "Source" is the table, and "Value" is the column name.

Custom functions can simplify complex data transformations and enhance the readability of your M code.

In addition to custom functions, M Language supports conditional logic, loops, and branching.

You can use "if" statements to implement conditional transformations based on specific criteria.

For example, you can filter rows based on a condition:

cssCopy code

```
let Source = Table.FromRecords({[Name: "Alice", Score: 85],
[Name: "Bob", Score: 92], [Name: "Charlie", Score: 78]}),
FilteredRows = Table.SelectRows(Source, each [Score] >= 90) in
FilteredRows
```

In this code, we use the "Table.SelectRows" function with a condition to keep only the rows where the "Score" column is greater than or equal to 90.

M Language also supports loops through the "each" keyword.

You can use "each" to apply transformations iteratively to elements within a table, list, or column.

For instance, you can create a custom column that applies a calculation to each row:

lessCopy code

```
let Source = Table.FromRecords({[Value: 10], [Value: 20],
[Value: 30]}), CustomColumn = Table.AddColumn(Source,
"SquaredValue", each [Value] ^ 2) in CustomColumn
```

134

In this example, the "each" keyword is used to iterate over each row in the "Value" column and calculate the square of each value.

M Language's flexibility in handling conditional logic and loops empowers you to perform intricate data transformations efficiently.

Error handling is another essential aspect of M Language.

When working with data, it's crucial to anticipate and handle potential errors gracefully.

M Language provides error handling functions like "try," "otherwise," and "error" to manage errors during data transformations.

Here's an example of using error handling to deal with division by zero:

javaCopy code

let Value = 10, Denominator = 0, Result = if Denominator = 0 then error "Division by zero is not allowed." else try Value / Denominator otherwise null in Result

In this code, we first check if the "Denominator" is zero and raise an error if it is, preventing division by zero.

If the "Denominator" is not zero, we use the "try" function to attempt the division, and the "otherwise" function specifies a fallback value (in this case, "null") if an error occurs.

This error handling approach ensures that your data transformations are robust and prevent unexpected failures.

M Language also allows you to work with tables, lists, and records directly, making it versatile for various data structures.

For example, you can create a list of records, transform it, and convert it back to a table seamlessly.

Understanding how to manipulate these data structures efficiently is essential for mastering M Language.

To concatenate tables, you can use the "Table.Combine" function, which merges multiple tables into one.

Here's an example:

lessCopy code

let Table1 = Table.FromRecords({ [Name: "Alice", Age: 30], [Name: "Bob", Age: 25] }), Table2 = Table.FromRecords({ [Name:

"Charlie", Age: 35], [Name: "David", Age: 28]}), CombinedTable
= Table.Combine({Table1, Table2}) in CombinedTable

In this code, we create two tables, "Table1" and "Table2," and then combine them into a single table using "Table.Combine."

This technique is useful when you need to merge data from multiple sources into one unified table for further analysis.

Understanding the nuances of working with data structures in M Language enables you to perform complex data manipulations effectively.

Power Query and M Language offer extensive support for working with various data sources, including databases, files, web services, and APIs.

To connect to different data sources, you can use the "Data Source Settings" in Power BI Desktop or the "Home" tab's options.

For instance, to connect to a SQL Server database, you can follow these steps:

Click on the "Home" tab in Power BI Desktop.

Select "Get Data."

Choose "Database" and then "SQL Server Database."

Enter the server details, database name, and authentication method.

Click "Connect" to establish the connection.

Power BI will prompt you to provide credentials if necessary.

Once connected, you can import data from tables, views, or custom SQL queries.

For web-based data sources or APIs, Power Query allows you to access data using the "Web" option.

Here's how to connect to a web service:

Click on the "Home" tab in Power BI Desktop.

Select "Get Data."

Choose "Web."

Enter the URL of the web service.

Click "OK" to retrieve data.

Power Query will connect to the web service and retrieve the available data.

For file-based data sources, you can import data from various formats, including Excel, CSV, JSON, XML, and more.

To import data from a file, follow these steps:
Click on the "Home" tab in Power BI Desktop.
Select "Get Data."
Choose the appropriate file format, such as "Excel" or "Text/CSV."
Locate and select the file from your local or network storage.
Click "Import" or "Load" to load the data into Power BI.
Power Query will import the data, and you can apply transformations as needed.
In addition to the built-in connectors, Power Query allows you to create custom connectors for proprietary or unique data sources.
Custom connectors are typically developed using the Power Query M language and can be shared with other users or reused across projects.
Creating a custom connector involves defining the data source's connection details, authentication methods, and any required transformations.
Once created, custom connectors can simplify the process of connecting to specific data sources and ensure consistency in data retrieval and transformation.
To create a custom connector, you can use the Power Query SDK (Software Development Kit), which provides tools and templates for connector development.
The Power Query SDK allows you to generate M code that encapsulates the logic for connecting to and retrieving data from your data source.
You can then package this M code into a connector, making it accessible through the Power Query interface.
Custom connectors offer flexibility and extend the capabilities of Power Query, allowing you to work with virtually any data source.
In addition to connecting to data sources, Power Query provides options for data shaping and transformation.
You can filter, sort, pivot, unpivot, aggregate, and perform various other operations to prepare your data for analysis.
One of the key features of Power Query is the ability to create reusable transformations using the "Query Editor."
The Query Editor provides a user-friendly interface for applying transformations to your data.

You can access it by clicking the "Edit Queries" button in Power BI Desktop.

Inside the Query Editor, you can perform a wide range of data transformations.

For example, you can remove duplicates, replace values, split columns, merge queries, or pivot data.

Each transformation step is recorded in the "Applied Steps" pane on the right, allowing you to review and modify the sequence of transformations.

To apply a transformation, select a column or data element, right-click, and choose the desired transformation action from the context menu.

For instance, to filter rows based on a condition, select a column, right-click, and choose "Filter Rows."

You can then specify the filter criteria in the dialog box that appears.

Power Query provides a rich set of transformation functions and expressions.

You can create custom calculations using M Language directly within the Query Editor.

To access the advanced editor for M code, click the "Advanced Editor" button in the Query Editor.

Inside the advanced editor, you can write M code to implement custom transformations.

Here's an example of creating a custom column that concatenates two columns:

mathematicaCopy code

```
let Source = Table.FromRecords({[First Name: "Alice", Last Name: "Smith"], [First Name: "Bob", Last Name: "Johnson"]}), CustomColumn = Table.AddColumn(Source, "Full Name", each [First Name] & " " & [Last Name]) in CustomColumn
```

In this code, we define a custom column named "Full Name" that combines the "First Name" and "Last Name" columns.

The "each" keyword is used to refer to each row in the table.

Once the custom column is created, you can see it in the table preview, and it becomes part of your data model.

The flexibility and capabilities of Power Query make it a powerful tool for data preparation and transformation.

It allows you to clean, reshape, and enrich your data from various sources, ensuring that your Power BI reports are built on accurate and well-structured data.

Furthermore, the ability to create custom transformations using M Language provides endless possibilities for tailoring your data to specific requirements.

In summary, connecting to different data sources in Power BI involves using a range of built-in connectors, creating custom connectors when necessary, and applying data transformations using Power Query and M Language.

By mastering these techniques, you can ensure that your data is ready for analysis and reporting, ultimately delivering valuable insights to your organization.

Combining advanced data sources with Power Query opens up a world of possibilities for gathering and transforming data in your Power BI projects.

As businesses increasingly rely on diverse data sets from various sources, the ability to integrate and process this data efficiently becomes crucial.

Next, we'll explore the techniques and strategies for connecting to and combining advanced data sources using Power Query, enabling you to harness the full potential of your data.

Power Query is a versatile tool that allows you to connect to a wide range of data sources, including databases, web services, APIs, and files.

However, working with advanced data sources often involves unique challenges and requirements.

Let's start by discussing some common advanced data sources and the techniques to connect to them effectively.

One common advanced data source is a REST API, which provides a programmatic interface to access data from web services.

To connect to a REST API in Power Query, you can use the "Web.Contents" function, which sends HTTP requests to the API endpoint and retrieves the response.

Here's an example of how to connect to a REST API:
bashCopy code

```
let apiUrl = "https://api.example.com/data", response =
Web.Contents(apiUrl), jsonData = Json.Document(response) in
jsonData
```

In this code, we specify the API URL, use "Web.Contents" to retrieve the data, and then parse the JSON response using "Json.Document."

This technique allows you to access data from web-based services and incorporate it into your Power BI reports.

Another advanced data source is a database, which can include SQL databases, NoSQL databases, and cloud-based databases like Azure SQL Database or Amazon Redshift.

To connect to a database in Power Query, you need to provide connection details such as the server address, credentials, and database name.

Here's an example of connecting to a SQL Server database:
bashCopy code

```
let server = "server-name.database.windows.net", database =
"database-name", username = "username", password =
"password", connectionString = "Provider=SQLOLEDB;Data
Source=" & server & ";Initial Catalog=" & database & ";User ID="
& username & ";Password=" & password, source =
Sql.Database(server, database, [Query="SELECT * FROM table"])
in source
```

In this code, we define the server, database, username, and password, and then create a connection string.

We use "Sql.Database" to connect to the database and specify a SQL query to retrieve data from a specific table.

Connecting to databases allows you to leverage structured and organized data for your Power BI reports.

Data lakes, such as Azure Data Lake Storage and Amazon S3, are becoming increasingly popular for storing large volumes of raw and unstructured data.

140

To connect to a data lake in Power Query, you can use the "Folder.Files" function to retrieve files and folders from a specified path.

Here's an example of connecting to a folder in a data lake:

bashCopy code

```
let                    dataLakePath                    =
"https://datalakestore.blob.core.windows.net/container-
name/folder/", source = Folder.Files(dataLakePath) in source
```

In this code, we specify the data lake path and use "Folder.Files" to retrieve a list of files and folders.

You can then apply further transformations to process the data stored in the data lake.

Connecting to data lakes provides access to a vast reservoir of data for analysis and reporting in Power BI.

Streaming data sources, such as Azure Stream Analytics and Apache Kafka, deliver real-time data that requires immediate processing and analysis.

To connect to streaming data sources in Power Query, you can use the "Stream.Contents" function, which allows you to retrieve data from a streaming endpoint.

Here's an example of connecting to a streaming data source:

arduinoCopy code

```
let streamUrl = "https://stream.example.com/data", response =
Stream.Contents(streamUrl) in response
```

In this code, we specify the stream URL and use "Stream.Contents" to fetch real-time data from the stream.

Streaming data can be ingested into Power BI for near-real-time analysis and visualization, providing valuable insights as events occur.

Power Query also offers native connectors for cloud-based data sources, such as Azure Blob Storage, Azure Data Factory, and Amazon S3.

These connectors simplify the process of connecting to cloud data sources by allowing you to authenticate using your cloud credentials and access data stored in the cloud.

For instance, you can connect to Azure Blob Storage to retrieve files and data stored in containers.

To do so, follow these steps:

Click on the "Home" tab in Power BI Desktop.

Select "Get Data."

Choose "Azure" and then "Azure Blob Storage."

Enter your Azure Storage account name and account key.

Browse and select the container and file you want to import.

Click "OK" to retrieve the data.

Power Query handles the authentication and retrieval process, making it easy to work with cloud-based data sources.

Now that we've explored various advanced data sources and how to connect to them, let's discuss techniques for combining data from multiple sources.

Power Query allows you to merge, append, or join data from different sources, providing a unified view of your data.

One common scenario is merging data from multiple tables or queries with similar structures.

To merge data in Power Query, you can use the "Table.Join" function, which allows you to specify the columns to join on and the type of join (inner, outer, left, right).

Here's an example of merging two tables:

lessCopy code

```
let table1 = Table.FromRecords({[ID: 1, Name: "Alice"], [ID: 2, Name: "Bob"]}), table2 = Table.FromRecords({[ID: 2, Age: 30], [ID: 3, Age: 25]}), mergedTable = Table.Join(table1, "ID", table2, "ID", JoinKind.LeftOuter) in mergedTable
```

In this code, we create two tables, "table1" and "table2," and then use "Table.Join" to merge them based on the "ID" column with a left outer join.

The resulting "mergedTable" contains the combined data from both tables.

Appending data from multiple tables or queries with identical structures is another common scenario.

To append data in Power Query, you can use the "Table.Combine" function, which combines tables vertically.

Here's an example of appending two tables:
lessCopy code

```
let table1 = Table.FromRecords({[ID: 1, Name: "Alice"], [ID: 2,
Name: "Bob"]}), table2 = Table.FromRecords({[ID: 3, Name:
"Charlie"], [ID: 4, Name: "David"]}), appendedTable =
Table.Combine({table1, table2}) in appendedTable
```

In this code, we create "table1" and "table2" and then use "Table.Combine" to append them into a single table.

The "appendedTable" contains all the rows from both tables.

Joining data from different sources with distinct structures requires careful consideration and transformation.

You may need to reshape and consolidate the data to align with the desired structure before performing the join.

Power Query provides tools for data transformations, such as pivoting, unpivoting, and renaming columns, to prepare data for joining.

To join data from different sources, you can follow these steps:

Load each data source into separate queries in Power Query.

Transform each query to ensure data compatibility and alignment.

Use the "Table.Join" function to join the queries based on common columns.

Specify the type of join (inner, outer, left, right) based on your requirements.

Merge the resulting joined queries into a single query or table.

This process allows you to combine data from diverse sources and create a consolidated data model for your Power BI reports.

Additionally, Power Query supports hierarchical data structures, which are common in scenarios involving parent-child relationships or organizational hierarchies.

You can work with hierarchical data by using functions like "Table.Group" and "Table.ExpandTableColumn."

Here's an example of working with hierarchical data:
phpCopy code

```
let employees = Table.FromRecords({[EmployeeID: 1, Name:
"Alice", ManagerID: null], [EmployeeID: 2, Name: "Bob",
ManagerID: 1], [EmployeeID: 3, Name: "Charlie", ManagerID:
```

```
2 ]}), groupedTable = Table.Group(employees, {"ManagerID"},
{{"Subordinates", each _, type table}}), expandedTable =
Table.ExpandTableColumn(groupedTable, "Subordinates",
{"EmployeeID", "Name"}, {"SubordinateID",
"SubordinateName"}) in expandedTable
```

In this code, we create an "employees" table with hierarchical data, where each employee has a ManagerID pointing to their manager.

We use "Table.Group" to group employees by their ManagerID, creating a hierarchy.

Then, we use "Table.ExpandTableColumn" to expand the "Subordinates" column and retrieve the EmployeeID and Name of each subordinate.

This technique enables you to work with hierarchical data structures effectively in Power Query.

When combining advanced data sources, it's essential to consider data refresh and update strategies.

Data from these sources may change frequently, requiring regular updates in your Power BI reports.

Power BI offers various options for scheduling data refresh, depending on your data source and licensing.

For cloud-based data sources, you can use Power BI's built-in refresh capabilities, allowing you to schedule automatic refreshes at specified intervals.

To schedule data refresh in Power BI, follow these steps:

Publish your Power BI report to the Power BI service.

In the Power BI service, go to the dataset settings for your report.

Configure the refresh settings, including the frequency and credentials required to access the data source.

Save the settings to enable automatic refresh.

Power BI will then refresh the data according to the defined schedule, ensuring that your reports are always up to date.

For on-premises data sources or other sources that are not natively supported for direct refresh in the Power BI service, you can use the Power BI Gateway.

The Power BI Gateway is an on-premises data gateway that acts as a bridge between your on-premises data sources and the Power BI service.

To set up data refresh for on-premises sources using the Power BI Gateway, follow these steps:

Install and configure the Power BI Gateway on a machine that can access your on-premises data.

In the Power BI service, go to the dataset settings for your report.

Configure the data source to use the gateway.

Set up refresh schedules as needed.

The Power BI Gateway allows you to keep your reports updated with data from on-premises or non-cloud sources, ensuring data accuracy.

When dealing with advanced data sources, it's crucial to consider data security and access control.

You must protect sensitive data and grant appropriate permissions to users who need access to specific data sets.

Power BI provides robust security and permission features to address these concerns.

One way to manage data security in Power BI is through Row-Level Security (RLS).

RLS allows you to restrict data access based on user roles and rules defined in your data model.

For example, you can create roles that limit access to specific regions, departments, or products within your organization.

To implement RLS in Power BI, you can follow these steps:

Define roles: In Power BI Desktop, go to the "Model" view and create roles for your data model.

Create rules: Define rules for each role to specify the data that users in that role can access.

Assign users: Assign users or groups to the appropriate roles in the Power BI service.

Publish and test: Publish your report to the Power BI service and test data access based on the defined roles.

RLS ensures that users only see the data relevant to their role, enhancing data security and confidentiality.

Additionally, Power BI offers encryption options to protect data both in transit and at rest.

For data sources that require authentication, you can store credentials securely using the Power BI service's built-in encryption features.

By encrypting sensitive information, you minimize the risk of data breaches and unauthorized access.

In summary, combining advanced data sources with Power Query in Power BI opens up opportunities for comprehensive data analysis and reporting.

You can connect to a variety of data sources, including REST APIs, databases, data lakes, and streaming data.

Using techniques like merging, appending, and handling hierarchical data, you can create a unified data model for your reports.

Consider data refresh and security when working with advanced data sources to ensure that your reports remain accurate and protected.

By mastering these techniques, you'll be well-equipped to harness the full potential of your data in Power BI and deliver valuable insights to your organization.

Chapter 8: Managing Large and Complex Data Sets

Handling big data with Power BI requires a strategic approach to ensure that your reports remain efficient and responsive.

As organizations accumulate vast amounts of data, the need to analyze and visualize this data efficiently becomes paramount.

Next, we'll explore techniques and best practices for handling big data in Power BI, allowing you to unlock insights from large and complex datasets.

Big data often comes from a variety of sources, including IoT devices, social media, logs, and more, generating massive volumes of data.

To effectively handle big data in Power BI, you need to consider data storage, data processing, and data visualization.

One of the first steps in dealing with big data is to select an appropriate storage solution that can accommodate the volume and velocity of incoming data.

For large-scale data storage, many organizations turn to cloud-based data lakes and data warehouses.

Popular choices include Azure Data Lake Storage, Amazon S3, Azure Synapse Analytics, and Google BigQuery.

These platforms offer scalable and cost-effective storage solutions for big data.

Once you've chosen a storage solution, you'll need to ingest data from various sources into your data lake or data warehouse.

Power BI provides native connectors for many of these data sources, making it relatively straightforward to extract and load data.

However, when dealing with big data, you must optimize data loading to minimize resource usage and reduce data latency.

One way to optimize data loading is to use Power Query's query folding capabilities, which push data transformations and filtering back to the data source.

Query folding can significantly improve performance when working with large datasets.

Here's an example of using query folding with a SQL database:
bashCopy code
let source = Sql.Database("server-name.database.windows.net", "database-name", [Query="SELECT * FROM large_table WHERE date_column >= '2022-01-01'"]), filteredData = Table.SelectColumns(source, {"column1", "column2", "column3"}) in filteredData
In this code, we filter the data at the source by specifying a date condition in the SQL query.

This reduces the amount of data transferred to Power BI and improves performance.

Another technique for handling big data is to implement data partitioning.

Data partitioning involves dividing large tables into smaller, more manageable partitions based on a specific column, such as date or region.

By doing this, you can query and load only the relevant partitions, reducing the overall data processing load.

For example, if you have a large sales data table, you can partition it by year or month.

Then, when querying the data, you can specify the specific partitions you want to work with.

Power BI supports data partitioning for some data sources, such as Azure Synapse Analytics and SQL Server.

To implement data partitioning, you'll need to set it up in your data source, and Power BI will automatically recognize and use the partitions.

In addition to optimizing data storage and loading, you'll need to consider data processing within Power BI.

Big data often requires complex calculations and transformations, which can impact report performance.

To address this, you can leverage Power BI's performance optimizations, such as aggregations and direct query mode.

Aggregations allow you to precompute and store summary data at different levels of granularity.

For example, you can precompute monthly sales totals from daily transaction data.

This reduces the need to perform complex calculations at query time and speeds up report rendering.

To set up aggregations in Power BI, follow these steps:

Create a summary table that contains the aggregated data.

Define relationships between the summary table and the detailed data table.

Configure aggregation tables in Power BI Desktop, specifying the granularity and aggregation functions.

Direct query mode allows you to offload data processing to the underlying data source, such as a data warehouse.

In direct query mode, Power BI sends queries directly to the data source, and the data source performs the calculations and transformations.

This can be beneficial for handling big data because it reduces the amount of data transferred to Power BI.

To enable direct query mode, you'll need to configure it in Power BI Desktop by selecting the appropriate data source connection type.

Keep in mind that direct query mode has limitations, such as limited support for complex calculations and visualizations.

You may need to strike a balance between using direct query mode and importing data into Power BI for optimal performance.

Another consideration when working with big data is data modeling and optimization.

Power BI's Data Analysis Expressions (DAX) language allows you to create calculated columns, measures, and complex calculations for your reports.

When dealing with large datasets, it's essential to write efficient DAX code to avoid performance bottlenecks.

Consider using techniques like calculated tables, summarization, and filter context optimization to enhance DAX query performance.

For example, you can create calculated tables that precompute specific calculations, reducing the need for real-time calculations during report rendering.

Additionally, you can use DAX functions like "SUMX" and "FILTER" to optimize calculations by applying filters at the most granular level possible.

Handling big data also involves effective data visualization.

Power BI's ability to create interactive and visually appealing reports is a significant advantage when dealing with large datasets.

However, overloading a report with too many visuals or displaying all data points can lead to sluggish performance.

To address this, consider techniques for data visualization optimization:

Implement drill-through and drill-down features to allow users to explore data hierarchies and details selectively.

Use visual-level filters to allow users to interactively filter data within visuals without affecting the entire report.

Limit the number of visuals on a single report page to maintain performance.

Implement responsive design principles to ensure that reports are user-friendly on various devices and screen sizes.

By following these best practices for data visualization, you can create engaging and performant reports, even with big data.

Lastly, when handling big data, it's essential to monitor and fine-tune your Power BI reports regularly.

Performance bottlenecks and data issues may arise over time, requiring adjustments and optimizations.

Power BI offers built-in monitoring and diagnostic tools, such as Query Diagnostics and Performance Analyzer, to help identify and resolve issues.

Regularly review query execution times, report rendering times, and resource usage to identify areas for improvement.

You can also use the Power BI Premium Capacity Metrics app to gain insights into report performance at the workspace level.

Consider setting up alerts or notifications to proactively address performance degradation or data quality concerns.

In summary, handling big data with Power BI requires a holistic approach that encompasses data storage, data processing, data modeling, and data visualization.

By optimizing data storage, leveraging query folding, implementing data partitioning, and using performance optimizations like aggregations and direct query mode, you can ensure that your reports remain responsive and efficient.

Efficient data modeling and visualization techniques, coupled with regular monitoring and fine-tuning, will allow you to unlock insights and make data-driven decisions from large and complex datasets.

Data partitioning and compression techniques are essential strategies for optimizing data storage and query performance in Power BI.

When working with large datasets, it's crucial to manage data efficiently to ensure that your reports remain responsive and scalable.

Next, we'll explore the concepts of data partitioning and compression and how to implement them effectively in Power BI.

Partitioning involves dividing a large table into smaller, more manageable sections based on a specific column, often referred to as the partitioning key.

The goal of partitioning is to reduce the amount of data that needs to be loaded and processed for each query, which can significantly improve query performance.

Partitioning is especially valuable when dealing with large fact tables in a data model, such as sales transactions or log data.

Power BI supports data partitioning for some data sources, such as Azure Synapse Analytics and SQL Server Analysis Services (SSAS) Tabular.

To implement data partitioning in Power BI, follow these steps:

Identify a suitable column to serve as the partitioning key. This column should have a logical and even distribution of data values, such as a date column for time-based data.

Configure partitioning in your data source. The process for setting up partitioning may vary depending on your data source, so consult the documentation for your specific data platform.

In Power BI Desktop, connect to your partitioned data source and load the data into your data model.

Set up relationships between the partitioned table and other related tables in your data model.

When querying data, specify the relevant partitions to query. Power BI will automatically filter the data at the source, retrieving only the necessary partitions.

By implementing data partitioning, you can reduce the data processing load on your data model, resulting in faster query performance and improved report responsiveness.

Another important consideration when working with large datasets is data compression.

Data compression techniques in Power BI reduce the amount of storage space required for your data model and can also lead to faster query performance.

Power BI uses columnar compression, which is a technique that stores data in columnar format rather than row-by-row.

Columnar compression allows for efficient storage and retrieval of data, especially when aggregations and filters are applied.

Additionally, Power BI employs a dictionary-based compression method for text values.

In this method, unique text values are stored in a dictionary, and each occurrence of a text value is replaced with a reference to the dictionary entry.

This reduces the storage space needed for repetitive text values.

While Power BI's compression techniques are automatic and generally highly efficient, there are cases where you can further optimize data compression.

One such technique is to leverage the "Data Analysis Expressions" (DAX) language to create calculated columns that store aggregated or summarized data.

By precomputing aggregations or summarizations in calculated columns, you can reduce the need for real-time calculations during query execution.

For example, instead of summing sales amounts for each row in a large fact table, you can create a calculated column that stores the total sales amount for each product or category.

Here's an example of a DAX formula to create a calculated column for total sales by product:

DAXCopy code

Total Sales = SUMX(FILTER(SalesTable, SalesTable[ProductID] = EARLIER(SalesTable[ProductID])), SalesTable[SalesAmount])

In this DAX formula, "Total Sales" is a calculated column that sums the "SalesAmount" for each product, using the FILTER and SUMX functions.

By creating calculated columns like this, you can improve both data compression and query performance.

Another technique to optimize data compression is to remove unnecessary columns from your data model.

If your dataset contains columns that are not used in your reports or calculations, consider removing them from the data model to reduce storage requirements.

You can do this by selecting the table in Power BI Desktop, going to the "Model" view, and unchecking the unnecessary columns.

Keep in mind that removing columns should be done carefully, as it may affect your ability to create certain reports or perform specific analyses.

Data partitioning and compression are powerful techniques for optimizing data storage and query performance in Power BI.

By partitioning large tables based on a suitable key and leveraging automatic and custom data compression methods, you can ensure that your reports remain efficient and responsive, even when dealing with vast amounts of data.

Additionally, using DAX to create calculated columns for aggregations and removing unnecessary columns from your data model can further enhance performance and reduce storage requirements.

These techniques, when applied thoughtfully, allow you to make the most of Power BI's capabilities and deliver valuable insights from your data.

Chapter 9: Advanced Data Security and Permissions

Role-Based Security (RBS) and Row-Level Security (RLS) are crucial components of data security in Power BI, allowing organizations to control and restrict access to data based on user roles and specific rules.

While RBS defines the roles that users can have, RLS focuses on determining which data users within those roles can access.

This chapter explores the concepts, implementation, and best practices for Role-Based Security and Row-Level Security in Power BI.

Role-Based Security (RBS) is the foundation for controlling data access in Power BI.

RBS defines roles, and roles, in turn, determine what a user can see and do within a Power BI dataset or report.

Roles can be created based on various criteria, such as department, job title, or function within the organization.

For instance, an organization may define roles like "Sales Manager," "Marketing Analyst," or "Finance Director."

To implement RBS in Power BI, you need to follow these steps:

Create Roles: Start by defining the roles within Power BI Desktop. Go to the "Model" view, select "Manage Roles," and then create the roles you need.

Assign Roles to Users: After defining roles, you must assign them to specific users or groups within the Power BI service. This is typically done by the Power BI administrator.

Define Role Filters: Within each role, you can specify role filters, which are DAX expressions that determine what data a role can access. These filters can be as simple as filtering data based on a department or more complex, depending on your requirements.

Publish and Test: Once roles are assigned and role filters are defined, publish your report to the Power BI service and test data access for each role.

Role-Based Security ensures that users are only able to see and interact with the data that is relevant to their role, maintaining data security and confidentiality.

Row-Level Security (RLS) is an extension of Role-Based Security and focuses on filtering data at a granular level.

With RLS, you can control access to individual rows of data within tables, ensuring that users within the same role only see the data that applies to them.

For example, if an organization has a "Sales" role, RLS can be used to ensure that each salesperson within that role can only access their own sales data.

To implement Row-Level Security in Power BI, you should follow these steps:

Define RLS Tables: Start by creating one or more RLS tables in Power BI Desktop. These tables typically contain the relationships between users (or roles) and the data they are allowed to access.

Create RLS Rules: Define RLS rules by creating relationships between the RLS tables and the data tables you want to secure. These relationships should be based on user identifiers or attributes, such as user email addresses or employee IDs.

Create RLS Filters: In the RLS tables, create DAX expressions that filter data based on user attributes or roles. These expressions determine which rows of data each user or role can access.

Apply RLS to Data Tables: Finally, apply the RLS filters to the data tables by creating relationships between the RLS tables and the data tables. Make sure to set the filter direction to "Both" to ensure that the filters apply in both directions.

RLS enables fine-grained control over data access, ensuring that users only see the specific data that pertains to their role or attributes.

One common use case for RLS is ensuring that employees can only access data related to their department or team.

Organizations can also use RLS to comply with regulatory requirements by restricting access to sensitive data, such as personal or financial information.

When implementing RLS, it's essential to thoroughly test your security rules to ensure they are correctly filtering data for each user or role.

Additionally, it's important to keep RLS rules up to date as user roles and data access requirements change within your organization.

Power BI provides auditing and monitoring capabilities to track user activity and security violations, helping you maintain data integrity.

In summary, Role-Based Security (RBS) and Row-Level Security (RLS) are essential features for controlling and securing data access in Power BI.

RBS defines user roles, while RLS enables fine-grained control over data access at the row level.

By implementing these security mechanisms, organizations can ensure that users only see the data relevant to their roles and responsibilities, protecting sensitive information and complying with data access regulations.

Careful planning, testing, and monitoring are key to successfully implementing RBS and RLS in Power BI and maintaining data security.

Data encryption and compliance are critical aspects of data security and governance in Power BI, ensuring that sensitive information is protected and that organizations meet regulatory requirements.

This chapter explores the concepts of data encryption, data compliance, and best practices for implementing these measures in Power BI.

Data encryption is the process of converting data into a coded form to prevent unauthorized access and protect data confidentiality.

Power BI employs multiple layers of encryption to safeguard data at rest and in transit, ensuring that sensitive information remains secure throughout its lifecycle.

At rest, Power BI uses data encryption technologies to protect data stored in its data centers.

Azure Data Encryption at Rest is one of the key encryption mechanisms used by Power BI, which encrypts data while it's stored on disk.

Additionally, Power BI implements role-based access control (RBAC) and data access policies to restrict access to authorized personnel.

Data in transit is also safeguarded through encryption protocols such as HTTPS and TLS/SSL.

When data is transmitted between the Power BI service and client devices, it's encrypted to prevent eavesdropping and data interception.

Organizations can further enhance data encryption in Power BI by using encryption features provided by their data sources and ensuring secure connectivity.

For example, if data is sourced from an on-premises SQL Server database, it's advisable to implement Transparent Data Encryption (TDE) on the SQL Server to encrypt data at rest.

Additionally, organizations can use Power BI Gateways to establish secure connections between Power BI and on-premises data sources, ensuring that data in transit remains encrypted.

Power BI also supports Azure Active Directory (Azure AD) integration for user authentication and access control.

Azure AD offers robust security features, including multi-factor authentication (MFA) and conditional access policies, to further protect user accounts and data access.

Organizations can leverage these features to enhance the security of their Power BI deployments.

Data compliance is another crucial aspect of data governance in Power BI, particularly for organizations subject to regulatory requirements such as GDPR, HIPAA, or SOC 2.

Power BI provides features and capabilities to assist organizations in achieving compliance with these regulations.

One fundamental aspect of compliance is data classification and labeling.

Power BI allows organizations to define data sensitivity labels based on their internal policies and regulatory requirements.

These labels can be applied to datasets, reports, and dashboards, indicating the level of sensitivity and access controls required.

For instance, organizations can classify data as "Public," "Confidential," or "Restricted," and define who can access and share each type of data.

Organizations can also use Power BI's audit and compliance logs to track user activity, data access, and report sharing.

The Power BI audit log records actions such as dataset access, report viewing, and data export, providing a comprehensive record of user interactions with data.

This audit trail is valuable for compliance reporting and investigating security incidents.

Additionally, Power BI integrates with Microsoft's compliance solutions, such as the Microsoft 365 Compliance Center and Azure Security Center, which provide advanced threat protection and compliance capabilities.

These integrations enable organizations to monitor and assess compliance across their entire Microsoft 365 ecosystem, including Power BI.

When dealing with sensitive data, organizations should consider implementing data loss prevention (DLP) policies.

Power BI allows organizations to define DLP policies that prevent the sharing of sensitive data with unauthorized individuals or external parties.

For example, organizations can configure DLP policies to block the export of datasets or reports containing sensitive information to unmanaged devices or external email addresses.

This ensures that sensitive data remains within the organization's boundaries and is shared only with authorized personnel.

Organizations should also regularly review and update their data governance and compliance policies in alignment with changing regulatory requirements.

Power BI's flexibility allows organizations to adapt to evolving compliance standards and data protection regulations.

In summary, data encryption and compliance are essential components of data security and governance in Power BI.

Data encryption protects data at rest and in transit, while compliance measures ensure that organizations meet regulatory requirements and maintain data integrity.

By implementing encryption technologies, classifying data sensitivity, and using audit logs and compliance features, organizations can enhance data security and demonstrate adherence to data protection standards.

Regularly reviewing and updating data governance policies is crucial for staying compliant with evolving regulations and protecting sensitive information effectively.

Chapter 10: Best Practices for Enterprise-Level Power BI Solutions

Scaling Power BI for enterprise deployments involves a strategic approach to ensure that the platform can handle large volumes of data, users, and complex reporting requirements.

As organizations grow, their data analytics needs often expand, and Power BI must be configured and optimized to meet these evolving demands.

This chapter explores the key considerations, best practices, and techniques for scaling Power BI for enterprise-level deployments.

One of the first considerations when scaling Power BI for the enterprise is choosing the right licensing model.

Power BI offers various licensing options, including Power BI Free, Power BI Pro, and Power BI Premium.

For smaller organizations or teams, Power BI Pro may be sufficient, but larger enterprises typically opt for Power BI Premium or Premium Per User (PPU) licensing.

Power BI Premium provides dedicated capacity, which means organizations have greater control over resource allocation and can handle larger datasets and more concurrent users.

Power BI PPU offers similar capabilities but on a per-user basis, making it suitable for organizations with varying user requirements.

Once the appropriate licensing model is selected, organizations should evaluate their data storage and processing needs.

Large datasets often require dedicated capacity, which can be allocated using Power BI Premium or Power BI Premium Per User.

Organizations can choose the appropriate Power BI Premium capacity size based on their data volume and performance requirements.

For example, Power BI Premium capacities range from A1 (small) to EM3 (extra-large), with each capacity providing different levels of resources.

Larger capacities offer more memory and processing power, allowing organizations to handle complex data models and support a larger user base.

Implementing a data refresh strategy is crucial when scaling Power BI for the enterprise.

Organizations must determine how often data should be refreshed and ensure that the refresh process is efficient and reliable.

To configure data refresh settings in Power BI, administrators can use Power Query Online and configure scheduled refresh options based on data source availability and data freshness requirements.

Additionally, organizations should consider using incremental data refresh to minimize data processing time and reduce the load on data sources.

Incremental data refresh allows only the changed or newly added data to be refreshed, rather than refreshing the entire dataset.

To configure incremental data refresh, you can follow these steps:

Identify the columns that can be used for partitioning the data, such as date or category.

In Power Query, create a partitioning query that splits the data based on the identified columns.

Configure incremental refresh settings in the Power BI service by specifying the partitioning column and the range of data to keep in cache.

Schedule regular refreshes to keep the data up to date.

Another critical aspect of enterprise-level Power BI deployments is managing data source connections and data security.

Power BI allows administrators to set up data source credentials, such as user names and passwords, securely.

It's essential to configure these credentials correctly to ensure that data sources can be accessed and refreshed without issues.

Organizations can also leverage Single Sign-On (SSO) and Azure Active Directory (Azure AD) integration for seamless and secure authentication.

Power BI's integration with Azure AD provides advanced identity and access management capabilities, allowing organizations to control data access based on user roles and permissions.

Managing data security at scale involves setting up role-based access control (RBAC) and row-level security (RLS) to ensure that users only see the data relevant to their roles and responsibilities.

Administrators can define roles, assign users or groups to roles, and configure role filters to control data access.

Role-based access control is particularly valuable in large enterprises with diverse user groups and varying data access requirements.

Monitoring and optimizing performance are ongoing tasks when scaling Power BI for the enterprise.

Organizations should regularly review usage metrics and query performance to identify bottlenecks and optimize data models.

Power BI offers performance monitoring capabilities, including the Power BI Premium Metrics app, which provides insights into resource consumption, query performance, and user activity.

Administrators can use these metrics to identify and address performance issues proactively.

Additionally, organizations can leverage Power BI's ability to use aggregations and composite models to optimize data query performance for large datasets.

Aggregations allow organizations to precompute summarized data, reducing the need for real-time calculations during query execution.

Composite models enable the combination of DirectQuery and import modes in a single report, providing flexibility and performance optimization options.

Scaling Power BI for enterprise deployments also involves implementing a disaster recovery and backup strategy.

Organizations should regularly back up Power BI workspaces, datasets, and reports to ensure data availability and resilience.

Power BI provides export and import capabilities for creating backups and restoring content when needed.

For advanced backup and recovery options, organizations can consider using Power BI Premium's automated deployment pipelines and APIs.

In summary, scaling Power BI for enterprise deployments requires careful planning, configuration, and ongoing management.

Organizations should select the appropriate licensing model, allocate dedicated capacity, configure data refresh strategies, and manage data source connections securely.

Role-based access control and row-level security should be implemented to ensure data security, and performance should be monitored and optimized regularly.

Disaster recovery and backup strategies should also be in place to safeguard data availability and resilience.

By following these best practices and techniques, organizations can effectively scale Power BI to meet the demands of large and complex enterprise analytics environments.

Governance and lifecycle management are critical aspects of maintaining a healthy and organized Power BI environment in any organization.

Governance ensures that the use of Power BI aligns with the organization's policies, regulatory requirements, and security standards.

Lifecycle management covers the planning, development, deployment, and maintenance of Power BI solutions over time.

This chapter explores best practices for governance and lifecycle management in Power BI.

One of the foundational aspects of governance in Power BI is defining roles and responsibilities within the organization.

This involves designating individuals or teams responsible for creating, publishing, and maintaining Power BI content.

For instance, organizations typically have Power BI administrators who manage security, data sources, and user access, while report authors are responsible for creating and updating reports and dashboards.

It's crucial to establish clear guidelines and communication channels between these roles to ensure effective collaboration and adherence to governance policies.

A governance center of excellence (CoE) can be established to oversee Power BI governance practices and provide guidance to report authors and administrators.

A CoE can define governance policies, standards, and best practices, and facilitate training and communication efforts.

In larger organizations, the CoE may include representatives from various departments to ensure that governance policies align with department-specific requirements.

To implement governance effectively, organizations should establish a robust data governance framework.

This framework includes defining data classifications, access controls, and data sensitivity labels, which indicate the level of confidentiality and access rights associated with each dataset or report.

Data classification helps organizations categorize data as public, internal, confidential, or restricted, and ensures that appropriate access controls are in place.

Power BI allows organizations to define and apply data sensitivity labels, which can be used to enforce access controls and data protection policies.

Power BI also supports integration with Azure Purview, a data governance and cataloging solution, to help organizations manage their data assets more comprehensively.

Another aspect of governance in Power BI is version control and content management.

Organizations should implement version control practices to track changes and revisions to reports and datasets.

This ensures that previous versions of content can be restored if needed and helps prevent accidental data loss or report corruption.

Power BI provides built-in version history and content restore capabilities, making it easier for report authors and administrators to manage content revisions.

Lifecycle management encompasses the entire lifecycle of Power BI content, from planning and development to deployment and maintenance.

Organizations should establish standardized processes for content development, including requirements gathering, design, data modeling, and report creation.

Using a project management approach, organizations can use tools like Microsoft Project or Azure DevOps to plan and track the progress of Power BI projects.

These tools help teams collaborate effectively, manage tasks, and ensure that projects are completed on time and within scope.

As part of the development process, organizations should promote best practices for data modeling, report design, and performance optimization.

This includes guidelines for data source connections, data transformation, DAX calculations, and visualization design.

Power BI report authors should be encouraged to follow these best practices to ensure the quality and performance of their reports.

Once content is developed, organizations need to establish a well-defined deployment process.

This involves moving content from development to testing and production environments while ensuring that data sources, security, and access controls are configured correctly.

Power BI offers deployment pipelines, which allow organizations to automate the deployment process, making it more efficient and less error-prone.

With deployment pipelines, organizations can promote content from one environment to another, making it easier to maintain consistency and manage updates.

Power BI's deployment pipelines also integrate with version control systems like Azure DevOps, enabling organizations to track changes and roll back deployments if necessary.

Organizations should establish a process for content review and validation before deploying reports and dashboards to production. This includes peer reviews, testing, and validation of data accuracy and performance.

Reviewers should ensure that reports meet business requirements, adhere to design standards, and are free of errors.

After deployment, organizations need to manage the ongoing maintenance and updates of Power BI content.

This includes monitoring data source refreshes, tracking user activity, and addressing any issues or enhancements as they arise.

Power BI provides monitoring capabilities through the Power BI Premium Metrics app and audit logs, allowing organizations to track usage, performance, and potential security concerns.

Regularly scheduled maintenance and updates are essential to keep reports and dashboards relevant and accurate.

Organizations should establish a process for handling user feedback and requests for changes or enhancements.

Power BI's comment and feedback features make it easy for users to provide input and report issues, helping organizations address user needs effectively.

In summary, governance and lifecycle management are essential components of a successful Power BI implementation.

Governance involves defining roles and responsibilities, establishing data classifications and access controls, and promoting best practices.

Lifecycle management covers the entire content development and deployment process, from planning to maintenance.

By implementing these best practices, organizations can ensure that Power BI is used effectively, efficiently, and in alignment with their business goals and governance policies.

BOOK 3
POWER BI DATA MODELING
BUILDING ROBUST DATASETS FOR EFFECTIVE ANALYSIS

ROB BOTWRIGHT

Chapter 1: Foundations of Data Modeling in Power BI

Data modeling plays a pivotal role in Power BI, serving as the foundation upon which meaningful insights and visualizations are built.

A well-structured data model defines how data is organized, related, and transformed within a Power BI dataset, enabling users to explore and analyze data effectively.

Next, we will delve into the importance of data modeling in Power BI and explore various techniques and best practices for creating robust data models.

Data modeling involves structuring data to facilitate efficient querying, reporting, and visualization.

At the heart of a Power BI data model are tables, which represent different entities or data sources, and relationships, which define how these tables are interconnected.

Tables in Power BI can be sourced from various data sources, including databases, Excel files, web services, and more.

Once data is imported or connected, it is essential to shape and transform it to align with your analytical objectives.

Power Query, an ETL (Extract, Transform, Load) tool within Power BI, provides a robust environment for data preparation and transformation.

Through Power Query, users can filter, merge, pivot, unpivot, and aggregate data to create a clean and structured dataset.

DAX (Data Analysis Expressions) is another integral part of data modeling in Power BI.

DAX is a formula language that enables users to create custom calculations, measures, and calculated columns within the data model.

DAX functions allow for complex calculations, time intelligence, and aggregations, enhancing the analytical capabilities of Power BI.

One of the key principles in data modeling is ensuring that data relationships are accurately defined.

Relationships establish the connections between tables, enabling users to combine and analyze data from multiple sources seamlessly.

To create relationships in Power BI, users should identify common fields (keys) between tables and define relationships as one-to-one or one-to-many based on the nature of the data.

Implementing relationships correctly is vital for accurate data analysis and visualizations.

Hierarchies play a significant role in data modeling by enabling users to drill down into data at different levels of granularity.

Power BI allows users to create hierarchies within tables, such as date hierarchies (year, quarter, month) or product hierarchies (category, subcategory, product).

These hierarchies enhance the user experience by providing flexibility in data exploration and reporting.

Calculations in Power BI are often reliant on time-based analysis, making time intelligence a critical aspect of data modeling.

Time intelligence functions in DAX facilitate the creation of measures for year-over-year comparisons, running totals, and other time-related calculations.

Effective data modeling should consider performance optimization.

As datasets grow in size and complexity, it becomes essential to optimize data models to ensure responsiveness and efficient querying.

Techniques such as creating calculated tables, using summary tables, and leveraging DirectQuery or Live Connection can help improve query performance.

Star schema and snowflake schema are common data modeling techniques used in Power BI.

Star schema structures data with a central fact table connected to dimension tables, simplifying data analysis and visualization.

Snowflake schema extends the star schema by normalizing dimension tables, reducing data redundancy.

Both schemas offer advantages depending on the specific analytical requirements.

Row-level security is another critical aspect of data modeling in Power BI.

It allows organizations to control access to data at the row level based on user roles and filters.

Row-level security ensures that users only see the data relevant to their role, maintaining data confidentiality and compliance.

Creating effective and user-friendly hierarchies is essential for a successful data model.

Power BI enables users to define custom hierarchies within tables, providing a structured way to explore data at different levels of detail.

Hierarchies enhance the user experience by enabling drill-down and summarization of data in visuals.

Another advanced data modeling technique in Power BI is the use of bidirectional filters.

Bidirectional filters allow relationships between tables to flow in both directions, enabling users to filter data in related tables based on selections made in a visual.

This technique provides more flexibility in creating interactive reports.

Advanced users may also explore advanced modeling scenarios, such as many-to-many relationships, role-playing dimensions, and custom tables for specific calculations.

Many-to-many relationships allow for modeling complex data scenarios, while role-playing dimensions enable the same dimension table to serve different roles in a data model.

Custom tables and functions can be created to address specific analytical needs, offering flexibility and customization.

Organizations should consider data model documentation as a fundamental practice in Power BI.

Documentation ensures that others can understand and work with the data model effectively.

Power BI allows users to add descriptions, comments, and annotations to tables, columns, and measures, making it easier to share knowledge and insights within the team.

In summary, data modeling is the backbone of effective data analysis and visualization in Power BI.

It involves structuring data, defining relationships, creating hierarchies, and implementing calculations to enable meaningful insights.

Data modeling is a dynamic process that requires continuous optimization and adherence to best practices to ensure responsive and efficient data models.

By mastering data modeling techniques in Power BI, users can unlock the full potential of their data and create impactful reports and dashboards.

Data modeling is a fundamental concept in the world of data analysis and business intelligence, and it serves as the foundation for organizing and structuring data for meaningful insights.

At its core, data modeling is the process of creating a visual representation of data structures and the relationships between them.

In the context of data modeling, a data model is essentially a blueprint that defines how data elements are related and how they should be organized within a database or data warehouse.

Data modeling is a crucial step in designing and building databases, data warehouses, and analytical systems because it ensures that data is structured in a way that aligns with the needs of the business and enables efficient data retrieval and analysis.

There are two main types of data models: conceptual data models and physical data models.

A conceptual data model focuses on high-level business concepts and relationships between them, often using non-technical language that is easily understood by business stakeholders.

It provides a broad overview of the data that will be captured and managed within an organization but doesn't go into specific technical details.

In contrast, a physical data model delves into the technical aspects of how data will be stored, including details such as database tables, columns, data types, and indexes.

Physical data models are used by database administrators and developers to implement the actual database structure based on the requirements defined in the conceptual data model.

One of the key components of a data model is an entity. An entity represents a real-world object or concept about which data is being captured and stored.

Entities are typically depicted as rectangles in a data model diagram, and each entity has attributes that describe the characteristics or properties of that entity.

For example, in a data model for a retail business, entities might include "Customer," "Product," and "Order," with attributes like "CustomerID," "ProductName," and "OrderDate."

Entities are connected by relationships, which define how data from one entity is related to data from another entity.

Relationships are represented by lines connecting the entities in a data model diagram, and they are essential for establishing the connections and dependencies between different pieces of data.

In addition to entities and relationships, data models often include constraints and business rules that define how data should be validated, enforced, and maintained.

Constraints can include rules like "each order must have a unique order number" or "a product must belong to at least one category."

These constraints help ensure data accuracy and consistency within the database.

There are several notations and methodologies for creating data models, including Entity-Relationship Diagrams (ERD), Unified Modeling Language (UML), and Data Definition Language (DDL).

Entity-Relationship Diagrams (ERD) are one of the most widely used notations for creating data models.

In an ERD, entities are represented as rectangles, relationships as lines connecting entities, and attributes as ovals connected to their respective entities.

This visual representation makes it easy to understand the structure and relationships of the data.

Unified Modeling Language (UML) is a more general-purpose modeling language that can be used for various types of modeling, including data modeling.

UML diagrams can represent data models using classes to represent entities, associations to represent relationships, and attributes to represent entity properties.

Data Definition Language (DDL) is a specific language used to define the structure of a database or data warehouse.

DDL statements are written in SQL (Structured Query Language) and include commands like CREATE TABLE, ALTER TABLE, and DROP TABLE to define tables, columns, indexes, and other database objects.

When working with databases, it's essential to consider the normalization of data, which is the process of organizing data in a way that minimizes redundancy and improves data integrity.

Normalization involves dividing a database into two or more tables and defining relationships between those tables.

The goal of normalization is to eliminate data redundancy and prevent data anomalies, such as update anomalies, insert anomalies, and delete anomalies.

Normalization is typically categorized into different levels or forms, from First Normal Form (1NF) to Fifth Normal Form (5NF).

Each level represents a higher degree of normalization, with 1NF being the least normalized and 5NF being the most normalized.

Normalization is an important consideration when designing a database schema to ensure that data is efficiently stored and maintained.

In addition to normalization, denormalization is another concept that is sometimes used to optimize query performance.

Denormalization involves intentionally introducing redundancy into a database schema to reduce the need for joins and improve query response times.

While denormalization can be effective for read-heavy workloads, it can also introduce complexity and the risk of data inconsistencies, so it should be used judiciously.

Another key concept in data modeling is the use of keys to uniquely identify rows in a table.

A primary key is a column or set of columns that uniquely identifies each row in a table.

Primary keys ensure that there are no duplicate rows in a table and are essential for maintaining data integrity.

A foreign key is a column or set of columns in one table that refers to the primary key of another table.

Foreign keys establish relationships between tables and are used to enforce referential integrity, ensuring that data remains consistent across related tables.

In summary, data modeling is a fundamental concept in data management and business intelligence, providing a structured framework for organizing and representing data.

Data models define entities, relationships, attributes, constraints, and business rules that guide how data is stored, validated, and maintained.

Normalization and denormalization are important considerations for optimizing data storage and query performance, while keys, including primary keys and foreign keys, play a crucial role in ensuring data integrity and establishing relationships between tables.

Understanding these key concepts is essential for effective data modeling and database design.

Chapter 2: Importing and Transforming Data for Modeling

Data import strategies are a critical component of any data-driven project, as they define how data is retrieved and loaded into a system for analysis and reporting purposes.

Choosing the right data import strategy can significantly impact the efficiency, accuracy, and timeliness of your data-driven processes.

Next, we will explore various data import strategies and best practices for effectively bringing data into your analytics environment.

One common data import strategy is batch processing, which involves collecting and importing data in predefined chunks or batches.

Batch processing is suitable for scenarios where data updates occur periodically and can be scheduled to minimize system resource usage during import.

To implement batch processing, you can use scripting languages like Python or PowerShell to automate the extraction and loading of data from source systems into your analytics platform.

For example, you might schedule a nightly batch job to retrieve the latest sales data from a remote database and load it into your data warehouse using SQL commands.

Batch processing can be particularly useful when dealing with large datasets, as it allows you to control the timing of data imports and optimize system resources.

Another data import strategy is real-time or near-real-time data streaming, which involves continuously ingesting and processing data as it becomes available.

This approach is suitable for scenarios where immediate access to fresh data is critical, such as monitoring systems, financial transactions, or sensor data from IoT devices.

To implement real-time data streaming, you can use specialized tools and technologies like Apache Kafka, Apache Flink, or cloud-based services like Amazon Kinesis and Azure Stream Analytics.

These platforms allow you to ingest, transform, and analyze streaming data in real-time, making it available for immediate insights and decision-making.

Real-time data streaming is well-suited for applications that require low-latency access to data, such as fraud detection, stock trading, or social media analytics.

In some cases, a hybrid approach that combines batch processing and real-time data streaming may be the most effective data import strategy.

For example, you might use batch processing to load historical data into your data warehouse and then switch to real-time streaming for incremental updates.

This hybrid approach provides a balance between historical analysis and real-time insights.

When working with data import strategies, it's essential to consider data quality and data cleansing processes.

Data quality refers to the accuracy, completeness, consistency, and reliability of the data being imported.

Before importing data, it's crucial to assess its quality and apply data cleansing and validation procedures to address any issues.

Common data quality tasks include removing duplicate records, correcting data anomalies, handling missing values, and validating data against predefined business rules.

Data cleansing can be performed using data integration and transformation tools, SQL queries, or custom scripts, depending on your data import strategy and requirements.

Data security and compliance are also important considerations when importing data.

Sensitive or confidential data must be protected during the import process to prevent unauthorized access or data breaches.

Encryption, access controls, and auditing mechanisms should be implemented to safeguard data during transmission and storage.

Furthermore, compliance with data protection regulations, such as GDPR or HIPAA, may require specific data handling procedures and documentation.

When importing data from external sources, it's essential to establish data lineage and documentation to track the source, transformations, and usage of the data.

Data lineage provides visibility into how data flows through your analytics environment and helps ensure data traceability and accountability.

Documentation should include metadata, data dictionaries, and data catalogs that describe the structure, meaning, and usage of imported data.

Version control is another critical aspect of data import strategies, especially when dealing with evolving data sources or data models.

Version control systems like Git can help manage changes to data import scripts, configurations, and data transformation logic.

By tracking and documenting changes, you can ensure that imported data remains consistent and reproducible over time.

Data import strategies also involve considerations related to data integration and data silos.

Data integration aims to unify data from various sources and make it available for analysis in a centralized location.

Data silos, on the other hand, occur when data is fragmented and isolated in different systems or departments.

Efforts should be made to break down data silos and establish data integration processes that bring together relevant data for analysis.

This may involve implementing data integration platforms, ETL (Extract, Transform, Load) tools, or data virtualization solutions to create a single source of truth for your analytics.

Data governance and data stewardship play essential roles in ensuring data import strategies are executed correctly and consistently.

Data governance defines the policies, procedures, and responsibilities for managing data throughout its lifecycle.

Data stewards are individuals or teams responsible for overseeing data quality, compliance, and data import processes.

By establishing clear data governance practices and involving data stewards, organizations can maintain data consistency and adhere to data import best practices.

Cloud-based data import services have gained popularity due to their scalability, flexibility, and ease of use.

Cloud providers like Amazon Web Services (AWS), Microsoft Azure, and Google Cloud offer a range of data import and ingestion services.

For example, AWS offers AWS Data Pipeline and AWS Glue, which can automate data import and transformation tasks.

Azure provides Azure Data Factory, Azure Data Lake, and Azure Stream Analytics for data import and processing.

Google Cloud offers Google Cloud Dataflow and Google Cloud Dataprep for data integration and cleansing.

These cloud services simplify data import and management, allowing organizations to focus on analytics rather than infrastructure.

To implement a cloud-based data import strategy, you can use CLI (Command Line Interface) commands provided by the cloud platform to configure and schedule data import pipelines.

For example, you might use the AWS CLI to create and manage data import jobs in AWS Data Pipeline.

Similarly, you can use the Azure CLI to define data import workflows in Azure Data Factory.

These CLI commands provide a programmatic way to automate data import tasks and integrate them into your data pipeline.

In summary, data import strategies are a crucial aspect of data-driven projects, impacting data quality, timeliness, and efficiency.

Choosing the right strategy, whether it's batch processing, real-time streaming, or a hybrid approach, depends on the specific requirements of your project.

Data quality, security, and compliance considerations are essential when importing data, along with data integration efforts to unify data from different sources.

Data governance, data stewardship, and version control practices contribute to the success of data import strategies.

Cloud-based data import services offer scalability and ease of use, and CLI commands can help automate and manage data import workflows within cloud platforms.

By carefully planning and executing data import strategies, organizations can ensure that their analytics processes are built on a solid foundation of accurate and reliable data.

Data transformation techniques are a critical aspect of data preparation and analysis, helping to convert raw data into a structured and usable format.

These techniques involve various operations and manipulations that cleanse, reshape, and enrich data to make it suitable for further analysis.

Next, we will explore different data transformation techniques and their significance in the data analysis process.

One fundamental data transformation technique is data cleaning, which focuses on identifying and correcting errors or inconsistencies in the data.

Data cleaning can involve tasks such as removing duplicate records, handling missing values, correcting typographical errors, and resolving inconsistent data formats.

For example, when dealing with a dataset containing customer information, data cleaning may include standardizing date formats, fixing misspelled names, and filling in missing phone numbers.

To implement data cleaning, you can use various tools and programming languages like Python or R to write scripts that automate the cleansing process.

Another essential data transformation technique is data aggregation, which involves summarizing data at a higher level of granularity.

Aggregation can be applied to numerical data, such as calculating sums, averages, or counts, and can also be used for categorical data by grouping and counting distinct values.

For instance, if you have a sales dataset with individual transactions, data aggregation can help calculate total sales revenue for each product category or the average order value for each customer.

To perform data aggregation, you can use SQL queries or data manipulation libraries in programming languages like Pandas in Python.

Data filtering is another data transformation technique used to select a subset of data based on specific criteria or conditions.

Filtering allows you to focus on relevant data and exclude irrelevant or noisy information from your analysis.

For example, in a dataset of e-commerce reviews, you might filter for reviews with a rating of four stars or higher to analyze positive feedback.

You can apply data filtering using SQL WHERE clauses or filter functions in data analysis tools like Microsoft Excel.

Data normalization is a technique used to scale numerical data to a common range, making it easier to compare variables with different units or magnitudes.

Normalization transforms data into a standard format, typically with a mean of zero and a standard deviation of one.

This technique is beneficial when working with machine learning algorithms or statistical analyses that rely on standardized data.

To normalize data, you can use mathematical formulas or libraries like Scikit-learn in Python, which provides various normalization techniques such as Min-Max scaling and Z-score normalization.

Data encoding involves converting categorical variables into a numerical format that can be used in statistical models or machine learning algorithms.

Many algorithms require numerical input, so encoding is necessary when dealing with features like product categories, geographic regions, or customer segments.

Common encoding methods include one-hot encoding, label encoding, and target encoding, depending on the nature of the categorical data.

For example, one-hot encoding represents each category as binary values (0 or 1) in separate columns, while label encoding assigns a unique numeric label to each category.

To apply data encoding, you can use libraries like Scikit-learn for machine learning tasks or Pandas for data manipulation.

Data imputation is a technique used to fill in missing values in a dataset to ensure completeness and accuracy.

Missing data can arise due to various reasons, such as data entry errors or incomplete records.

Imputation methods include mean imputation, median imputation, mode imputation, or more advanced techniques like regression imputation or k-nearest neighbors imputation.

For example, if you have missing values in a dataset of employee salaries, you can impute missing values by replacing them with the median salary of all employees.

To perform data imputation, you can use libraries like Pandas or specialized imputation functions in machine learning frameworks like Scikit-learn.

Data pivot and unpivot are techniques used to reshape data by changing its structure from a wide format to a long format or vice versa.

Pivoting is useful when you want to aggregate data by different categories or variables, and unpivoting is helpful when you want to convert aggregated data back into its original format.

For instance, if you have a dataset with sales data where each column represents a month, you can pivot it to have a single column for months and another column for sales values.

To pivot or unpivot data, you can use data manipulation functions in tools like Microsoft Excel, SQL pivoting queries, or specialized functions in programming languages like Python.

String manipulation is a data transformation technique used to manipulate and extract information from text data.

This technique is especially valuable when dealing with unstructured or semi-structured data sources, such as text documents, web pages, or log files.

String manipulation operations include text extraction, text parsing, substring extraction, regular expression matching, and text concatenation.

For example, if you have a dataset containing email addresses, you can extract the domain names from each email address using string manipulation techniques.

To perform string manipulation, you can use programming languages like Python or libraries like regular expressions in JavaScript.

Data transformation techniques are essential for preparing data for analysis, modeling, and visualization.

These techniques allow data analysts and data scientists to work with clean, structured, and relevant data, leading to more accurate and insightful results.

Whether it's cleaning, aggregating, filtering, normalizing, encoding, imputing, pivoting, unpivoting, or performing string manipulation, understanding and applying these techniques is crucial for successful data analysis projects.

To implement these techniques effectively, practitioners can leverage a combination of data manipulation tools, programming languages, and libraries tailored to their specific needs and requirements.

By mastering data transformation techniques, data professionals can unlock the full potential of their data and uncover valuable insights that drive informed decision-making and business success.

Chapter 3: Understanding Relationships in Power BI

Creating and managing relationships between data tables is a fundamental aspect of database design and data modeling, essential for constructing meaningful and insightful data analyses.

Next, we will delve into the concepts and techniques involved in establishing and maintaining relationships within your data.

At the heart of data relationships lies the concept of a relational database, where data is organized into tables, each containing a specific type of information.

Tables are designed to be related to one another based on shared attributes or keys, creating a structured framework for storing and retrieving data.

For example, in a retail database, you may have separate tables for customers, products, and orders, and these tables can be linked through common keys like customer IDs and product IDs.

The primary key of a table uniquely identifies each record within that table, ensuring that each row has a distinct identifier.

In contrast, a foreign key is a field in one table that refers to the primary key of another table, establishing a connection between the two tables.

To illustrate, in the aforementioned retail database, the customer ID in the orders table would be a foreign key referencing the customer's primary key in the customers table.

This relationship allows you to associate each order with a specific customer.

Relationships can be categorized into several types, primarily one-to-one, one-to-many, and many-to-many.

A one-to-one relationship means that each record in the first table corresponds to one and only one record in the second table, and vice versa.

In contrast, a one-to-many relationship indicates that each record in the first table can have multiple corresponding records in the second table, but each record in the second table can only relate to one record in the first table.

For instance, in a university database, a student may have one student ID, and that ID is unique, representing a one-to-one relationship between students and student IDs.

On the other hand, a one-to-many relationship exists between courses and students, where one course can have multiple students, but each student is enrolled in only one course.

Many-to-many relationships are more complex and are typically implemented using a junction table or associative entity.

In this type of relationship, each record in the first table can be associated with multiple records in the second table, and vice versa.

For instance, in a music database, a song can be associated with multiple genres, and each genre can be linked to multiple songs.

To represent this many-to-many relationship, you would create a junction table that includes the primary keys of both the songs and genres tables.

Establishing relationships within a database requires careful planning and attention to data integrity.

Referential integrity is a crucial concept that ensures the consistency and accuracy of data relationships.

It dictates that foreign keys must always reference a valid primary key value in the related table.

For example, if an order references a customer through a foreign key, that foreign key should always point to an existing customer record.

Maintaining referential integrity is essential to prevent data inconsistencies and anomalies.

When creating relationships in relational database management systems (RDBMS), you use SQL statements to define foreign keys and constraints.

For example, in SQL Server, you can create a foreign key constraint like this:

sqlCopy code

```
ALTER TABLE Orders ADD CONSTRAINT FK_CustomerID
FOREIGN KEY (CustomerID) REFERENCES
Customers(CustomerID);
```

This SQL statement adds a foreign key constraint to the Orders table, linking the CustomerID column to the CustomerID column in the Customers table.

In addition to referential integrity, it's vital to consider the cascading options associated with foreign keys.

These options define the actions that should occur when a referenced record in the parent table is modified or deleted.

Common cascading options include cascading updates and cascading deletes.

Cascading updates ensure that changes in the parent table's primary key values are reflected in the corresponding foreign key values in child tables.

Cascading deletes, on the other hand, specify that when a parent record is deleted, all related child records should also be deleted to maintain data consistency.

While cascading options can simplify data management, they should be used cautiously to avoid unintended data loss or cascading updates that affect a large number of records.

In addition to traditional relational databases, relationship management is also integral to data modeling in tools like Power BI and Excel.

These tools allow users to establish relationships between data tables without requiring SQL queries or database management expertise.

For example, in Power BI, you can create relationships by simply dragging and dropping fields from different tables onto each other.

The tool automatically detects matching columns and establishes relationships based on user interactions.

However, it's essential to understand the underlying concepts of relationships and referential integrity, even when working in user-friendly environments, to design effective data models.

Maintaining and managing relationships is an ongoing process in data management and analytics.

As data evolves and new records are added, relationships may need to be updated or refined to accommodate changing requirements.

Proper documentation of relationships and data lineage can help ensure that all stakeholders understand the structure of the data model and how tables are related.

Documentation should include descriptions of each relationship, the purpose it serves, and any business rules associated with it.

Moreover, regular validation and testing of relationships can uncover issues with data integrity, such as orphaned records or broken links.

It's crucial to conduct data validation checks periodically to confirm that the relationships within your data are consistent and accurate.

In database systems, you can use SQL queries to verify the integrity of relationships and identify any data anomalies.

For example, you can write a SQL query that identifies records in the child table with missing or invalid foreign key references.

In data modeling tools like Power BI, you can utilize features such as modeling view, diagram view, or the relationship view to visualize and manage relationships in your data model.

These tools provide a user-friendly interface for exploring, modifying, and validating relationships within your data.

In summary, creating and managing relationships is a foundational skill in the world of data modeling and database design.

Understanding the types of relationships, referential integrity, and cascading options is essential for building accurate and reliable data models.

Whether you're working with relational databases, data modeling tools, or spreadsheet applications, the principles of data relationships remain consistent.

By mastering the art of creating and managing relationships, data professionals can ensure that their data models serve as a solid foundation for meaningful and impactful data analysis and decision-making.

Handling many-to-many relationships in data modeling and database design is a complex but crucial task, as many real-world scenarios involve entities that can be associated with multiple instances of another entity, creating intricate connections.

A many-to-many relationship exists when multiple records in one table are related to multiple records in another table, and vice versa.

For example, consider a database for a library where books can have multiple authors, and authors can write multiple books.

In this scenario, each book is related to multiple authors, and each author is related to multiple books, forming a many-to-many relationship.

To handle many-to-many relationships effectively, you typically employ an intermediary table, often referred to as a junction table or associative table.

This intermediary table acts as a bridge between the two related tables, allowing you to manage the relationship and avoid data duplication.

In the case of the library database, the junction table would store pairs of book IDs and author IDs, indicating which books are written by which authors.

When creating a junction table, you include foreign keys that reference the primary keys of the two related tables.

For example, if you have a Books table and an Authors table, the junction table might be named BookAuthors and include two foreign keys: BookID and AuthorID.

To establish a many-to-many relationship in a database, you define the necessary foreign key constraints, ensuring that the values in the junction table's foreign key columns reference valid records in the associated tables.

In a relational database management system (RDBMS), you can use SQL statements to create the junction table and define the foreign key constraints.

Here's an example of SQL code to create a junction table for a many-to-many relationship between books and authors:

sqlCopy code

```
CREATE TABLE BookAuthors ( BookID INT, AuthorID INT,
CONSTRAINT FK_BookID FOREIGN KEY (BookID) REFERENCES
Books (ID), CONSTRAINT FK_AuthorID FOREIGN KEY (AuthorID)
REFERENCES Authors (ID) );
```

This SQL code creates the BookAuthors table with two foreign keys, one referencing the Books table and the other referencing the Authors table.

It enforces referential integrity by ensuring that only valid book and author combinations can be stored in the junction table.

In addition to creating the junction table, you must populate it with data that represents the relationships between books and authors.

This data insertion process typically occurs when adding new books or authors to the database or when specifying authorship for each book.

For example, to associate a book with one or more authors, you insert corresponding records into the BookAuthors table.

Here's an example of SQL code to insert a record into the BookAuthors table, linking a book with ID 1 to an author with ID 2: sqlCopy code

```
INSERT INTO BookAuthors (BookID, AuthorID) VALUES ( 1, 2);
```

This SQL statement inserts a record indicating that book ID 1 is authored by author ID 2.

To handle many-to-many relationships in non-relational databases or data modeling tools, you follow a similar approach of using an intermediary structure.

For example, in a NoSQL database, you might create a collection or document that represents the relationship between books and authors, storing the relevant book and author IDs.

In data modeling tools like Power BI or Excel, you establish many-to-many relationships by defining the appropriate connections between tables and specifying how they relate to each other.

Handling many-to-many relationships requires careful consideration of data integrity, as it's possible for records in the junction table to become orphaned if not properly managed.

Orphaned records occur when a record in one of the related tables is deleted without removing the corresponding records in the junction table.

To prevent orphaned records and maintain referential integrity, you can use cascading delete options or implement business logic that ensures proper data handling.

In SQL databases, you can configure cascading delete actions to automatically remove related records in the junction table when a parent record is deleted.

For example, if an author is deleted from the Authors table, the database can automatically delete all entries in the BookAuthors table that reference that author's ID.

Here's an example of SQL code to configure cascading deletes for a foreign key constraint:

sqlCopy code

```
ALTER TABLE BookAuthors ADD CONSTRAINT FK_AuthorID
FOREIGN KEY (AuthorID) REFERENCES Authors (ID) ON DELETE
CASCADE;
```

This SQL statement specifies that when an author is deleted from the Authors table, all corresponding records in the BookAuthors table should be deleted as well.

In data modeling tools, you can define similar cascading behaviors to handle many-to-many relationships effectively.

Another consideration when working with many-to-many relationships is querying and reporting.

To retrieve meaningful insights from data with many-to-many relationships, you often need to perform complex queries and aggregations that involve multiple tables.

In SQL databases, you can use JOIN operations to combine data from multiple tables and extract relevant information.

For example, to retrieve a list of books authored by a specific author, you might use a SQL query like this:

sqlCopy code

```
SELECT Books.Title FROM Books JOIN BookAuthors ON Books.ID
= BookAuthors.BookID WHERE BookAuthors.AuthorID = 2;
```

This SQL query joins the Books table with the BookAuthors table, filtering by the AuthorID to retrieve books authored by the specified author (AuthorID = 2).

In data modeling tools, you can create relationships between tables and use calculated columns or measures to perform complex calculations and aggregations that involve many-to-many relationships.

Overall, handling many-to-many relationships is a fundamental skill in database design and data modeling, as these relationships are prevalent in various domains and scenarios.

By understanding the concept of junction tables, establishing foreign key constraints, managing data integrity, and performing effective queries, data professionals can effectively model and work with complex data structures that involve many-to-many relationships, unlocking valuable insights and enhancing decision-making processes.

Chapter 4: Advanced Techniques for DAX Modeling

Advanced Data Analysis Expressions (DAX) functions play a pivotal role in enhancing the capabilities of Power BI and other business intelligence tools, enabling data professionals to perform complex calculations and modeling tasks.

Next, we will explore a range of advanced DAX functions that empower analysts and data modelers to solve intricate business problems and gain deeper insights from their data.

One of the fundamental concepts in DAX is the idea of calculated columns, which allow you to create new columns in your data model based on custom expressions or formulas.

While basic calculations are straightforward, advanced DAX functions provide the flexibility to perform more sophisticated operations.

For instance, the SWITCH function is a powerful tool for creating conditional expressions within calculated columns.

With SWITCH, you can evaluate a series of conditions and return different results based on the first condition that evaluates to true.

Here's an example of how you might use SWITCH to categorize sales transactions into different revenue bands:

daxCopy code

Revenue Band = SWITCH (TRUE (), [Sales Amount] <= 1000, "Low", [Sales Amount] <= 5000, "Medium", [Sales Amount] > 5000, "High")

In this DAX formula, the SWITCH function evaluates the sales amount and assigns it to one of three revenue bands: Low, Medium, or High.

Another advanced function, SUMMARIZECOLUMNS, allows you to create summary tables or virtual tables that aggregate data based on specific columns and expressions.

This function is particularly useful when you need to generate custom aggregations or perform calculations on filtered subsets of your data.

For example, you can use SUMMARIZECOLUMNS to create a summary table that calculates the total sales amount for each product category:

daxCopy code

Product Category Sales = SUMMARIZECOLUMNS (Products[Category], "Total Sales", [Sales Amount])

The resulting summary table provides a concise view of total sales for each product category.

Advanced DAX functions also include time intelligence functions, which enable you to perform complex calculations involving dates and time periods.

Functions like DATESYTD (Year-to-Date), TOTALYTD (Total Year-to-Date), and SAMEPERIODLASTYEAR facilitate comparisons and trend analysis.

For instance, you can use TOTALYTD to calculate the cumulative sales amount year-to-date, considering a specified date column:

daxCopy code

Total Sales YTD = TOTALYTD ([Sales Amount], Dates[Date])

This DAX formula computes the cumulative sales amount from the beginning of the year up to the selected date.

Furthermore, advanced DAX functions provide enhanced statistical and mathematical capabilities.

For example, the RANKX function enables you to rank data based on specified columns and expressions.

You can use RANKX to determine the rank of products by sales amount, allowing you to identify top-performing items.

daxCopy code

Product Rank = RANKX (ALL (Products), [Sales Amount])

In this DAX expression, the RANKX function ranks products based on their sales amounts across all products in the data model.

Additionally, DAX offers functions for working with advanced filtering and iterating logic.

The FILTER function allows you to create dynamic filters on tables or columns, enabling complex filtering criteria.

For example, you can use FILTER to extract all sales transactions where the sales amount exceeds a certain threshold:

daxCopy code

High Sales Transactions = FILTER (Sales, [Sales Amount] > 10000)

This DAX formula filters the Sales table to include only transactions with sales amounts greater than $10,000.

Another valuable function is ALLSELECTED, which can be used to remove filters applied to a specific column while preserving other filters.

Suppose you want to calculate the total sales amount for a selected product category without being affected by other filters on the report. In that case, you can utilize the ALLSELECTED function:

daxCopy code

Total Sales for Selected Category = CALCULATE ([Sales Amount],

ALLSELECTED (Products[Category]))

This DAX expression removes filters applied to the Products[Category] column, allowing you to compute the total sales for the selected category independently.

Moreover, DAX provides functions for handling parent-child hierarchies, such as PATH and PATHCONTAINS, which assist in navigating hierarchical structures.

These functions enable you to traverse paths within hierarchies and analyze data at different levels of granularity.

For instance, you can use PATHCONTAINS to determine whether a specific product category is part of a selected hierarchy path:

daxCopy code

Is Selected Category in Path = PATHCONTAINS (Products, [Category], "Electronics")

In this example, the PATHCONTAINS function checks if the "Electronics" category is included in the hierarchy path defined by the Products table's [Category] column.

Advanced DAX functions are also indispensable for solving complex business scenarios involving time intelligence, forecasting, and advanced calculations.

Functions like DAX Studio allow you to explore and debug DAX formulas in your data model.

DAX Studio provides a comprehensive environment for writing and testing DAX expressions, helping you gain a deeper understanding of your data and ensuring the accuracy of your calculations.

To use DAX Studio, you can download and install it, connect it to your Power BI file or Analysis Services model, and then start writing and evaluating DAX expressions.

Additionally, DAX functions can be combined and nested to create more intricate calculations.

For example, you can nest functions like SUMMARIZECOLUMNS within other DAX functions to perform multi-step calculations and generate sophisticated reports.

In summary, advanced DAX functions empower data professionals to tackle complex data modeling, calculations, and analysis tasks in Power BI and similar business intelligence tools.

These functions offer a wide range of capabilities, from conditional logic to time intelligence, statistical analysis, and filtering control.

By mastering advanced DAX functions, data modelers and analysts can harness the full potential of their data and deliver valuable insights that drive informed business decisions.

In the world of data modeling and analysis with tools like Power BI and DAX, understanding the concepts of filter context and row context is essential for creating accurate and meaningful reports and calculations.

Filter context and row context are two fundamental aspects of DAX (Data Analysis Expressions) that govern how calculations are performed and data is filtered within a data model.

Filter context refers to the set of filters or criteria applied to a calculation or measure in a data model.

These filters can come from various sources, such as slicers, filters on visualizations, or even implicit filters based on relationships between tables.

For example, if you have a table of sales transactions and a slicer that allows users to filter data by a specific year, the filter context for any calculation or measure will include that selected year.

When you create a measure, such as "Total Sales," DAX considers the filter context in which it is evaluated.

The measure will return the total sales amount considering only the data that meets the applied filters.

So, if a user selects the year 2023 in the slicer, the "Total Sales" measure will show the total sales amount for the year 2023.

Understanding and managing filter context is crucial because it ensures that your calculations are context-aware and provide the correct results based on user interactions.

To further illustrate the concept of filter context, let's consider an example where you have a table of products and a table of sales transactions.

You want to create a measure that calculates the total sales amount for a selected product category.

In this scenario, the filter context is determined by the user's selection of a specific product category.

DAX allows you to work with this filter context seamlessly by referencing columns from related tables, like Product Category from the Products table.

This way, your measure can adapt to different user selections and provide accurate results based on the current filter context.

Now, let's explore row context, which is another critical aspect of DAX calculations.

Row context defines the context in which DAX calculations are performed for individual rows of data.

When you create a calculated column or use a DAX function that iterates through rows, such as SUMX or AVERAGEX, row context comes into play.

Row context is established for each row in a table, and DAX formulas evaluate within that context for each row individually.

For instance, if you have a table of products with a calculated column that computes the profit margin for each product, row context determines how the profit margin is calculated for each product row.

Row context can be thought of as a temporary context for a single row during calculations.

It enables you to perform row-level calculations that depend on the values in that specific row.

To work effectively with row context, you need to be aware of how DAX functions handle it.

Some functions, like FILTER and SUMX, iterate through rows and apply calculations within the row context.

For example, if you want to calculate the total revenue for each product based on the quantity sold and the unit price, you can use the SUMX function to iterate through each row and compute the revenue for that specific row.

daxCopy code

Total Revenue = SUMX (Sales, Sales[Quantity] * Sales[Unit Price])

In this formula, the SUMX function iterates through the rows in the Sales table, and for each row, it calculates the revenue by multiplying the quantity and unit price within the row context.

It then aggregates these individual row-level results to provide the total revenue.

One common scenario where understanding both filter context and row context is crucial is when creating measures that involve complex calculations.

For example, if you want to calculate the year-over-year growth in sales, you need to consider filter context to ensure that the calculation considers the selected time period.

At the same time, you also need to be aware of row context when performing calculations for individual sales transactions within the selected time period.

DAX provides functions like CALCULATE and FILTER to manipulate filter context within measures, allowing you to override or modify the existing filters based on specific criteria.

For instance, you can use CALCULATE to change the filter context for a measure temporarily.

Let's say you want to calculate the total sales for a specific product category regardless of the current filter context.

You can achieve this by using CALCULATE to remove any filters applied to the Product Category column:

daxCopy code

Total Sales for Category = CALCULATE ([Total Sales], ALL (Products[Category]))

In this formula, CALCULATE modifies the filter context by removing all filters applied to the Products[Category] column, effectively calculating the total sales for the selected category independently of other filters.

When working with DAX, it's essential to be mindful of the interplay between filter context and row context, as well as how functions manipulate these contexts.

This understanding allows you to create robust calculations and measures that produce accurate results in various scenarios.

Furthermore, DAX provides extensive capabilities for managing and manipulating both filter context and row context to meet the specific requirements of your data analysis and reporting tasks.

In summary, filter context and row context are foundational concepts in DAX that govern how calculations and measures are evaluated within a data model.

Filter context is determined by applied filters or criteria, while row context defines the context for individual rows during calculations. By mastering these concepts and using DAX functions effectively, you can create powerful and context-aware calculations that provide valuable insights from your data.

Chapter 5: Hierarchies and Time Intelligence in Data Models

Hierarchies are a fundamental component of data modeling and analysis, enabling you to organize and structure data in a meaningful way within tools like Power BI and other business intelligence platforms.

Next, we will explore the concepts of hierarchies, how to create them, and the various ways to manage hierarchies effectively to enhance your data analysis capabilities.

A hierarchy is a structured arrangement of data elements or attributes in a way that represents a parent-child relationship.

Hierarchies are particularly valuable when dealing with categorical or dimensional data, such as product categories, geographical regions, organizational structures, or time periods.

One of the primary benefits of hierarchies is that they allow you to drill down or roll up data to different levels of granularity, providing users with the flexibility to explore data at various levels of detail.

For example, consider a geographical hierarchy that includes continents, countries, states, and cities.

Users can start by viewing data at the continent level, then drill down to countries, states, and cities to gain a deeper understanding of regional data patterns.

Creating hierarchies in Power BI or similar tools is a straightforward process that involves defining the relationships between attributes or columns.

In Power BI, you can create hierarchies by selecting the relevant columns in your data model and configuring their hierarchy settings.

Let's take a closer look at how to create a hierarchy step by step:

Open your Power BI Desktop file and navigate to the Data view.

Identify the columns that you want to include in your hierarchy. In this example, let's say you have a table with geographical data containing columns for Continent, Country, State, and City.

Select the columns in the order you want them to appear in the hierarchy. Click and drag the Continent column to the top, followed by Country, State, and City.

Right-click on one of the selected columns and choose "Create Hierarchy" from the context menu.

Give your hierarchy a meaningful name, such as "Geographical Hierarchy."

Your hierarchy is now created and can be found in the Fields pane under the Tables section. You can expand or collapse the hierarchy levels as needed.

Once you have created a hierarchy, you can use it in your visualizations to provide users with the ability to drill down or roll up data effortlessly.

For example, you can add a visual, such as a table or chart, to your report canvas and drag the Geographical Hierarchy onto the visual's Axis field well.

Users can then interact with the hierarchy by expanding or collapsing levels to explore data at different levels of the geographical hierarchy.

In addition to creating hierarchies, it's essential to manage and customize them to meet your specific reporting and analysis requirements.

Power BI and similar tools offer various options for managing hierarchies, including sorting, defining default levels, and setting drill-through actions.

Sorting hierarchies allows you to control the order in which hierarchy levels are displayed.

You can choose to sort levels alphabetically, numerically, or based on custom criteria to ensure that the hierarchy presents data in a logical and user-friendly manner.

For instance, if you have a time hierarchy with levels for Year, Quarter, Month, and Day, you may want to sort the months chronologically within each quarter.

Power BI provides sorting options within the hierarchy settings to achieve this.

Defining default levels for hierarchies determines the initial state of the hierarchy when a report is loaded or when a visual is created.

You can set a default level to ensure that users start their analysis at a specific hierarchy level.

For instance, in a product hierarchy with levels for Category, Subcategory, and Product, you can set the default level to Category to provide an overview of product categories when users first access the report.

Drill-through actions are another valuable feature for enhancing the interactivity of hierarchies.

With drill-through actions, you can specify which hierarchy levels users can drill into to access more detailed information.

For instance, you can enable drill-through actions from a table visualization that allows users to click on a specific category and drill into the subcategories for more granular insights.

Configuring drill-through actions in Power BI involves defining which fields or columns should be included in the drill-through context and specifying the visuals or pages that users can navigate to when drilling through.

Hierarchies can also be customized in terms of formatting and appearance to align with the overall design and branding of your reports.

You can adjust fonts, colors, and spacing for hierarchy levels to make them visually appealing and easy to navigate.

In addition to standard hierarchies, Power BI allows you to create custom hierarchies, which are user-defined hierarchies that combine attributes from different tables.

Custom hierarchies provide flexibility in organizing and exploring data beyond the natural relationships defined in your data model.

For example, you can create a custom hierarchy that combines product attributes from both a Products table and a Categories table, allowing users to drill down into products based on different criteria.

To create a custom hierarchy in Power BI, you can follow these steps:

In the Fields pane, select the table containing the attributes you want to include in the custom hierarchy.

Choose the attributes you want to add to the hierarchy by dragging them into the Values section of a new table visual.

In the visual, right-click on one of the attributes and select "Create Hierarchy" from the context menu.

Give your custom hierarchy a meaningful name.

Your custom hierarchy is now available in the Fields pane and can be used in your visuals like any other hierarchy.

Custom hierarchies provide users with additional flexibility to explore data and create tailored analysis paths.

In summary, hierarchies are a powerful tool in data modeling and analysis, offering a structured way to organize and navigate data in a meaningful manner.

Creating hierarchies involves defining relationships between columns, and they allow users to drill down or roll up data to different levels of detail.

Managing hierarchies includes sorting, setting default levels, defining drill-through actions, and customizing appearance to enhance user experience and interactivity.

Custom hierarchies provide even greater flexibility by allowing you to combine attributes from different tables.

By effectively creating and managing hierarchies, you can empower users to explore data, uncover insights, and make informed decisions within your reports and dashboards.

Time Intelligence functions are a crucial component of data modeling and analysis when dealing with temporal data, such as sales over time, stock prices, or user activity tracking.

Next, we will explore the concepts of time intelligence, the importance of time-based calculations, and how to implement Time Intelligence functions effectively in tools like Power BI.

Time Intelligence functions provide the ability to perform calculations and aggregations based on dates and time-related dimensions, such as years, quarters, months, weeks, and days.

These functions enable users to gain valuable insights into trends, patterns, and seasonality within their data, making them essential for any time-series analysis.

One common use case for Time Intelligence functions is calculating year-over-year growth, which helps businesses understand how their performance compares to the same period in the previous year.

For instance, a retail company may want to determine the year-over-year growth in sales for each month to assess their sales performance trends.

Time Intelligence functions in Power BI, such as SAMEPERIODLASTYEAR and TOTALYTD, make it easy to compute these types of comparisons.

Implementing Time Intelligence functions typically involves creating measures that utilize these functions within your data model.

Let's take a closer look at some key Time Intelligence functions and how to use them effectively:

YTD (Year-to-Date): This function allows you to calculate values for a specific measure from the beginning of the year up to the selected date. It's useful for tracking cumulative performance throughout the year. To implement it, you can create a measure like:

mathematicaCopy code

YTD Sales = TOTALYTD([Total Sales], 'Date'[Date])

This measure computes the year-to-date sales by summing up the total sales from the beginning of the year up to the selected date.

QTD (Quarter-to-Date): Similar to YTD, this function calculates values for a specific measure from the beginning of the quarter up to the selected date. You can create a measure like:

mathematicaCopy code

QTD Revenue = TOTALQTD([Total Revenue], 'Date'[Date])

This measure computes the quarter-to-date revenue based on the total revenue from the start of the quarter to the chosen date.

MOM (Month-over-Month): This function helps you compare values between different months. It's particularly useful for identifying trends and seasonality. To implement it, you can create a measure like:

mathematicaCopy code

MOM Sales Growth = [Total Sales] - CALCULATE([Total Sales], DATEADD('Date'[Date], -1, MONTH))

This measure calculates the month-over-month sales growth by subtracting the total sales for the previous month from the current month's total sales.

YOY (Year-over-Year): This function is essential for assessing annual growth or changes in performance. You can create a measure like:

mathematicaCopy code

YOY Revenue Growth = [Total Revenue] - CALCULATE([Total Revenue], SAMEPERIODLASTYEAR('Date'[Date]))

This measure computes the year-over-year revenue growth by subtracting the total revenue for the same period in the previous year from the current year's total revenue.

Running Totals: Time Intelligence functions can also help you calculate running totals, which provide a cumulative view of a measure over time. For instance:

mathematicaCopy code

Running Total Sales = TOTALMTD([Total Sales], 'Date'[Date])

This measure computes the running total of sales from the beginning of the data up to the selected date.

It's important to note that to use Time Intelligence functions effectively, you should have a well-structured date table in your data model.

A date table is a dedicated table that contains a complete range of dates, along with various attributes like year, quarter, month, week, and day.

In Power BI, you can create a date table by importing or generating date data, ensuring it covers the entire time range of your dataset.

Once you have a date table, you can establish relationships between it and other tables in your data model based on date-related fields.

These relationships enable Time Intelligence functions to work seamlessly, as they rely on the date hierarchy defined in your date table.

In Power BI, you can create a relationship by navigating to the "Model" view, selecting the date fields in both tables, and specifying the type of relationship (e.g., one-to-many).

Furthermore, Time Intelligence functions can be combined with other DAX functions to perform complex calculations and gain deeper insights.

For example, you can use the AVERAGEX function along with Time Intelligence functions to compute the moving average of a measure over a specific period.

The flexibility and versatility of Time Intelligence functions make them indispensable for data analysts and business intelligence professionals when analyzing time-series data.

Time Intelligence functions not only simplify the process of creating meaningful reports and visualizations but also empower users to explore data dynamically by selecting different time periods and comparing trends effortlessly.

In addition to calculations, Time Intelligence functions enable you to create compelling visuals that showcase temporal data effectively.

For instance, you can use line charts, bar charts, or area charts to visualize time-series data and highlight specific points of interest, such as spikes or dips in performance.

To summarize, Time Intelligence functions are a vital tool for analyzing temporal data in Power BI and similar tools.

By creating well-structured date tables, establishing relationships, and implementing Time Intelligence measures, you can unlock the power of time-based analysis and provide valuable insights to your organization.

Whether you're tracking sales, monitoring website traffic, or assessing user engagement, Time Intelligence functions help you make data-driven decisions by revealing trends, patterns, and seasonality in your data.

Chapter 6: Calculated Tables and Columns for Enhanced Insights

Calculated tables are a valuable feature in Power BI and other data analysis tools that enable you to generate new tables dynamically based on your existing data and calculations.

Next, we will delve into the concept of calculated tables, their significance in advanced analysis, and how to create and utilize them effectively in your data models.

Calculated tables are tables generated within your data model using Data Analysis Expressions (DAX) formulas.

Unlike regular tables that are loaded directly from your data source, calculated tables are computed on-the-fly based on your specified calculations and criteria.

These tables offer tremendous flexibility and can be employed for a wide range of advanced analysis scenarios.

One of the primary reasons for using calculated tables is to extend the capabilities of your data model by creating additional dimensions or aggregations that are not present in your original data source.

Consider a scenario where you have sales data, and you want to perform analyses based on the day of the week, but your data source only contains date information.

A calculated table can be generated to extract the day of the week from the date column, allowing you to explore and visualize sales trends by day.

Creating a calculated table starts with defining a DAX formula that specifies the logic for generating the table.

Let's examine the steps involved in creating a calculated table:

**Open your Power BI Desktop file and navigate to the "Model" view.

In the "Model" view, right-click on the empty space in the "Fields" pane, and select "New Table" from the context menu.

A formula bar will appear where you can enter your DAX formula for the calculated table. For instance, to create a table that lists unique values of product categories, you can use the following formula:

javaCopy code

```
Product Categories = VALUES( 'Sales' [Category])
```

This formula creates a calculated table named "Product Categories" that contains a distinct list of product categories from the 'Sales' table.

Press "Enter" to confirm the formula, and the calculated table will be added to your data model.

Once the calculated table is created, you can utilize it just like any other table in your data model. You can drag and drop its columns into visuals, create relationships with other tables, and use it as a dimension for slicing and dicing data.

Calculated tables offer several advantages, including the ability to:

Simplify complex calculations: Calculated tables can precompute results of complex calculations, making it easier to build meaningful visuals and measures.

Extend data models: You can use calculated tables to add new dimensions or hierarchies to your data model, enhancing its analytical capabilities.

Enhance performance: By reducing the need for real-time calculations, calculated tables can improve query and report performance.

Create custom aggregations: You can create calculated tables to aggregate data in a customized way that isn't possible with standard aggregation functions.

Accommodate business-specific needs: Calculated tables allow you to cater to unique business requirements by generating tables tailored to your analysis.

Beyond basic calculated tables, there are advanced scenarios where you can leverage calculated tables for more sophisticated analysis.

For example, you can create calculated tables to implement advanced time intelligence calculations, such as rolling averages, moving sums, or cumulative totals, which may not be available directly from your data source.

In addition to enhancing your data model's analytical capabilities, calculated tables are instrumental in addressing specific business requirements.

Consider a scenario where your organization wants to categorize customers into different segments based on their purchase behavior.

You can create a calculated table that uses DAX functions to classify customers into segments such as "High Value," "Medium Value," and "Low Value" based on their total purchase amounts.

By utilizing calculated tables, you can automate this segmentation process, ensuring that it stays up-to-date as new data is added to your model.

Moreover, calculated tables can be employed for scenario modeling and "what-if" analysis. You can create tables that simulate different business scenarios by adjusting parameters in your DAX formulas.

For example, you can create a calculated table to project future sales based on different growth rates, enabling you to evaluate the impact of various growth scenarios on your business.

Another advanced application of calculated tables is in handling complex filtering and security requirements. You can generate calculated tables that dynamically filter data based on specific user roles or conditions.

For instance, you can create a calculated table that restricts access to sensitive information, ensuring that only authorized users can view certain data elements.

Calculated tables also play a significant role in accommodating dynamic hierarchies within your data models. You can use calculated tables to create hierarchies that adapt to user selections and provide a tailored view of data.

For instance, you can create a calculated table that generates a dynamic time hierarchy allowing users to drill down from years to quarters to months based on their preferences.

In summary, calculated tables are a powerful tool for advanced analysis and modeling in Power BI and other data analysis platforms.

They offer flexibility in extending data models, automating complex calculations, addressing specific business requirements, and enabling scenario modeling and security implementations.

By mastering the creation and utilization of calculated tables, you can enhance your data modeling skills and provide valuable insights to your organization through more sophisticated and customized data analysis. Calculated columns are a fundamental concept in Power BI and other data analysis tools that enable you to create new columns in your dataset by defining expressions or calculations. Next, we will explore the significance of calculated columns in data analysis, how to create them effectively, and how they can provide valuable insights for your reports and visualizations.

Calculated columns allow you to extend your dataset with new data derived from existing columns, apply business rules, and perform calculations that are not directly available in your source data. The primary difference between calculated columns and calculated tables, as discussed in the previous chapter, lies in their scope.

While calculated tables generate new tables within your data model, calculated columns create new columns within existing tables.

This distinction is crucial because calculated columns become part of your dataset and can be used for filtering, sorting, and aggregating data.

To illustrate the importance of calculated columns, let's consider a practical scenario:

Imagine you have a dataset containing sales transactions with columns for 'ProductID,' 'Quantity Sold,' and 'Unit Price.' You want to calculate the 'Total Sales' for each transaction by multiplying the quantity sold by the unit price.

Creating a calculated column is an efficient way to achieve this without modifying your source data. Here's how you can do it:

Open your Power BI Desktop file and navigate to the "Model" view.

In the "Fields" pane, select the table where you want to create the calculated column. In this case, it's the 'Sales' table.

Right-click on the selected table and choose "New Column" from the context menu.

A formula bar will appear, allowing you to enter the DAX formula for the calculated column. To calculate 'Total Sales,' you can use the following formula:

javaCopy code

Total Sales = 'Sales'[Quantity Sold] * 'Sales'[Unit Price]

This formula multiplies the 'Quantity Sold' by the 'Unit Price' for each row, resulting in the 'Total Sales' for each transaction.

Press "Enter" to confirm the formula, and the calculated column 'Total Sales' will be added to your 'Sales' table.

Now, your dataset includes the 'Total Sales' column, which is automatically calculated based on the existing data whenever you refresh or modify your report.

Calculated columns offer several advantages in data analysis:

Custom Data Enhancements: You can create calculated columns to add custom dimensions, metrics, or classifications to your data. For instance, you can categorize products into different price tiers or assign customers to specific segments based on their purchase behavior.

Advanced Filtering: Calculated columns allow you to apply complex filtering and sorting operations based on the calculated values. You can use these columns to create slicers, apply visual-level filters, and perform row-level security based on custom criteria.

Enhanced Visualizations: Calculated columns provide additional data points that can be used in visualizations. You can create visuals that utilize these columns to uncover patterns, trends, and relationships in your data.

Dynamic Metrics: Calculated columns enable you to calculate dynamic metrics that adapt to user selections. For example, you can create a calculated column to compute the rolling average of sales over a selected time period.

Scenario Analysis: Calculated columns are valuable for scenario modeling and "what-if" analysis. You can create columns that simulate different scenarios by adjusting parameters in your DAX formulas. This allows you to explore the impact of various scenarios on your data.

In addition to basic calculations, calculated columns can be used for more advanced data transformations and pattern recognition.

For example, you can create calculated columns to identify outliers, detect seasonality in time-series data, or perform sentiment analysis on textual data by analyzing keywords and sentiment scores.

Furthermore, calculated columns are particularly useful when working with data that requires custom transformations, such as financial data that needs to be converted into specific formats or geographical data that requires coordinate calculations.

One important consideration when using calculated columns is their impact on data model size and performance.

Calculated columns increase the size of your data model because they store the calculated values for each row, potentially consuming more memory and storage.

However, they can also improve query performance by precomputing values, especially when dealing with complex calculations or aggregations.

To mitigate the impact on data model size, it's essential to use calculated columns judiciously and consider the trade-off between improved performance and increased storage requirements.

In some cases, calculated columns may not be the best choice, and you may opt for measures or calculated tables instead, depending on your specific analysis needs.

In summary, calculated columns are a fundamental tool in data analysis, providing the means to extend your dataset with custom calculations, dimensions, and metrics.

They offer flexibility in enhancing your data model, enabling advanced filtering and visualizations, supporting dynamic metrics, and facilitating scenario analysis.

By mastering the creation and utilization of calculated columns, you can gain deeper insights into your data, uncover hidden patterns, and create more informative and interactive reports and visualizations.

Chapter 7: Managing and Optimizing Data Models

Optimizing your data model is a critical aspect of Power BI development, ensuring that your reports and dashboards deliver excellent performance and a smooth user experience.

Next, we will explore various data model optimization strategies, techniques, and best practices that can help you create efficient and responsive Power BI solutions.

Data model optimization involves fine-tuning your Power BI data model to enhance query performance, reduce resource consumption, and improve the overall responsiveness of your reports.

A well-optimized data model not only delivers faster query results but also enables you to work with larger datasets and more complex reports.

Let's dive into some key strategies for optimizing your Power BI data model:

Data Source Optimization: Start by optimizing your data source queries. Use direct query connections or data source-specific optimizations to fetch only the necessary data, minimizing data transfer and processing.

Data Cleansing: Ensure that your data is clean and free of inconsistencies. Use Power Query's data transformation capabilities to clean, filter, and shape your data before it enters the data model.

Data Compression: Power BI employs efficient data compression techniques to reduce the memory footprint of your data model. Utilize summarized tables and aggregations to further optimize data storage.

Column Selection: Be selective in choosing which columns to load into your data model. Only include columns that are essential for your analysis, as unnecessary columns consume memory.

Relationship Optimization: Carefully design and optimize relationships between tables. Use a single-directional filter flow and define relationships with minimal cardinality to improve query performance.

Use Measures: Instead of calculated columns, consider using measures for calculations. Measures are computed on-the-fly, reducing the need for additional storage.

Model Simplification: Keep your data model as simple as possible. Avoid unnecessary hierarchies, tables, or calculated tables that may add complexity without providing significant value.

Partitioning: Implement data partitioning where applicable, especially for large datasets. Partition tables based on date or other logical criteria to improve query performance.

Aggregations: Create aggregations for frequently used measures, allowing Power BI to use summarized data for quicker responses to queries.

Indexing: Optimize table indexing for improved query performance. Utilize column indexing and sort by columns that are frequently used for filtering and sorting.

Avoid Overloading: Be mindful of overloading visuals with data. Limit the number of visuals and data points on a single page to avoid performance bottlenecks.

Report-Level Optimization: Optimize your reports by minimizing the use of high-cardinality visuals, reducing the number of slicers, and avoiding complex custom visuals that can slow down rendering.

Cross-Filtering: Limit the use of bidirectional cross-filtering, as it can introduce performance issues. Utilize one-way filtering whenever possible.

Memory Management: Monitor and manage memory usage in Power BI Desktop. Avoid unnecessary data loading and data model expansion that can lead to memory-related performance problems.

Performance Analyzer: Use Power BI's built-in Performance Analyzer tool to identify bottlenecks and areas for improvement in your reports and data models.

Query Folding: Ensure that data source queries are folded whenever possible, allowing the database engine to perform data transformations and filtering before bringing data into Power BI.

Data Refresh: Schedule data refresh during off-peak hours to reduce the impact on system resources and ensure timely data updates.

Use of Parameters: Implement query parameters to enable dynamic filtering and reduce the need for multiple similar queries.

Advanced Techniques: Consider advanced optimization techniques such as query reduction, star schema modeling, and row-level security optimizations for enterprise-level solutions.

Testing and Monitoring: Regularly test and monitor your Power BI solutions for performance issues. Use tools like Query Diagnostics and Performance Analyzer to identify and address problems.

Documentation: Document your data model, including relationships, calculations, and optimizations. This helps in maintaining and troubleshooting the model over time.

User Training: Provide training to report consumers on best practices for interacting with reports to minimize unnecessary data loading and filtering.

By implementing these data model optimization strategies, you can create Power BI solutions that are both efficient and responsive, delivering a seamless user experience and enabling users to derive insights from data quickly.

Remember that optimization is an iterative process, and ongoing monitoring and refinement of your data model are essential to maintain peak performance as data and report requirements evolve.

Performance tuning and troubleshooting are essential skills for Power BI developers and administrators to ensure that reports and dashboards deliver optimal performance and respond efficiently to user interactions.

Next, we will explore various performance tuning techniques and troubleshooting methods to identify and address common performance bottlenecks in your Power BI solutions.

Performance tuning involves optimizing the performance of your Power BI reports and data models to provide users with a responsive and seamless experience.

Whether you are working on a small-scale project or an enterprise-level solution, performance tuning plays a crucial role in ensuring that your reports load quickly, respond to user interactions promptly, and efficiently handle large datasets.

Here are some key performance tuning techniques:

Query Optimization: Start by optimizing your queries. Use the "Query Diagnostics" feature in Power Query to identify slow-loading queries and optimize them for faster data retrieval.

Data Model Optimization: Review and optimize your data model for better query performance. Consider using aggregations, summarized tables, and calculated tables to reduce the amount of data that needs to be processed.

DAX Optimization: Optimize DAX calculations by using measures instead of calculated columns wherever possible. Use DAX functions that are more efficient for specific calculations.

Indexing: Implement indexing on columns that are frequently used for filtering and sorting. This can significantly improve query performance.

Data Partitioning: If you are working with large datasets, consider partitioning your data tables by date or another logical criterion. Partitioning can speed up query performance by limiting the amount of data that needs to be scanned.

Aggregations: Create aggregations to precompute and store summarized data. This allows Power BI to use summarized data when appropriate, reducing query times.

Visual-Level Optimization: Optimize visuals by reducing the number of data points displayed, using slicers and filters effectively, and limiting the use of complex custom visuals.

Report-Level Optimization: Minimize the use of high-cardinality visuals and visuals that require intensive calculations. Keep an eye on the performance analyzer to identify potential bottlenecks.

Data Refresh: Schedule data refresh during non-peak hours to avoid resource contention and ensure that data is up-to-date when users access the reports.

Memory Management: Monitor and manage memory usage in Power BI Desktop. Avoid loading unnecessary data and visuals that can strain system resources.

Parameterization: Use query parameters to enable dynamic filtering and reduce the need for multiple similar queries. This can lead to more efficient query execution.

Caching: Leverage Power BI's caching mechanisms to store query results and visuals. Cached data can be reused for faster loading times.

Data Compression: Use data compression techniques to reduce the memory footprint of your data model. Compressed data loads faster and consumes fewer resources.

Troubleshooting is an essential part of performance tuning. Even with the best optimization practices in place, you may encounter performance issues that require investigation and resolution.

Here are some troubleshooting techniques:

Performance Analyzer: Use Power BI's Performance Analyzer tool to identify bottlenecks in your reports and data models. It provides detailed information about query execution times, visuals, and data sources.

Query Diagnostics: Enable query diagnostics to capture query execution details, including query plans and query folding. Analyze this information to optimize slow queries.

DAX Studio: DAX Studio is a powerful tool for analyzing and optimizing DAX queries and calculations. Use it to profile DAX queries and identify performance bottlenecks.

Monitoring Tools: Implement monitoring tools and alerts to track system performance, resource utilization, and data refresh schedules. This helps in identifying issues proactively.

Query Folding: Ensure that query folding is occurring wherever possible. Query folding allows the data source to perform data transformations and filtering, reducing the amount of data transferred to Power BI.

Data Source Profiling: Profile your data sources to understand the structure and distribution of your data. This can help identify potential issues with data quality and distribution.

Error Handling: Implement error handling and logging mechanisms in your data transformation processes to capture and analyze errors during data refresh.

Data Source Optimization: If you are using custom connectors or complex data sources, ensure that they are optimized for performance and compatibility with Power BI.

Resource Monitoring: Monitor system resources, such as CPU, memory, and disk usage, to identify resource constraints that may impact performance.

User Feedback: Gather feedback from users to identify specific performance issues they encounter. Use this feedback to prioritize and address performance improvements.

In addition to these techniques, it's essential to stay updated with the latest Power BI updates and features, as Microsoft continuously releases enhancements that can impact performance and troubleshooting capabilities.

Finally, remember that performance tuning and troubleshooting are ongoing processes. Regularly monitor and review the performance of your Power BI solutions, make adjustments as needed, and stay vigilant for potential bottlenecks as your data and user requirements evolve.

Chapter 8: Aggregations and Summarization for Large Datasets

Implementing aggregations is a critical technique in Power BI to improve query performance and ensure that your reports and dashboards are responsive even when dealing with large datasets.

Aggregations allow you to precompute and store summarized data that can be used to answer common queries quickly, reducing the need to scan and aggregate large volumes of raw data.

Next, we will explore how to implement aggregations in Power BI to achieve better query performance and deliver a smoother user experience.

Aggregation Basics:

Aggregations work by creating smaller, summarized versions of your data that can answer specific types of queries efficiently. These summarized versions are stored alongside your detailed data and are used when appropriate to speed up query execution.

When to Use Aggregations:

You should consider implementing aggregations when dealing with large datasets that have multiple dimensions and hierarchies. Aggregations are particularly useful when your reports require quick responses to aggregation queries like sums, averages, or counts.

The Aggregation Process:

Implementing aggregations involves the following steps:

Identify Measures: Begin by identifying the measures in your data model that are candidates for aggregation. These are typically numerical calculations like sales totals or averages.

Select Dimensions: Determine which dimensions or attributes will be used to slice and dice the data in your reports. These dimensions will be used to create aggregations.

Create Aggregation Tables: Build aggregation tables that summarize the data at different levels of granularity. For example, you may create an aggregation table that stores monthly sales totals for each product and region.

Define Relationships: Establish relationships between your aggregation tables and the detailed data tables in your data model. These relationships allow Power BI to automatically switch between detailed and aggregated data as needed.

Configure Storage Modes: Configure the storage mode for your aggregation tables. You can choose between Import and DirectQuery storage modes based on your requirements.

Import Storage Mode:

In Import mode, the aggregated data is imported into the Power BI dataset, allowing for extremely fast query performance. To configure an aggregation table in Import mode, follow these steps:

Open Power BI Desktop.

Create a new table or query that contains the aggregated data. You can use Power Query to build this table.

In the Power Query editor, load the aggregation table into the data model.

Create relationships between the aggregation table and the relevant detailed data tables.

Set the storage mode of the aggregation table to "Import" in the "Model" view of Power BI Desktop.

Configure the aggregation options for measures in your report visuals to use the aggregation tables when appropriate.

DirectQuery Storage Mode:

In DirectQuery mode, the aggregated data remains in the source database, and Power BI sends queries to the database for real-time aggregation. To configure an aggregation table in DirectQuery mode, follow these steps:

Create a database view or a materialized view in your source database that contains the aggregated data.

Connect Power BI to the database and create a connection to the view.

Establish relationships between the DirectQuery tables and the detailed data tables.

Configure the measures in your report visuals to use the DirectQuery tables when appropriate.

Query Folding and Performance:

When using DirectQuery mode, it's essential to ensure that query folding is happening effectively. Query folding means that as much of the data processing as possible occurs within the source database, reducing data transfer and processing in Power BI.

Optimizing Aggregations:

To optimize aggregations for improved performance:

Keep aggregation tables as small as possible while still providing value.

Monitor query performance and adjust aggregation levels based on usage patterns.

Consider creating multiple aggregation tables with different granularities to cater to different reporting needs.

Test and iterate on your aggregation design to ensure optimal query performance.

In summary, implementing aggregations is a powerful technique for improving query performance in Power BI. By creating summarized versions of your data and intelligently configuring storage modes, you can deliver responsive reports and dashboards even when working with large and complex datasets.

Data summarization techniques are fundamental in data analysis and reporting, as they allow you to distill large volumes of data into concise, meaningful insights that can drive informed decision-making.

Next, we will explore various data summarization techniques and their applications in the context of Power BI and data analysis.

Aggregation: One of the most common data summarization techniques is aggregation, which involves combining data values into a single value based on a specific criterion. For example, you can aggregate sales data to calculate the total revenue for a specific period.

Summarization Levels: Data can be summarized at different levels of granularity. For instance, you can summarize sales data at the daily, monthly, or yearly level, depending on your reporting needs. Power BI provides flexibility in defining summarization levels.

Grouping: Grouping is a technique used to categorize and summarize data by common attributes. In Power BI, you can group data using the "Group By" feature, which allows you to create custom groupings based on specific columns or calculations.

Pivoting and Unpivoting: Pivoting involves reorganizing data to view it from a different perspective. Unpivoting, on the other hand, is the process of transforming columns into rows. These techniques are useful for summarizing data in a more structured format.

Filtering and Slicing: Data summarization can also be achieved by applying filters or slicers to your visualizations. This allows users to focus on specific subsets of data, effectively summarizing the information presented.

Rolling Totals and Moving Averages: Rolling totals involve calculating cumulative sums or averages over a specific time period. This technique is valuable for analyzing trends and patterns in time-series data.

Percentiles and Quartiles: Percentiles and quartiles are summary statistics that provide insights into the distribution of data. Power BI includes functions like "PERCENTILEX.INC" and "QUARTILE.INC" for calculating these values.

Top N Analysis: Top N analysis is a summarization technique used to identify the top or bottom items based on a specific measure. For example, you can determine the top-selling products or lowest-performing employees.

Hierarchy Summarization: Hierarchies are commonly used in data summarization. They allow you to drill down from higher-level summaries to more detailed information. Power BI supports hierarchies in data modeling.

Custom Calculations: Data summarization often involves creating custom calculations and measures. Power BI's DAX (Data Analysis Expressions) language is a powerful tool for defining complex custom calculations to summarize data.

Data Modeling Techniques: Effective data modeling is crucial for data summarization. Power BI's modeling capabilities, including relationships, hierarchies, and calculated tables, enable you to structure data for efficient summarization.

Cross-Filtering and Highlighting: Cross-filtering and highlighting techniques allow users to interactively summarize data by selecting data points within visualizations. This provides a dynamic way to explore and summarize data.

Parameterization: Parameterization is a technique that allows users to change certain inputs or criteria, which can affect data summarization. Parameters can be used to create dynamic reports that adapt to user preferences.

Time Intelligence: Summarizing data over time is a common requirement. Power BI offers time intelligence functions like "TOTALYTD" and "SAMEPERIODLASTYEAR" to facilitate summarization based on date and time dimensions.

Conditional Summarization: Conditional summarization involves applying summarization techniques based on specific conditions or criteria. For example, you can summarize sales data differently for different regions or product categories.

Statistical Summarization: Statistical techniques like mean, median, standard deviation, and variance are valuable for summarizing data distribution and variability.

Data Profiling: Data profiling tools can automatically generate summary statistics and insights about your data, helping you understand its quality and characteristics.

Data Visualization: Data visualization is a powerful way to summarize data visually. Charts, graphs, and dashboards enable users to grasp key insights quickly.

In Power BI, you can leverage these summarization techniques within visualizations, measures, and calculated columns to create meaningful reports and dashboards. Additionally, Power Query provides a robust environment for data transformation and summarization before data enters the data model.

Effective data summarization is a skill that requires a balance between simplicity and informativeness. The goal is to present data in a way that is easy to understand and actionable for decision-makers while retaining essential details.

As you explore data summarization techniques in Power BI, consider the specific requirements of your reports and the preferences of your audience. Tailoring your summarization approaches to the unique characteristics of your data and the needs of your users will result in more impactful insights and reports.

Handling advanced business logic in Power BI models is essential to create robust and insightful reports and dashboards that cater to specific business requirements.

Custom Measures and Calculations: One way to handle advanced business logic is by creating custom measures and calculations using the DAX (Data Analysis Expressions) language. DAX provides a powerful set of functions and operators that allow you to define complex calculations tailored to your business needs. For example, you can calculate year-to-date sales, growth rates, or customer churn rates.

Time Intelligence: Time intelligence is a critical aspect of handling advanced business logic, especially for organizations that rely heavily on time-based data. Power BI offers various time-related functions like "TOTALYTD," "SAMEPERIODLASTYEAR," and "DATESBETWEEN" to enable time-based calculations. These functions are vital for analyzing trends, seasonality, and year-over-year performance.

Parameterization: Parameterization is a technique that allows users to change certain inputs or criteria dynamically. It is particularly useful for creating versatile reports that adapt to user preferences or varying business scenarios. For instance, you can use parameters to change date ranges, filter criteria, or comparison periods interactively.

Advanced Filtering Techniques: Power BI provides advanced filtering capabilities that enable you to apply complex filters to your data. You can use techniques like relative date filtering, top N filtering, and advanced filtering expressions to refine data presentation based on specific business logic.

Conditional Formatting: Conditional formatting is a powerful tool for highlighting data points based on predefined conditions or rules. This technique is valuable for emphasizing critical information in your reports. For example, you can use conditional formatting to highlight underperforming products or outstanding invoices.

Data Modeling: Effective data modeling is crucial for handling advanced business logic. Properly defining relationships, hierarchies, and calculated tables in your data model ensures that your measures and calculations function correctly. A well-structured data model simplifies the implementation of complex business logic.

Advanced DAX Functions: Power BI offers a wide range of advanced DAX functions that facilitate complex calculations. Functions like "EARLIER," "FILTER," "ALL," and "SWITCH" allow you to address intricate business requirements. These functions are essential for scenarios involving advanced filtering, row-level security, and conditional calculations.

Parameter Tables: Parameter tables are tables in your data model that store values or configurations used for calculations. You can create parameter tables to store constants, thresholds, or reference data that your measures and calculations rely on. This approach simplifies maintenance and ensures consistency across reports.

Handling Hierarchies: Many businesses deal with hierarchical data structures. Power BI supports hierarchies in data modeling, allowing you to handle advanced business logic related to hierarchical relationships. Hierarchies are essential for drilling down from summary levels to detailed data and vice versa.

Advanced Data Transformations: Power Query, the data transformation engine in Power BI, enables advanced data transformations. You can use custom functions, conditional transformations, and merging techniques to shape your data according to intricate business requirements.

Advanced Joining and Merging: Combining data from multiple sources or tables often requires advanced joining and merging techniques. Power Query offers capabilities to perform complex joins and transformations, ensuring that data integration aligns with your business logic.

Handling Data Quality: Advanced business logic often includes data quality considerations. Power Query provides tools for data profiling, cleansing, and transformation to address data quality issues. Techniques like data validation and error handling are crucial for maintaining data accuracy.

Handling Large Datasets: For organizations dealing with large datasets, optimizing data loading and query performance becomes paramount. Power BI offers techniques like data partitioning and aggregations to handle large datasets efficiently.

Iterative Calculations: Some advanced business logic requires iterative calculations, where a calculation depends on its own output. Power BI supports iterative functions like "SUMX" and "AVERAGEX" for such scenarios.

Scenario Analysis: Handling different business scenarios is a common requirement. You can use techniques like "What-If" parameters and scenario analysis to evaluate the impact of various assumptions and decisions on your data.

Advanced Visualization Customization: To convey complex business insights effectively, you may need to customize visualizations extensively. Power BI provides a wide range of customization options, including custom visuals and themes, to tailor your reports to specific business needs.

Dynamic Reporting: Dynamic reporting involves creating reports that adapt to user interactions or changing data conditions. Techniques like bookmarks, drill-through actions, and interactive visuals enable dynamic reporting in Power BI.

Handling advanced business logic in Power BI models requires a deep understanding of the DAX language, data modeling concepts, and the specific requirements of your organization. It involves a combination of data transformation, calculation, visualization, and user interaction techniques to create reports and dashboards that provide valuable insights for decision-makers.

Complex business scenarios demand sophisticated solutions in Power BI, as organizations seek to extract valuable insights from their data.

Hierarchical Data Analysis: Many industries deal with hierarchical data structures, such as organizational hierarchies, product categories, or geographical regions. To address complex business scenarios involving hierarchies, Power BI allows users to create custom hierarchies within the data model. These hierarchies facilitate drill-down and roll-up operations, enabling users to analyze data at different levels of granularity.

Multi-Source Data Integration: In real-world scenarios, data often originates from multiple sources, including databases, spreadsheets, web services, and cloud platforms. Power BI's data integration capabilities allow organizations to connect to and consolidate data from diverse sources seamlessly. The Power Query tool, for instance, enables data transformation, cleansing, and enrichment, ensuring that data from various sources can be harmonized for analysis.

Cross-Functional Analysis: Power BI supports cross-functional analysis by enabling users from different departments to collaborate and gain insights from the same dataset. Cross-functional dashboards can provide a holistic view of the organization's performance, allowing stakeholders from various departments, such as sales, marketing, finance, and operations, to access and analyze relevant data in one place.

Real-Time Data Analysis: In today's fast-paced business environment, real-time data analysis is essential. Power BI offers streaming capabilities that enable organizations to ingest and analyze streaming data sources, such as IoT devices or social media feeds, in real time. This allows for immediate decision-making and monitoring of dynamic business processes.

Advanced Analytics Integration: Complex business scenarios often require advanced analytics, including predictive modeling, machine learning, and statistical analysis. Power BI can integrate with advanced analytics tools like R and Python, enabling data scientists and analysts to leverage predictive models and algorithms within their reports and dashboards. This integration empowers organizations to make data-driven predictions and forecasts.

Custom Data Connectors: Sometimes, businesses work with specialized data sources that aren't supported out-of-the-box by Power BI. In such cases, organizations can create custom data connectors using the Power Query M language or leverage existing custom connectors developed by the community. These connectors enable the seamless integration of unique data sources into Power BI.

Row-Level Security: Maintaining data security and privacy is critical, especially when dealing with sensitive information. Power BI offers row-level security, allowing organizations to implement fine-grained access control. This feature ensures that users only see the data relevant to their roles and responsibilities, even within a shared report or dashboard.

Advanced Data Transformations: Complex business scenarios often require intricate data transformations, such as merging, unpivoting, or pivoting data tables. Power Query provides a user-friendly interface for performing these transformations and automating data cleaning processes, saving valuable time and effort.

Custom Visualizations: To address unique business requirements, Power BI enables users to create custom visualizations using technologies like D3.js. Custom visuals allow organizations to display data in innovative ways that standard visuals might not support.

Scenario Analysis: Organizations frequently need to perform scenario analysis to assess the potential impact of different decisions or external factors on their operations. Power BI supports scenario analysis through techniques like parameterization and "What-If" analysis. Users can create scenarios by adjusting parameters or assumptions and instantly see how those changes affect their data and key performance indicators.

Natural Language Processing (NLP): Power BI incorporates NLP capabilities, such as Q&A and Quick Insights, which enable users to interact with their data using natural language queries and receive automated insights. NLP features make it easier for non-technical users to explore data and uncover valuable insights.

Enterprise-Level Deployments: For large organizations, deploying Power BI at an enterprise level involves considerations such as scalability, governance, and performance optimization. Organizations can deploy Power BI in the cloud, on-premises, or in a hybrid environment, depending on their specific needs and data security policies.

Extensibility: Power BI's extensibility options allow organizations to tailor the platform to their specific business scenarios. This includes developing custom visuals, integrating with external applications, and automating tasks through APIs and scripting.

Data Storytelling: In complex business scenarios, effectively communicating insights is crucial. Power BI offers data storytelling capabilities, enabling users to create compelling narratives that guide decision-makers through the data-driven insights and recommendations.

Audit and Compliance: Organizations in highly regulated industries must adhere to strict audit and compliance requirements. Power BI provides auditing and compliance features that allow organizations to track user activity, secure sensitive data, and meet regulatory standards.

Global Collaboration: In today's globalized business environment, collaboration across geographical boundaries is essential. Power BI facilitates global collaboration by enabling users to share reports and dashboards with stakeholders worldwide. The platform supports multiple languages and allows for data localization.

Machine Learning Integration: Advanced business scenarios often involve leveraging machine learning models for predictive analytics and anomaly detection. Power BI can integrate with machine learning platforms like Azure Machine Learning, making it easier to incorporate machine learning capabilities into reports and dashboards.

Custom Data Refresh Schedules: Complex scenarios may require customized data refresh schedules to ensure that data is up-to-date when needed. Power BI allows users to define refresh schedules based on business requirements, ensuring timely access to the latest data.

Data Distribution and Subscriptions: Distributing insights to a broad audience is a key aspect of addressing complex business scenarios. Power BI offers options for sharing reports and dashboards with users both inside and outside the organization, including automated report subscriptions via email or other channels.

In summary, Power BI's versatility and capabilities make it a powerful tool for addressing complex business scenarios. By leveraging its features, organizations can navigate intricate data challenges, uncover insights, and drive informed decision-making in today's competitive business landscape.

Chapter 10: Data Model Documentation and Maintenance Strategies

Documenting your data model in Power BI is a crucial step in ensuring that your reports and dashboards are well-understood, maintainable, and compliant with organizational standards.

Why Document Your Data Model: Documenting your data model serves several essential purposes. First and foremost, it provides a clear and comprehensive reference for anyone working with your Power BI project, whether they are the original creator or a colleague. It also helps ensure consistency and adherence to best practices, making it easier to troubleshoot issues and onboard new team members. Additionally, documentation is essential for data governance and compliance, helping organizations meet regulatory requirements and maintain data quality.

Documenting Tables and Fields: A fundamental part of data model documentation is describing each table and its fields. For each table, you should provide a detailed explanation of its purpose and the source of the data it contains. Additionally, document each field's name, data type, and any calculations or transformations applied to it. This information helps users understand the content and context of the data.

Describing Relationships: Relationships between tables are a critical aspect of a data model. Document the relationships between tables, specifying the type (e.g., one-to-many, many-to-many), the fields involved, and the purpose of each relationship. This clarity helps users navigate the model's structure and ensures accurate data retrieval.

Explaining Calculations: If your data model includes calculated columns or measures, document these calculations thoroughly. Explain the purpose of each calculation, the formula used, and any specific business logic applied. This documentation aids in understanding how data is derived and helps users leverage calculations effectively in their reports.

Providing Examples: Whenever possible, include examples and use cases for tables, fields, relationships, and calculations. Real-world examples make the documentation more relatable and illustrate how the data model is intended to be used.

Metadata and Annotations: Power BI allows you to add metadata and annotations directly to tables and fields within the Power Query Editor. Take advantage of this feature to provide additional context and explanations for data elements. Annotations can include descriptions, data source information, and any relevant notes.

Data Dictionary: Create a data dictionary as part of your documentation. A data dictionary is a centralized reference that lists all tables and fields in your data model along with their descriptions, data types, and other relevant information. It acts as a quick reference guide for users and developers.

Data Lineage: Documenting data lineage is especially important for understanding how data flows through your data model. Use visual representations or diagrams to illustrate the flow of data from source to destination, including any transformations or calculations along the way. This provides a high-level view of the data's journey.

Version History: Keep a version history of your data model documentation. This helps track changes over time and allows users to access previous versions of the documentation if needed. Version history is essential for maintaining data lineage and auditability.

User and Security Documentation: If your data model includes row-level security or user-specific considerations, document these aspects thoroughly. Describe the roles and their associated filters, as well as any security policies in place. This documentation ensures that data access and security are well-understood.

Collaboration and Sharing: Consider using collaboration tools or platforms to share and collaborate on data model documentation. This can include Microsoft Teams, SharePoint, or dedicated documentation platforms. Collaborative documentation ensures that multiple stakeholders can contribute and stay up-to-date with changes.

Documentation as a Living Resource: Treat your data model documentation as a living resource that evolves with your project. Update it as the data model changes, new fields are added, or business requirements evolve. Regularly review and revise documentation to ensure accuracy and relevance.

Using CLI Commands for Documentation: While Power BI does not provide a command-line interface (CLI) specifically for documentation, you can integrate CLI commands into your documentation process. For example, you can use PowerShell scripts to automate tasks like exporting metadata, refreshing data, or generating documentation files. These scripts can be part of your documentation workflow, ensuring consistency and efficiency.

Deploying Documentation: To make documentation accessible to your team, consider deploying it in a central location accessible to authorized users. This could be a shared folder, a document management system, or a dedicated web portal. Ensure that documentation is organized and easily navigable, making it convenient for users to find the information they need.

In summary, documenting your data model in Power BI is an essential practice for enhancing data understanding, collaboration, and compliance. By providing clear and comprehensive documentation for tables, fields, relationships, calculations, and other aspects of your data model, you empower users to make informed decisions and maintain data quality. Utilize metadata, data dictionaries, data lineage, and version history to create a valuable resource that evolves with your project's needs.

Maintaining your Power BI data model is a crucial aspect of ensuring its long-term effectiveness and reliability in delivering insights to your organization. Next, we will explore the best practices for model maintenance and provide guidance on how to keep your data model in optimal condition.

Regular Data Refresh: One of the fundamental aspects of model maintenance is ensuring that your data is up to date. Schedule regular data refreshes to keep your reports and dashboards current. You can configure data refresh settings in Power BI Service or by using PowerShell scripts.

Monitoring Data Quality: Implement data quality checks as part of your maintenance routine. This involves monitoring for missing, inaccurate, or inconsistent data. Power BI provides features like data profiling and data lineage to help you identify and address data quality issues.

Automated Testing: Consider implementing automated testing procedures to validate your data model and calculations. Tools like DAX Studio and custom scripts can be used to automate testing scenarios, ensuring that changes to your data model do not introduce errors.

Version Control: Use version control systems like Git to manage changes to your Power BI files (.pbix). Version control allows you to track modifications, collaborate with team members, and roll back to previous versions if issues arise. You can use Git through the command line or integrate it with Power BI Desktop.

Documentation Maintenance: As your data model evolves, update your documentation to reflect the changes. Ensure that descriptions, calculations, and relationships are accurately documented. This ongoing documentation process helps new team members understand the model and its intricacies.

Security Review: Periodically review your security settings and row-level security rules to ensure they align with current business requirements. Remove unnecessary or outdated security roles and refine the existing ones.

Performance Monitoring: Keep an eye on the performance of your data model. Use tools like Performance Analyzer for Power BI to identify bottlenecks and slow-performing visuals. Address performance issues promptly to maintain a responsive user experience.

Backup Strategy: Implement a robust backup strategy for your Power BI files and datasets. Regularly back up your .pbix files and datasets to prevent data loss in case of unexpected issues. Use PowerShell or other automation tools to schedule backups.

Optimization for Large Datasets: If your data model grows significantly, consider partitioning tables, using incremental refresh, or aggregating data to improve query performance. These techniques are especially beneficial for large datasets that may become unwieldy over time.

Data Purging and Archiving: Define data retention policies and archiving processes to manage historical data. This ensures that your data model remains manageable and doesn't become cluttered with obsolete information.

Collaboration and Communication: Maintain open channels of communication within your team. Regularly discuss changes, updates, and issues related to the data model. Encourage collaboration and knowledge sharing to collectively address maintenance tasks.

User Feedback: Solicit feedback from end-users to identify areas for improvement. Users often have valuable insights into what is working well and where enhancements are needed. Incorporate user feedback into your maintenance plan.

Testing in Staging Environments: Before applying changes to a production data model, thoroughly test them in a staging or development environment. This minimizes the risk of introducing errors into live reports and dashboards.

Data Governance and Compliance: Ensure that your data model adheres to data governance and compliance standards. Stay informed about relevant regulations and update your model accordingly to maintain data privacy and security.

Training and Skill Development: Invest in ongoing training for your team to keep them up to date with Power BI best practices and new features. A well-trained team is better equipped to handle model maintenance effectively.

Performance Tuning: Continuously fine-tune your data model's performance by optimizing DAX calculations, data transformations, and data loading processes. Use tools like Query Diagnostics to identify and resolve performance bottlenecks.

User Education: Educate end-users on best practices for interacting with reports and dashboards. Provide guidelines on filtering, slicing, and navigating to ensure that they make the most of the data model without causing unnecessary strain on it.

Communication of Changes: Clearly communicate any changes or updates to the data model to all relevant stakeholders. This includes notifying users of scheduled maintenance windows or updates to reports.

Disaster Recovery Plan: Develop a disaster recovery plan that outlines how you would recover from critical data model failures or data loss scenarios. Regularly test your disaster recovery procedures to ensure they are effective.

Documentation as a Living Resource: Treat your data model documentation as a living resource that evolves with your project. Update it as the data model changes, new fields are added, or business requirements evolve.

Incorporating these best practices into your model maintenance strategy will help you keep your Power BI data model in excellent condition, ensuring its continued usefulness and reliability for delivering insights to your organization.

BOOK 4
EXPERT POWER BI
ADVANCED ANALYTICS AND CUSTOM VISUALIZATIONS MASTERY

ROB BOTWRIGHT

Chapter 1: Advanced Analytics with Power BI

Predictive analytics and machine learning integration in Power BI represent a powerful capability for organizations seeking to derive deeper insights and make data-driven decisions. This chapter explores the techniques, tools, and best practices for seamlessly incorporating predictive analytics and machine learning into your Power BI reports and dashboards.

The integration of predictive analytics and machine learning (ML) into Power BI is a testament to the platform's versatility and ability to provide advanced analytical capabilities to business users. By leveraging these technologies, organizations can enhance their decision-making processes, uncover hidden patterns, and forecast future trends with greater accuracy.

Machine Learning in Power BI: Power BI incorporates machine learning through its integration with Azure Machine Learning, an industry-leading platform for building, training, and deploying machine learning models. This integration allows users to harness the power of Azure Machine Learning directly within their Power BI projects.

Predictive Analytics and Machine Learning Use Cases: Predictive analytics and machine learning find applications across various domains, such as sales forecasting, customer churn prediction, fraud detection, inventory optimization, and more. These techniques enable organizations to make data-driven predictions and recommendations to drive business growth.

Data Preparation: Effective predictive analytics and machine learning require clean, well-structured data. Before integrating ML into Power BI, ensure that your data is prepared and cleaned appropriately. Power Query and Power BI's data transformation capabilities can be used for data preparation.

Azure Machine Learning Integration: To integrate Azure Machine Learning into Power BI, you can use the "Azure Machine Learning" custom visual. This visual allows you to embed machine learning models created in Azure Machine Learning directly into your

Power BI reports. You'll need to provide the necessary API endpoints and authentication details.

Building Machine Learning Models: Azure Machine Learning offers a wide range of tools and libraries for building machine learning models, including regression, classification, clustering, and more. You can use popular ML libraries like scikit-learn or TensorFlow within Azure Machine Learning to create custom models tailored to your business needs.

Data Visualization: Once you've integrated machine learning models into Power BI, visualize the results effectively using Power BI's native visualizations. The results of your predictive models can be displayed alongside other data visualizations, providing a comprehensive view of your data.

Interactivity and User Engagement: Power BI's interactivity features allow users to interact with predictive results dynamically. Users can slice and filter data to see how predictions change based on different criteria, enhancing their understanding of the data.

Real-time Predictions: For real-time predictive analytics, consider using Azure Stream Analytics in conjunction with Power BI. This allows you to make predictions on streaming data and visualize the results in Power BI dashboards in near real-time.

Model Evaluation and Validation: It's crucial to evaluate and validate your machine learning models to ensure their accuracy and reliability. Techniques like cross-validation, confusion matrices, and ROC curves can help assess model performance.

Continuous Model Monitoring: Machine learning models should be monitored continuously to ensure that they remain accurate over time. Set up alerts and notifications to trigger model retraining when performance metrics fall below predefined thresholds.

Security and Compliance: When integrating predictive analytics and machine learning into Power BI, pay attention to security and compliance requirements. Ensure that sensitive data is handled and stored securely, and that models adhere to regulatory standards.

Model Deployment: Azure Machine Learning provides options for model deployment, including Azure Kubernetes Service (AKS) and Azure Functions. Deploying models to a production environment allows your Power BI reports to consume predictions in real-world scenarios.

Custom Machine Learning in Power Query: For users comfortable with R or Python, Power Query supports custom scripting for data transformation. You can incorporate custom machine learning code into Power Query to enrich your data with predictions or classifications.

CLI Commands and Automation: Use Azure Command-Line Interface (CLI) commands to automate tasks such as model deployment, data ingestion, and model retraining. Automation ensures that your predictive analytics processes remain efficient and consistent.

User Training: To maximize the benefits of predictive analytics and machine learning integration, provide training and resources to your Power BI users. Ensure that they understand how to interpret and utilize the predictive insights generated by machine learning models.

Documentation and Knowledge Sharing: Maintain documentation that details the machine learning models, data sources, and methodologies used in your Power BI projects. Encourage knowledge sharing within your organization to foster collaboration and best practice adoption.

Feedback Loop: Establish a feedback loop between data analysts, data scientists, and business users. Regularly gather feedback on the predictive results and incorporate it into model refinement and improvement efforts.

In summary, the integration of predictive analytics and machine learning in Power BI opens up a world of possibilities for organizations looking to gain deeper insights from their data. Whether you're forecasting sales, predicting customer behavior, or optimizing operations, the seamless integration of Azure Machine Learning and Power BI empowers you to harness the full potential of your data to make informed decisions and drive business growth. By following best practices, staying vigilant about data quality, and fostering collaboration, you can successfully leverage predictive analytics and machine learning to stay ahead in today's data-driven world.

Statistical analysis and hypothesis testing play a crucial role in data-driven decision-making, helping organizations extract meaningful insights and draw reliable conclusions from their data. Next, we delve into the world of statistical analysis within the context of Power BI, exploring how to apply statistical techniques, interpret results, and make informed decisions based on data.

Importance of Statistical Analysis: Statistical analysis is the foundation of data-driven decision-making. It allows organizations to move beyond descriptive statistics and uncover hidden patterns, relationships, and trends in their data. By applying statistical techniques, businesses can make more informed choices, optimize processes, and gain a competitive edge.

Statistical Functions in Power BI: Power BI offers a rich set of built-in statistical functions that enable users to perform a wide range of analyses. These functions include measures for central tendency (mean, median, mode), dispersion (variance, standard deviation), and distribution (normality tests, skewness, kurtosis).

Descriptive vs. Inferential Statistics: Descriptive statistics provide a summary of data, while inferential statistics are used to make inferences or predictions about a population based on a sample. Both types of statistics have their place in data analysis, depending on the objectives of the analysis.

Hypothesis Testing: Hypothesis testing is a fundamental concept in statistical analysis. It involves formulating a null hypothesis (H0) and an alternative hypothesis (Ha) and then conducting tests to determine whether there is enough evidence to reject the null hypothesis in favor of the alternative. Common hypothesis tests include t-tests, chi-squared tests, ANOVA, and more.

Practical Application: Let's consider a practical scenario. Imagine you are analyzing sales data for a retail business. You want to determine whether a recent marketing campaign has had a significant impact on sales. You formulate the null hypothesis (H0) that the campaign had no effect and the alternative hypothesis

(Ha) that it did. You then conduct a hypothesis test to evaluate the campaign's impact.

Data Preparation: Before performing any statistical analysis in Power BI, it's essential to ensure that your data is clean, complete, and properly structured. Use Power Query for data cleaning and transformation tasks to prepare your data for analysis.

Sampling Techniques: In cases where analyzing the entire dataset is impractical, sampling techniques can be employed to select a representative subset of data for analysis. Power BI supports random sampling and stratified sampling through the Power Query Editor.

Visualizations for Statistical Analysis: Power BI offers a range of visualizations that can aid in statistical analysis. Histograms, box plots, scatter plots, and time series plots can help you visualize the distribution and relationships within your data.

Regression Analysis: Regression analysis is a powerful statistical technique for exploring relationships between variables. Power BI supports linear regression, allowing you to model and analyze how one or more independent variables influence a dependent variable.

Statistical Significance: When conducting hypothesis tests, it's essential to understand the concept of statistical significance. A result is considered statistically significant if the p-value is below a predefined significance level (usually 0.05). If the p-value is less than the significance level, you can reject the null hypothesis.

Effect Size: In addition to statistical significance, consider the effect size, which measures the practical or clinical significance of an observed effect. A small p-value may indicate significance, but a small effect size may not have practical implications.

Interpreting Results: When performing statistical analysis in Power BI, carefully interpret the results of hypothesis tests. Understand what the p-value means and whether it supports the rejection or acceptance of the null hypothesis. Consider the confidence intervals for parameter estimates.

Confounding Variables: Be aware of confounding variables that can introduce bias or distort the results of your analysis. Power

BI's capabilities for data exploration and visualization can help you identify potential confounders.

Statistical Modeling: For more advanced statistical modeling, consider using R or Python scripts within Power BI. These languages offer extensive libraries for statistical analysis and can be seamlessly integrated into your Power BI reports.

CLI Commands and Automation: To automate statistical analyses in Power BI, you can use the Power BI PowerShell cmdlets. These cmdlets allow you to create and manage datasets, reports, and dashboards programmatically.

Data Validation: Ensure that the data used for statistical analysis is accurate and reliable. Implement data validation checks and data quality rules to minimize errors that could impact the results.

Model Documentation: Document your statistical models, hypothesis tests, and assumptions thoroughly. This documentation helps ensure transparency, reproducibility, and collaboration within your organization.

Real-world Applications: Statistical analysis in Power BI can be applied to a wide range of business scenarios. Whether you're analyzing customer satisfaction surveys, A/B testing website variations, or predicting equipment failures, statistical techniques empower data professionals to extract actionable insights.

Continuous Learning: Stay updated with the latest developments in statistical analysis and data science. Online courses, books, and communities can provide valuable resources for enhancing your statistical analysis skills.

In summary, statistical analysis is a vital component of data-driven decision-making in Power BI. By understanding the principles of statistical testing, effectively applying statistical techniques, and interpreting results correctly, organizations can gain deeper insights from their data and make informed choices that drive business success. Statistical analysis in Power BI is a powerful tool for uncovering patterns, testing hypotheses, and extracting meaningful insights that lead to smarter, data-driven decisions.

Chapter 2: Mastering Advanced DAX Formulas

Next, we dive into the world of advanced time-intelligence functions within Power BI, exploring how these functions can take your data analysis to the next level.

Advanced time-intelligence functions are essential for handling complex scenarios that involve dates and time-related data, such as year-over-year comparisons, rolling averages, and dynamic date ranges.

One of the most commonly used advanced time-intelligence functions in Power BI is the TOTALYTD function, which stands for "Total Year-to-Date." This function allows you to calculate cumulative values for a measure over time, starting from the beginning of a specified year.

TOTALYTD can be particularly useful when analyzing financial data, as it helps you track the cumulative performance of key metrics, such as revenue or profit, throughout the year.

Another powerful time-intelligence function is SAMEPERIODLASTYEAR, which enables you to compare data from the current period to the same period in the previous year.

For example, if you want to analyze the year-over-year growth in sales for each month, you can use SAMEPERIODLASTYEAR to calculate the sales for the corresponding months in the previous year and then calculate the growth percentage.

The DATESYTD function is another essential tool for time-intelligence analysis. It allows you to filter a table to include only the rows that are within the year-to-date range based on a specified date column.

This function is particularly valuable when you want to create visualizations or measures that focus on the performance of your data within a specific time frame, such as the current year.

In addition to these functions, Power BI provides a range of other advanced time-intelligence functions, including DATESQTD (Quarter-to-Date), DATEADD (Add or Subtract Time Periods), and DATESBETWEEN (Filter Dates Between Two Dates).

These functions enable you to perform advanced calculations and create dynamic reports that adapt to changing date selections.

When working with advanced time-intelligence functions in Power BI, it's crucial to have a well-structured date table. A date table is a dedicated table in your data model that contains a continuous sequence of dates, along with various attributes such as year, quarter, month, and day.

The date table serves as the foundation for time-intelligence calculations and allows you to create meaningful visualizations that slice and dice your data by date-related attributes.

To create a date table in Power BI, you can use the "CALENDAR" function in DAX (Data Analysis Expressions). Here's an example of how to create a simple date table using DAX:

scssCopy code

```
DateTable = CALENDAR(DATE(2020, 1, 1), DATE(2025, 12, 31))
```

This DAX formula generates a date table with dates ranging from January 1, 2020, to December 31, 2025.

Once you have a date table in your data model, you can leverage its attributes and relationships with other tables to perform advanced time-intelligence calculations.

For example, you can create a measure that calculates the year-to-date total sales by using the TOTALYTD function and referencing the date column from your date table.

scssCopy code

```
YTD Sales = TOTALYTD(SUM(Sales[Amount]), DateTable[Date])
```

This measure calculates the cumulative total sales from the beginning of the year up to the selected date in your report.

When deploying advanced time-intelligence functions in Power BI, it's essential to consider the context in which your calculations are evaluated.

Power BI uses a concept called "filter context" and "row context" to determine how calculations should be applied.

Filter context refers to the filters applied to your report or visualizations, such as date filters or slicers. These filters influence which data is included in your calculations.

Row context, on the other hand, is the context within each individual row of a table. It's essential to understand how DAX functions interpret both filter and row context to ensure that your time-intelligence calculations produce accurate results.

For example, when you create a measure to calculate year-to-date sales, Power BI evaluates the measure in the context of each row in your data. The filter context determines which rows are considered in the calculation, while the row context specifies the date for each row.

To gain a deeper understanding of the filter and row context, you can use the "Evaluate" feature in Power BI to see how DAX expressions are evaluated step by step.

To access the "Evaluate" feature, select a measure in Power BI Desktop, go to the "Modeling" tab, and click on "Evaluate."

Using this feature, you can observe how the filter and row context interact with your DAX calculations, helping you troubleshoot and fine-tune your time-intelligence functions.

Another important consideration when working with advanced time-intelligence functions is the handling of non-standard fiscal years.

Many organizations have fiscal years that don't align with the calendar year. In such cases, you can use DAX functions like "FiscalYearStart" and "FiscalYearEnd" to define your custom fiscal year.

For instance, if your fiscal year starts in July and ends in June, you can define it as follows:

```
sqlCopy code
FiscalYearStart    =    DATE ( YEAR (DateTable[ Date ])    -
IF( MONTH (DateTable[ Date ]) < 7, 1, 0), 7, 1) FiscalYearEnd =
DATE ( YEAR (DateTable[ Date ])    +    IF( MONTH (DateTable[ Date ])
>= 7, 1, 0), 6, 30 )
```

These DAX calculations ensure that your fiscal year aligns correctly with your organization's financial calendar.

In summary, advanced time-intelligence functions in Power BI are powerful tools for analyzing and visualizing time-related data. By mastering these functions and understanding the interplay between filter and row context, you can create sophisticated reports and dashboards that provide valuable insights into your data.

With a well-structured date table and a grasp of DAX expressions, you can tackle complex time-intelligence challenges, whether you're dealing with year-to-date calculations, rolling averages, or custom fiscal years.

As you continue your journey with Power BI, explore the possibilities of advanced time-intelligence functions and their applications in various business scenarios. Whether you're a business analyst, data scientist, or Power BI enthusiast, these functions will enhance your data analysis capabilities and empower you to make data-driven decisions with confidence.

Next, we delve into the world of DAX (Data Analysis Expressions) optimization techniques within the Power BI ecosystem.

DAX optimization is crucial for ensuring that your Power BI reports and dashboards perform efficiently, especially when dealing with large datasets and complex calculations.

One of the fundamental principles of DAX optimization is to reduce the number of calculations performed by your measures. This can significantly improve query performance and responsiveness.

To achieve this, consider using the EVALUATE command in DAX Studio or Query Diagnostics in Power BI Desktop to identify measures with high query times.

Once you've identified performance bottlenecks, explore techniques to optimize your DAX calculations, starting with the use of SUMMARIZECOLUMNS.

SUMMARIZECOLUMNS is a powerful DAX function that allows you to create summary tables, reducing the need for expensive filter context calculations. You can use it to pre-aggregate data and improve query response times.

For example, suppose you have a table of sales transactions with millions of rows. Instead of calculating the total sales amount for each row in a visual, you can use SUMMARIZECOLUMNS to calculate the total sales amount by product category in advance and then visualize this summarized data.

Here's an example of how you can use SUMMARIZECOLUMNS:

DAXCopy code

SummaryTable = SUMMARIZECOLUMNS ('Product'[Category], "Total Sales", SUM ('Sales'[Amount]))

This DAX expression creates a summary table that groups sales data by product category and calculates the total sales amount for each category.

Another optimization technique is the use of iterator functions like FILTER and ALL. While these functions are powerful, they can be resource-intensive when applied to large tables.

To optimize iterator functions, consider using the ADDCOLUMNS function to create calculated columns that store pre-filtered values. This reduces the need to apply filters repeatedly, improving query performance.

For example, instead of using FILTER to calculate the number of products with sales exceeding a certain threshold, you can create a calculated column using ADDCOLUMNS:

DAXCopy code

Product['High Sales'] = ADDCOLUMNS (Product, "High Sales Count", CALCULATE (COUNTROWS (Sales), Sales[Amount] > 10000))

This DAX expression creates a calculated column in the Product table that stores the count of products with sales exceeding $10,000, reducing the need for real-time filtering during queries.

Another critical aspect of DAX optimization is the efficient use of time-intelligence functions. Time-intelligence calculations can be resource-intensive, especially when dealing with large date ranges.

To optimize time-intelligence functions, leverage calculated tables to pre-calculate necessary values. For example, you can create a calculated table that contains pre-computed rolling averages for different time periods.

By using a calculated table, you eliminate the need to perform complex calculations on the fly during queries, resulting in faster response times.

Additionally, consider using the "Mark as Date Table" feature in Power BI to designate a date table in your model. This allows Power BI to recognize the date table and optimize queries related to date calculations automatically.

To mark a table as a date table, right-click on the date table in the Power BI Model view, select "Mark as Date Table," and choose the appropriate date column.

Another DAX optimization technique is the use of query folding. Query folding occurs when Power BI pushes some data transformation operations back to the data source, reducing the amount of data transferred to your model.

To enable query folding, avoid using complex DAX expressions within Power Query Editor. Instead, perform data transformations at the source, such as SQL Server, and utilize calculated columns or measures for advanced calculations in Power BI.

By optimizing your DAX calculations and leveraging advanced techniques, you can create high-performance Power BI reports and dashboards that provide rapid insights into your data.

One of the critical aspects of DAX optimization is understanding the filter context and row context. Filter context is the set of filters applied to your data, such as slicers or visuals, which can significantly impact DAX calculations.

To optimize filter context, use functions like CALCULATE and FILTER sparingly. These functions introduce additional filters that can slow down query performance.

Instead, leverage the power of measures and calculated columns to create reusable calculations that minimize the need for recalculating the same values repeatedly.

For instance, rather than using CALCULATE to apply filters to every measure individually, you can create a measure that encapsulates the filter logic and then reference that measure in other calculations.

Here's an example of optimizing filter context:

DAXCopy code

Total Sales = SUM (Sales[Amount])

In this case, the Total Sales measure doesn't apply additional filters, relying on the existing filter context from visuals or slicers. This approach can enhance query performance.

Another optimization technique is the use of table variables. Table variables allow you to store intermediate results and reuse them within a DAX calculation, reducing redundant calculations.

To declare a table variable in DAX, use the VAR keyword, followed by the variable name and assignment. You can then reference the variable in subsequent expressions.

Here's an example of using a table variable to optimize a calculation:

DAXCopy code

Total Sales = VAR FilteredSales = FILTER (Sales, Sales[Year] = 2023

) RETURN SUMX (FilteredSales, Sales[Amount])

In this example, the VAR statement creates a table variable called FilteredSales, which filters the Sales table for the year 2023. The subsequent expression then uses the filtered table, reducing the need to apply the filter multiple times.

Additionally, consider optimizing your DAX measures by using the "Optimize for Q&A" feature in Power BI Desktop. This feature allows you to specify synonyms and phrasings for your measures, making them more accessible and user-friendly.

By providing clear and intuitive names for your measures, you enhance the user experience and encourage self-service exploration of your data.

To optimize your measures for Q&A, go to the Modeling tab in Power BI Desktop, select the measure, and click on "Optimize for Q&A."

In summary, DAX optimization is essential for maximizing the performance of your Power BI reports and dashboards. By adopting best practices, leveraging calculated tables, and understanding filter and row context, you can create highly responsive and efficient data models.

Remember that optimizing DAX calculations is an iterative process, and continuous monitoring and refinement are key to maintaining optimal performance as your data grows and evolves. Whether you're a seasoned Power BI professional or just getting started, mastering DAX optimization techniques is crucial for delivering impactful data insights to your organization.

Chapter 3: Advanced Data Mining and Forecasting

Next, we dive into the fascinating world of data mining algorithms and techniques, which play a pivotal role in extracting valuable patterns and insights from vast datasets.

Data mining is the process of discovering meaningful and previously unknown patterns, correlations, or trends within data. It involves the application of various algorithms and methodologies to uncover hidden knowledge.

One of the most widely used data mining techniques is clustering. Clustering algorithms group similar data points together based on certain attributes or features.

K-Means clustering is a popular example. It partitions data into clusters, where each cluster represents a group of data points that are close to each other in terms of similarity.

To implement K-Means clustering, you can use a variety of programming languages and tools, such as Python with libraries like scikit-learn or R. Here's an example of how to use K-Means in Python:

pythonCopy code

```
from sklearn.cluster import KMeans # Create a K-Means model
with 3 clusters kmeans = KMeans(n_clusters=3) # Fit the model
to your data kmeans.fit(X) # Get the cluster assignments for each
data point cluster_labels = kmeans.labels_
```

Another essential data mining technique is classification. Classification algorithms are used to categorize data points into predefined classes or labels based on their features.

Decision trees, support vector machines (SVM), and logistic regression are commonly used classification algorithms. These algorithms can be applied to various domains, such as spam email detection, image recognition, and customer churn prediction.

Here's an example of using a decision tree classifier in Python:

pythonCopy code

```
from sklearn.tree import DecisionTreeClassifier # Create a
decision tree classifier clf = DecisionTreeClassifier() # Fit the
classifier to your training data clf.fit(X_train, y_train) # Make
predictions on new data predictions = clf.predict(X_test)
```

Association rule mining is another valuable technique used to uncover relationships between items in transactional data. It's widely used in market basket analysis to discover patterns of items that are often purchased together.

One well-known algorithm for association rule mining is the Apriori algorithm. It identifies frequent itemsets and generates association rules based on the support and confidence of item combinations.

In Python, you can use libraries like mlxtend to implement the Apriori algorithm:

pythonCopy code

```
from mlxtend.frequent_patterns import apriori,
association_rules # Create a DataFrame with transactional data
transactions = pd.DataFrame(data) # Use Apriori to find frequent
itemsets frequent_itemsets = apriori(transactions,
min_support=0.01, use_colnames=True) # Generate association
rules rules = association_rules(frequent_itemsets, metric="lift",
min_threshold=1.0)
```

Time series forecasting is a critical data mining technique for predicting future values based on historical data points. It's commonly used in financial forecasting, demand forecasting, and weather prediction.

Exponential smoothing methods, autoregressive integrated moving average (ARIMA), and machine learning models like recurrent neural networks (RNNs) are frequently employed for time series forecasting.

For example, you can use Python's statsmodels library to fit an ARIMA model to your time series data:

pythonCopy code

```python
from statsmodels.tsa.arima.model import ARIMA # Create an
ARIMA model (p, d, q) model = ARIMA(data, order=(2, 1, 1)) #
Fit the model to your time series data results = model.fit() # Make
future predictions forecast = results.predict(start=len(data),
end=len(data) + 10, typ='levels')
```

Text mining is another fascinating area within data mining that focuses on extracting meaningful insights from unstructured text data. Techniques like natural language processing (NLP) and sentiment analysis are commonly used in text mining.

NLP libraries like NLTK (Natural Language Toolkit) and spaCy in Python provide tools and resources to process and analyze text data. Sentiment analysis can help you determine the sentiment or emotional tone of text documents, which is valuable for social media monitoring and customer feedback analysis.

Here's a simplified example of sentiment analysis using the NLTK library in Python:

pythonCopy code

```python
import nltk from nltk.sentiment.vader import
SentimentIntensityAnalyzer # Initialize the sentiment analyzer
nltk.download('vader_lexicon') sia =
SentimentIntensityAnalyzer() # Analyze sentiment for a text
sentiment_scores = sia.polarity_scores(text) # Determine the
sentiment (positive, neutral, negative) if
sentiment_scores['compound'] >= 0.05: sentiment = 'positive'
elif sentiment_scores['compound'] <= -0.05: sentiment =
'negative' else: sentiment = 'neutral'
```

Data mining techniques are not limited to standalone analysis; they can also be integrated into Power BI for enhanced data exploration and visualization. Power BI supports various data mining algorithms through its R and Python integration.

You can use R or Python scripts within Power BI to perform advanced analytics, create custom visualizations, and generate insights from your data. By combining the power of data mining with Power BI's interactive dashboards and reports, you can create compelling data-driven stories that drive decision-making within your organization.

In summary, data mining techniques are essential tools for extracting valuable insights and patterns from complex datasets. Whether you're clustering similar data points, classifying data into categories, finding association rules, forecasting future values, analyzing text sentiment, or using other data mining methods, these techniques empower you to unlock the hidden knowledge within your data. Incorporating data mining into your data analytics toolbox can elevate your ability to make informed decisions and gain a competitive edge in the data-driven world.

Time series forecasting is a vital aspect of data analysis, and it plays a significant role in helping organizations make informed decisions based on historical data trends.

Power BI, a powerful business intelligence tool, offers robust features for time series forecasting, enabling users to predict future values based on historical data points.

One of the primary advantages of using Power BI for time series forecasting is its integration with R and Python, two widely-used programming languages for data analysis and machine learning.

To leverage time series forecasting in Power BI, you can use R or Python scripts within the Power Query Editor. These scripts allow you to apply various forecasting models to your data and visualize the results seamlessly.

For example, suppose you have historical sales data and want to predict future sales figures. You can use the Power Query Editor to import your data, and then apply forecasting models using R or Python scripts.

In R, you can use the "forecast" package to perform time series forecasting. Here's an example of how to do it:

RCopy code

```
# Load the forecast package library(forecast) # Create a time series object from your data ts_data <- ts(your_data, frequency = 12) # Assuming monthly data with a frequency of 12 # Fit a forecasting model (e.g., ARIMA) forecast_model <-
```

auto.arima(ts_data) # Generate forecasts for future periods
forecasts <- forecast(forecast_model, h = 12) # Forecasting 12 periods ahead

In this example, the "auto.arima" function automatically selects the best ARIMA model for your time series data, and the "forecast" function generates forecasts for the next 12 periods.

Power BI also offers custom visuals and custom scripting options, allowing you to create interactive visualizations and dashboards that display your time series forecasts.

Moreover, you can use Python within Power BI for time series forecasting. Python provides various libraries for time series analysis and forecasting, such as "statsmodels" and "Prophet."

Here's an example of using the "statsmodels" library in Python for time series forecasting within Power BI:

PythonCopy code

```
# Load the necessary Python libraries import pandas as pd
import statsmodels.api as sm # Load your time series data into a
DataFrame data = pd.read_csv('your_data.csv') # Create a time
series model (e.g., SARIMA) model =
sm.tsa.SARIMAX(data['sales'], order=(1, 1, 1),
seasonal_order=(1, 1, 1, 12)) # Assuming monthly data with
seasonality # Fit the model to your data results = model.fit() #
Generate forecasts for future periods forecasts =
results.get_forecast(steps=12) # Forecasting 12 periods ahead
```

In this Python example, we load the time series data, create a SARIMA model, and generate forecasts for the next 12 periods, considering seasonality.

Additionally, Power BI offers the Forecasting feature in its visualization tools, which simplifies the process of generating forecasts. Users can select the time series data and apply forecasting algorithms directly within the Power BI interface.

To use the Forecasting feature in Power BI:

Import your time series data into Power BI.

Create a line chart visualization with your time series data.

Select the line chart, go to the "Analytics" pane, and enable the "Forecast" option.

Adjust the settings, such as the forecast horizon, confidence intervals, and algorithm used.

Power BI will automatically generate and display the forecasts on your line chart.

This built-in forecasting feature simplifies the process for users who may not have extensive programming experience in R or Python.

Furthermore, Power BI allows you to customize the visualizations and dashboards to present your time series forecasts effectively. You can add slicers, filters, and drill-through actions to provide interactive exploration of your forecasted data.

In summary, time series forecasting is a crucial aspect of data analysis, and Power BI provides a powerful platform for performing such tasks. With the integration of R and Python scripts, custom visualizations, and the Forecasting feature, Power BI empowers users to create accurate and insightful time series forecasts, aiding in data-driven decision-making for businesses and organizations.

Chapter 4: Advanced Data Transformation Techniques

Advanced data cleansing and preparation are essential steps in the data analysis process, ensuring that your data is accurate, consistent, and ready for meaningful insights. Next, we will delve into advanced techniques and best practices for cleansing and preparing data in Power BI.

One powerful tool in Power BI for advanced data cleansing is the Power Query Editor, which allows users to perform a wide range of transformations on their data. To open the Power Query Editor, you can follow these steps within Power BI Desktop:

Load your data into Power BI.

In the "Home" tab, click on "Edit Queries."

Once in the Power Query Editor, you can apply various cleansing and preparation techniques to your data. One common task is dealing with missing or erroneous values. Power BI offers multiple options to handle missing data, such as removing rows with missing values, filling missing values with default values, or imputing missing values based on specific criteria.

For example, you can use the "Replace Values" transformation in Power Query to replace missing values in a column with a default value or a calculated value based on other columns in your dataset. The following CLI command demonstrates how to replace missing values in a column named "Sales" with zeros:

PowerQueryCopy code

```
Table.ReplaceValue(#"PreviousStep",    0,    each    [Sales],
Replacer.ReplaceValue, {"Sales"})
```

Another crucial aspect of advanced data cleansing is data deduplication. In Power Query, you can identify and remove duplicate rows based on specific columns. This ensures that your analysis is based on unique records, avoiding any skew in your results. To perform deduplication, use the "Remove Duplicates" transformation in Power Query.

PowerQueryCopy code

```
Table.Distinct(#"PreviousStep", {"Column1", "Column2", ...})
```

Power Query also offers capabilities for data normalization, which involves transforming data into a consistent format. This is especially important when dealing with data from various sources that may have different structures or units of measurement. Techniques like scaling, standardization, and conversion can be applied using Power Query functions.

Another advanced data cleansing technique is data profiling, which involves analyzing the quality and consistency of your data. Power BI provides various data profiling options, such as calculating summary statistics, identifying outliers, and checking for data distribution. The results of data profiling can help you understand the characteristics of your data and make informed decisions on how to clean and prepare it effectively.

Power Query also supports data enrichment through merging and appending tables. You can merge tables based on common columns to combine data from multiple sources or add additional information to your dataset. The "Join" and "Append Queries" options in Power Query Editor facilitate these operations.

To implement a left join between two tables in Power Query, you can use the following CLI command:

PowerQueryCopy code

```
Table.NestedJoin(#"PreviousStep1", {"CommonColumn"}, #"PreviousStep2", {"CommonColumn"}, "NewColumn", JoinKind.LeftOuter)
```

Handling date and time data is another crucial aspect of data cleansing and preparation. Power Query offers functions for parsing, formatting, and manipulating date and time values. You can convert text-based date formats into proper date data types and extract components like year, month, and day for further analysis.

Additionally, Power Query provides capabilities for data transformation using custom functions. You can create custom functions in Power Query's M language to perform specific data cleansing and preparation tasks tailored to your dataset's needs.

For instance, if you have complex data validation rules to apply to your data, you can create a custom function to check and clean data based on those rules. The custom function can then be applied to multiple columns or tables, ensuring consistency and accuracy.

Here's an example of creating a custom function in Power Query's M language to remove special characters and spaces from a text column:

PowerQueryCopy code

```
let RemoveSpecialCharacters = (text) => Text.Replace(Text.Remove(text, {" ", ".", ",", "-", "_", "!"}), " ", "") in RemoveSpecialCharacters
```

Once you've created a custom function, you can use it in Power Query Editor to transform your data. This approach is especially useful for enforcing data quality standards and ensuring that your data is in a consistent format.

In summary, advanced data cleansing and preparation are critical steps in the data analysis process, and Power BI provides a robust set of tools and techniques to facilitate these tasks. From handling missing data and deduplication to data profiling, normalization, and custom function creation, Power Query Editor empowers users to transform their data into a clean and well-prepared state for effective analysis and visualization. By mastering these advanced data cleansing techniques, you can unlock the full potential of your data in Power BI and drive data-driven decision-making within your organization.

Custom data transformation scripts offer a powerful way to perform advanced data manipulations and calculations in

Power BI, allowing you to tailor your data transformation process to specific requirements. These scripts are typically written in the M language or R, and they extend the capabilities of Power Query Editor to handle complex transformations that cannot be achieved through standard visual tools alone.

To create a custom data transformation script in Power BI, you need to access the Power Query Editor. Once you have loaded your data, follow these steps to open the editor:

In the Power BI Desktop application, select "Edit Queries" from the "Home" tab.

This will launch the Power Query Editor, where you can perform various data transformation tasks, including custom scripting.

In the Power Query Editor, you can apply custom transformation scripts to your data using the "Advanced Editor" option. The "Advanced Editor" allows you to write and execute custom scripts in the M language, which is the primary scripting language for Power Query.

For instance, suppose you want to create a custom column that calculates the total sales by multiplying the "Quantity" and "Unit Price" columns. You can achieve this by writing a custom M script:

PowerQueryCopy code

```
let Source = YourDataSource, CustomColumn = Table.AddColumn(Source, "Total Sales", each [Quantity] * [Unit Price]) in CustomColumn
```

In this script, "Source" represents your data source, and "CustomColumn" is a new column that calculates the total sales for each row by multiplying the "Quantity" and "Unit Price" columns.

Power Query's M language provides a wide range of functions and operations for data manipulation, such as filtering rows, aggregating data, and performing complex transformations. You can use these functions within your custom scripts to achieve specific data transformation goals.

Additionally, Power BI also supports custom data transformation scripts written in R, a programming language commonly used for statistical analysis and data manipulation. To leverage R scripts in Power Query, follow these steps:

In the Power Query Editor, select the column or table you want to apply the R script to.

Go to the "Transform" tab and click on "Run R script."

This will open a dialog where you can write and execute your custom R script. For example, you might want to perform a sentiment analysis on a text column using an R script:

RCopy code

```
library(sentimentr)          output          <- sentiment(get_data_from_column)
```

In this script, you first load the "sentimentr" library, then apply sentiment analysis to the data in the selected column, storing the results in the "output" variable.

Custom data transformation scripts in R are especially valuable when you need to integrate external libraries or perform specialized analytical tasks beyond the capabilities of the M language.

Furthermore, Power BI allows you to manage and reuse custom functions and scripts across multiple queries and reports. By creating functions within the "Shared" section of the Power Query Editor, you can build a library of custom functions that can be easily applied to various datasets and reports.

To deploy custom data transformation scripts effectively, it's essential to follow best practices:

Document Your Scripts: Provide clear and concise comments within your scripts to explain the purpose of each step, making it easier for others to understand and maintain them.

Test Thoroughly: Before deploying custom scripts in production reports, thoroughly test them on sample data to ensure they work as expected and produce accurate results.

Version Control: If you're working in a team, consider using version control systems to track changes to your custom scripts and collaborate effectively.

Monitor Performance: Custom scripts can impact report performance, so regularly monitor the performance of your reports and optimize scripts if necessary.

Keep Scripts Modular: Break down complex transformations into smaller, modular scripts or functions to enhance reusability and maintainability.

By mastering the use of custom data transformation scripts in Power BI, you can unlock advanced data transformation capabilities and tailor your data preparation process to meet specific business requirements. Whether you choose the M language or R, custom scripting empowers you to handle complex data transformations and achieve deeper insights from your data sources.

Chapter 5: Creating Custom Visualizations with Power BI

Building custom visuals using D3.js is an exciting and powerful way to enhance your data storytelling and analysis within Power BI. D3.js, short for Data-Driven Documents, is a JavaScript library that provides a flexible and versatile framework for creating interactive and dynamic data visualizations. Next, we'll explore how you can leverage D3.js to build custom visuals that go beyond the standard offerings in Power BI.

Before diving into the world of custom visuals with D3.js, it's essential to understand the concept and significance of custom visuals. Custom visuals allow you to extend the capabilities of Power BI by designing unique, user-specific visualizations that cater to your data analysis needs. While Power BI provides a wide range of built-in visualizations, there may be instances where your data demands a custom visualization tailored to your specific requirements.

To get started with building custom visuals using D3.js in Power BI, you'll need to follow a series of steps:

Enable Custom Visuals: Before you can create custom visuals, you need to enable the custom visuals feature in Power BI. To do this, open Power BI Desktop, go to "File" > "Options and settings" > "Options" > "Security," and then enable the option to "Allow custom visuals."

Familiarize Yourself with D3.js: To build custom visuals, it's crucial to have a solid understanding of D3.js. D3.js is a JavaScript library that provides a robust set of tools for creating data visualizations. If you're not already familiar with D3.js, you may want to invest some time in learning its fundamentals.

Create a Custom Visual Template: Start by creating a custom visual template in Power BI. You can use the "Power BI Custom Visual Tool" (pbiviz) to scaffold a basic visual structure. The command to create a new custom visual template is as follows:

arduinoCopy code

pbiviz new customVisualName

Replace "customVisualName" with the name of your custom visual. This will generate a folder structure containing the necessary files for your visual.

Develop Your Custom Visual: Once you have your template in place, you can start developing your custom visual using D3.js. You'll typically work with HTML, CSS, and JavaScript files within the template folder to build your visual.

Leverage D3.js: Use D3.js to create the core functionality of your custom visual. D3.js provides a wide array of methods for selecting, binding, and manipulating data to create stunning and interactive visualizations.

Testing and Debugging: It's essential to thoroughly test and debug your custom visual as you build it. You can use Power BI Desktop's developer tools to troubleshoot issues and ensure your visual functions as expected.

Packaging Your Visual: Once your custom visual is complete, you'll need to package it into a .pbiviz file, which is the format Power BI uses for custom visuals. Use the following command to package your visual:

goCopy code

```
pbiviz package
```

Import into Power BI: To use your custom visual in Power BI reports, you'll need to import it into your Power BI Desktop file. Open your Power BI report, go to the "Visualizations" pane, click on the ellipsis (...) menu, and select "Import a custom visual." Then, choose the .pbiviz file you created in the previous step.

Add Data and Configure: With your custom visual added to the report, you can drag and drop fields from your data model onto the visual to configure it. Customize the visual's appearance and behavior according to your requirements.

Publish and Share: Once your report is ready, you can publish it to the Power BI service or export it for sharing with others. Your custom visual will be available in the published report, allowing others to interact with it.

Building custom visuals using D3.js in Power BI opens up a world of possibilities for creating unique and engaging data visualizations. Whether you need to visualize complex data structures, display data in a specific way, or tell a data-driven story with precision, custom visuals empower you to achieve your goals. However, building custom visuals with D3.js requires a solid understanding of web technologies, JavaScript, HTML, CSS, and D3.js itself. It's a creative and technical endeavor that allows you to bring your data to life in ways that standard visualizations may not permit.

As you embark on your journey to master custom visuals with D3.js, don't hesitate to explore D3.js documentation, tutorials, and community resources. These can be invaluable in helping you grasp the intricacies of D3.js and unlocking its full potential within Power BI.

In summary, custom visuals with D3.js provide a bridge between the rich world of web-based data visualization and the analytical power of Power BI. By combining these technologies, you can create custom visuals that not only convey your data insights effectively but also elevate the overall impact of your reports and dashboards.

In the world of data visualization and analytics, customization is often the key to presenting information effectively and making data-driven decisions. Power BI offers a range of built-in visualizations, but sometimes you need a visual that is tailored to your exact requirements. This is where the Custom Visual SDK comes into play, allowing you to create advanced custom visuals that go beyond what's possible with the out-of-the-box options.

Before diving into the advanced customization capabilities of the Custom Visual SDK, it's important to have a clear understanding of what custom visuals are and why they are valuable. Custom visuals are unique data visualizations created to address specific data analysis needs or to provide a unique perspective on data. They can be designed to tell a story, highlight critical insights, or present data in a visually appealing manner.

To begin harnessing the full power of the Custom Visual SDK, follow these essential steps:

Setting up the Development Environment: First, you need to set up your development environment to work with the Custom Visual SDK. This involves installing Node.js, npm (Node Package Manager), and the Power BI Custom Visual CLI (Command Line Interface).

To install Node.js and npm, visit the official Node.js website (https://nodejs.org/) and follow the installation instructions for your operating system.

To install the Power BI Custom Visual CLI, open your command prompt or terminal and run the following command:

Copy code

```
npm install -g powerbi-visuals-tools
```

This CLI tool is essential for creating, packaging, and testing custom visuals.

Creating a Custom Visual Project: Once your development environment is set up, you can create a new custom visual project using the CLI tool. Run the following command, replacing "CustomVisualName" with your desired project name:

arduinoCopy code

```
pbiviz new CustomVisualName
```

This command will generate a project folder with the necessary files and templates to get you started.

Designing Your Custom Visual: Now comes the creative part. You can start designing your custom visual using HTML, CSS, and TypeScript. The Custom Visual SDK provides a set of tools and components that make it easier to create interactive and engaging visuals. You can leverage D3.js, Chart.js, or other libraries to enhance your visualizations further.

Testing Your Custom Visual: It's crucial to thoroughly test your custom visual to ensure it works as expected. You can use the "powerbi-visuals-tools" package to test your visual locally. Run the following command within your project folder:

sqlCopy code

```
pbiviz start
```

This will launch a local development server where you can preview your custom visual and make real-time adjustments.

Configuring Your Visual: Custom visuals often require configuration options to allow users to customize their experience. You can define settings that control the visual's appearance, behavior, and data sources. These settings can be exposed to users in the Power BI service.

Packaging Your Custom Visual: Once you're satisfied with your custom visual, you need to package it into a .pbiviz file, which is the format used by Power BI for custom visuals. Run the following command to create the package:

goCopy code

```
pbiviz package
```

This command will generate a .pbiviz file that you can import into your Power BI reports.

Importing into Power BI: To use your custom visual in Power BI reports, open your Power BI Desktop file, go to the "Visualizations" pane, click on the ellipsis (...) menu, and select "Import a custom visual." Then, choose the .pbiviz file you created in the previous step.

Customizing in Power BI: With your custom visual added to the report, you can configure it by dragging and dropping fields from your data model onto the visual. Customize the visual's appearance, interactivity, and behavior according to your data analysis needs.

Publishing and Sharing: Once your report is complete, you can publish it to the Power BI service or export it for sharing with others. Your custom visual will be available in the published report, allowing others to interact with it.

Community and Resources: Custom visuals are a thriving community within Power BI. You can find a wealth of resources, tutorials, and support from the Power BI community and Microsoft's documentation. Don't hesitate to explore these resources to enhance your custom visual development skills.

The Custom Visual SDK opens up a world of possibilities for advanced customization within Power BI. You have the freedom to design visuals that precisely meet your analytical and reporting needs, making your data storytelling more effective and engaging.

Whether you're creating custom charts, maps, infographics, or interactive dashboards, the Custom Visual SDK empowers you to bring your data to life.

One of the key benefits of using the Custom Visual SDK is the ability to leverage external libraries and frameworks like D3.js, Three.js, or any other JavaScript library. This allows you to create visuals with advanced animations, complex interactivity, and unique aesthetics.

Additionally, custom visuals are not limited to a single chart or visualization type. You can create multi-faceted visuals that combine various elements, such as charts, tables, images, and narratives, to provide a comprehensive view of your data.

Moreover, custom visuals can enhance user interaction by offering features like tooltips, selection, filtering, and drill-through actions. These interactive capabilities enable users to explore data in-depth and gain deeper insights.

In summary, the Custom Visual SDK is a powerful tool for advanced customization and creativity within Power BI. It empowers you to design visuals that go beyond the standard offerings, catering to your specific data analysis requirements. With the ability to integrate external libraries, test locally, and customize interactions, you have the tools you need to create compelling and impactful data visualizations.

As you explore the world of custom visuals with the Custom Visual SDK, keep in mind that practice and experimentation are key to mastering this skill. With dedication and creativity, you can create visuals that not only convey data insights effectively but also captivate your audience and elevate your data storytelling to the next level.

Chapter 6: Advanced Interactivity and Drill-Through Actions

Creating dynamic interactions between visuals in Power BI is a powerful technique that enhances the user experience and enables more profound data exploration. It allows users to interact with one visual element, affecting the behavior or appearance of other visuals on the same report page. This interactivity can lead to more insightful data analysis and a better understanding of the data's underlying patterns and trends.

To implement dynamic interactions between visuals in Power BI, you'll need to follow these fundamental steps:

Design Your Report Page: Before you can create dynamic interactions, you must design the report page that will contain the visuals you want to connect. Consider the layout, the choice of visuals, and the overall story you want to convey through your report.

Add Visuals to the Page: Populate the report page with the visuals you intend to connect. These can include charts, tables, matrices, and other Power BI visuals that display your data.

Select the Source Visual: Choose the visual that will trigger the dynamic interaction. This source visual will be the one users interact with to influence other visuals on the page. Click on the source visual to select it.

Configure the Interaction: In Power BI Desktop, go to the "Format" pane and select the "Edit interactions" icon. This opens the interaction editing mode, allowing you to define how the selected source visual interacts with other visuals on the page.

Define the Target Visuals: Within the interaction editing mode, you'll see a list of all visuals on the report page. Each visual can be configured as either "None," "Filter," or "Highlight." Here's what each option means:

None: Choosing "None" means that the source visual's interactions won't affect the target visual in any way.

Filter: Selecting "Filter" means that when you interact with the source visual (e.g., selecting a data point or applying a filter), the target visual will update to display data that matches the selected criteria. This is a common interaction type used for drilling down into specific data points.

Highlight: Opting for "Highlight" means that when you interact with the source visual, the target visual will emphasize data points that align with the selection, making them stand out. This is often used for comparisons or emphasizing specific data points.

Set Interaction Behavior: For each target visual, select the interaction type that best suits your analysis goals. You can have different interactions for each target visual, allowing for fine-grained control over how visuals respond to user actions.

Test and Refine: After configuring the interactions, test your report to ensure that the dynamic interactions behave as intended. Check that selecting, filtering, or highlighting in the source visual appropriately affects the target visuals. Make adjustments as needed to refine the interactions.

Add User Guidance: To enhance the user experience, consider adding tooltips, explanations, or guidance to your report to help users understand how to interact with the visuals and interpret the results.

Publish and Share: Once you're satisfied with your interactive report, publish it to the Power BI service or export it for sharing. Users can then access and explore the report online, benefiting from the dynamic interactions you've implemented.

Iterate and Improve: Data analysis is an iterative process. Continuously gather feedback from users and stakeholders to improve the dynamic interactions and refine your report's design for better data exploration.

Dynamic interactions can be applied in various scenarios, such as:

Drill-Through: When users click on specific data points in a chart, they can drill down into more detailed information, navigating to another report page or revealing additional data in a table or matrix.

Cross-Filtering: Interactions can be set up to filter other visuals on the same page based on the selection in the source visual. For example, selecting a specific category in a bar chart can filter a table to display only data related to that category.

Cross-Highlighting: This interaction type can be used to emphasize data points that align with the selection in the source visual. For instance, selecting a region in a map can highlight corresponding data points in a scatter plot.

Parameterized Interactions: You can create more advanced interactions by using parameters and measures in Power BI. This allows you to dynamically change the behavior of visuals based on user selections or calculated measures.

Dynamic Titles and Labels: Another way to create dynamic interactions is by using dynamic titles and labels in your visuals. These can change based on user selections, providing context and guidance.

In Power BI, dynamic interactions can be a game-changer for data exploration and storytelling. They enable users to interact with data in a meaningful way, gaining deeper insights and making more informed decisions. By following the steps outlined above, you can harness the full potential of dynamic interactions to create engaging and informative reports that empower users to explore data on their terms.

As you become more proficient in creating dynamic interactions, you'll find that the flexibility and interactivity they offer can transform your Power BI reports into dynamic, user-friendly data analysis tools. Whether you're designing reports for internal stakeholders, clients, or the general public, these interactive features can make your reports more engaging and insightful.

When deploying reports with dynamic interactions to the Power BI service, keep in mind that users accessing the report online will have the same interactive capabilities as those using Power BI Desktop. This means that they can explore and interact with the report's visuals, apply filters, drill down into details, and gain a deeper understanding of the data presented.

Furthermore, Power BI's sharing and collaboration features make it easy to share your reports with others in your organization or with external stakeholders. You can publish reports to the Power BI service, share them with specific users or groups, and even embed them in websites or applications for wider accessibility.

In summary, dynamic interactions are a valuable technique in Power BI that allows you to create reports that engage users and provide them with the flexibility to explore data interactively. By following the steps outlined Next, you can design and implement dynamic interactions effectively, enhancing the overall user experience and delivering more meaningful insights through your reports.

Advanced drill-through configurations in Power BI offer the ability to create highly customized and interactive experiences for users seeking deeper insights into their data. While basic drill-through allows users to navigate from one visual to another, advanced configurations enable more sophisticated interactions and tailor the drill-through experience to specific use cases.

To implement advanced drill-through configurations effectively, it's essential to understand the underlying concepts and the steps involved in setting up these interactions. Next, we will explore advanced drill-through configurations, providing insights into their significance and practical implementation.

Understanding the Significance:

Advanced drill-through configurations enhance the analytical capabilities of Power BI reports by enabling users to perform intricate investigations into their data. Rather than relying on predefined drill-through paths, advanced configurations allow you to control the flow of data exploration, offering a more personalized and insightful experience.

Key Concepts:

Before delving into the implementation details, let's clarify some key concepts related to advanced drill-through configurations:

Source Visual: The source visual is the visual element in your report that triggers the drill-through action. It's the visual users interact with to initiate the drill-through process.

Drill-Through Page: A drill-through page is a dedicated report page that displays detailed information related to the selection made in the source visual. This page typically contains visuals, tables, or charts that provide a closer look at the selected data points.

Fields and Filters: Fields are the data columns or measures used in your report, and filters are conditions or criteria applied to those fields to refine the data displayed. When a user initiates drill-through, the selected fields and filters are passed to the drill-through page.

Custom Buttons or Links: Advanced drill-through often involves creating custom buttons or links in the source visual. These buttons or links can be designed to trigger specific drill-through actions, such as navigating to different drill-through pages or changing the context of the drill-through.

Implementation Steps:

Now, let's explore the practical steps involved in setting up advanced drill-through configurations:

Design Drill-Through Pages: Start by creating one or more dedicated drill-through pages in your Power BI report. These pages should be designed to present detailed information and insights related to specific data points.

Identify Drill-Through Scenarios: Determine the scenarios in which advanced drill-through will be most beneficial. Consider which visuals and data points users are likely to want to explore further.

Create Custom Buttons or Links: To offer more control over drill-through actions, design custom buttons or links in your source visual. These buttons can trigger specific drill-through scenarios or navigate to different drill-through pages.

Define Drill-Through Filters: Configure the filters and fields that will be passed to the drill-through pages. You can use the "Drillthrough filters" option in Power BI to specify which fields should be passed and how they should filter the drill-through pages.

Set Drill-Through Actions: Define the drill-through actions for each custom button or link. Specify the target drill-through page and the fields and filters that should be applied when users click on these elements.

Test and Refine: Thoroughly test your advanced drill-through configurations to ensure that they behave as intended. Check that the source visual correctly passes the selected data, filters are applied accurately, and drill-through pages provide meaningful insights.

Examples of Advanced Drill-Through Configurations:

Let's explore some examples of advanced drill-through configurations and their use cases:

Multi-Level Drill-Through: Create a source visual with custom buttons that allow users to drill through data at multiple levels of granularity. For example, in a sales report, users can start by drilling into regions, then into individual stores, and finally into specific products.

Conditional Drill-Through: Implement drill-through buttons that appear conditionally based on user selections. For instance, if a user selects a specific product category, a custom button may appear to provide drill-through details related to that category.

Contextual Drill-Through: Use drill-through filters to apply context-specific filters on drill-through pages. For example, if a user drills through from a visual showing monthly sales, the drill-through page can display detailed information for that specific month.

Custom Interactions: Design custom buttons or links that not only trigger drill-through actions but also change the behavior of visuals on the drill-through page. This allows for more dynamic and interactive drill-through experiences.

Deploying Advanced Drill-Through Configurations:

Deploying reports with advanced drill-through configurations follows the same process as deploying standard Power BI reports. You can publish the report to the Power BI service or export it for sharing with others.

When sharing reports with advanced drill-through configurations, it's essential to communicate how users can make the most of these interactions. Provide documentation or guidance on the specific drill-through scenarios available, the custom buttons or links they can use, and the insights they can gain through advanced drill-through.

In the Power BI service, users can access and interact with reports that include advanced drill-through configurations just as they would with standard reports. They can click on the source visuals, use custom buttons or links, and explore the drill-through pages to extract deeper insights from the data.

In summary, advanced drill-through configurations in Power BI empower users to perform more customized and insightful data exploration. By understanding the key concepts, following the implementation steps, and considering various use cases, you can leverage this feature to create reports that offer a richer and more interactive experience for your audience.

Chapter 7: Geographic Mapping and Spatial Analysis

Advanced geographic visualizations in Power BI allow you to unlock the full potential of location-based data, providing deeper insights and more engaging experiences for users. These visualizations go beyond basic maps and charts, enabling you to create compelling stories and uncover hidden patterns in your spatial data.

To harness the power of advanced geographic visualizations, it's crucial to understand the concepts, tools, and techniques available within Power BI. Next, we will explore the significance of advanced geographic visualizations and how to effectively implement them in your reports.

Significance of Advanced Geographic Visualizations:

Advanced geographic visualizations play a vital role in data analysis and decision-making across various industries. They allow you to represent spatial data in meaningful ways, helping users gain a better understanding of location-based insights. Here's why these visualizations are significant:

Spatial Context: Advanced geographic visualizations provide spatial context to your data, allowing users to see how data points relate to each other on a map. This context is essential for making informed decisions.

Pattern Recognition: With advanced geographic visualizations, you can identify patterns, trends, and clusters in your data that may not be apparent in traditional charts or tables. This is particularly valuable in fields like retail, real estate, and healthcare.

Storytelling: Geographic visualizations can tell compelling stories. You can use them to show the progression of events, changes over time, or the impact of geographical factors on your data.

Engagement: Maps and interactive geographic visuals enhance user engagement by providing an intuitive way to explore data. Users can interact with maps, zoom in, and click on data points for more details.

Key Concepts in Advanced Geographic Visualizations:

Before diving into the practical implementation, let's clarify some key concepts related to advanced geographic visualizations:

Geocoding: Geocoding is the process of converting addresses or place names into geographical coordinates (latitude and longitude) that can be plotted on a map. Power BI supports various geocoding services and custom geocoding for precise location data.

Shapefiles: Shapefiles are a common format for storing geographic and spatial data. They consist of multiple files that contain geometry, attributes, and other information about geographical features like boundaries, roads, or regions. Power BI can import and use shapefiles to enhance your visualizations.

Map Visuals: Power BI offers different map visuals, such as basic maps, filled maps, and custom visuals, to represent geographic data. Each type has unique features and use cases, so understanding when to use which one is crucial.

Custom GeoJSON Files: GeoJSON is another format for encoding geographical data. You can import custom GeoJSON files to create custom geographic visuals in Power BI.

Implementing Advanced Geographic Visualizations:

To implement advanced geographic visualizations effectively, follow these steps:

Prepare Your Data: Ensure that your dataset includes location data in a format that Power BI can use. This may involve geocoding addresses or using latitude and longitude coordinates.

Select the Right Visualization Type: Choose the most suitable map visualization type for your data and objectives. Basic maps are ideal for showing point data, while filled maps work well for regional or thematic data.

Customize Visuals: Customize your map visuals to enhance the user experience. You can adjust colors, add data labels, and use tooltips to provide additional information.

Layering and Overlays: Use layering and overlays to display multiple data sets on a single map. This allows you to compare and contrast different aspects of your spatial data.

Time-Based Analysis: If your data includes temporal elements, consider implementing time-based analysis in your geographic visualizations. This can reveal trends and changes over time.

Custom Geographic Data: Import custom shapefiles or GeoJSON files to include specific geographical boundaries or regions that are relevant to your analysis.

Interactivity: Make your geographic visualizations interactive. Allow users to zoom in and out, click on data points for details, and filter data based on their selections.

Examples of Advanced Geographic Visualizations:

Here are some examples of advanced geographic visualizations and their use cases:

Heatmaps: Heatmaps can represent data density or concentration in a particular area. They are useful for visualizing the distribution of crimes in a city, population density, or customer hotspots for a retail business.

Path Analysis: Path analysis visualizations show the paths taken by objects or entities over a geographical area. They are valuable for tracking the movement of vehicles, wildlife, or even customer journeys within a store.

Custom Map Overlays: Create custom map overlays to show specific regions, boundaries, or areas of interest. This is beneficial for illustrating sales territories, political districts, or service coverage areas.

Flow Maps: Flow maps depict the movement of goods, people, or information between locations. They are essential for logistics and supply chain analysis, as well as migration studies.

Deploying Advanced Geographic Visualizations:

Once you have created advanced geographic visualizations in Power BI, deploying your reports follows the standard process for sharing Power BI content. You can publish reports to the Power BI service, share them with colleagues or stakeholders, and schedule data refreshes to keep the information up to date.

Additionally, you can embed your Power BI reports with advanced geographic visualizations in websites or applications using Power BI Embedded, enabling a wider audience to access and interact with your spatial data.

In summary, mastering advanced geographic visualizations in Power BI opens up a world of possibilities for data analysis and storytelling. By understanding the significance, key concepts, and implementation steps, you can leverage the full potential of location-based data to make informed decisions and engage your audience effectively.

Spatial data analysis and mapping techniques are powerful tools for extracting valuable insights from geospatial data, enabling businesses and organizations to make informed decisions based on location-related information. Next, we will delve into the world of spatial data analysis and mapping, exploring various techniques and methodologies for harnessing the full potential of geographical data.

At its core, spatial data analysis involves examining and interpreting data that has a geographical or spatial component, such as latitude and longitude coordinates, postal codes, addresses, or region names. This type of data is prevalent in diverse fields, including urban planning, environmental science, logistics, marketing, and more.

One of the fundamental concepts in spatial data analysis is the notion of spatial relationships. Spatial relationships refer to the connections and associations between geographical features or data points. These relationships can be categorized into three main types:

Spatial Autocorrelation: Spatial autocorrelation measures the similarity of values for a variable at nearby locations. It helps identify whether neighboring areas exhibit similar characteristics or if there are spatial patterns in the data.

Spatial Dependence: Spatial dependence examines how one variable's value at a given location is influenced by the values of the same variable at nearby locations. It is essential for understanding the spread of phenomena like diseases, pollution, or crime.

Spatial Heterogeneity: Spatial heterogeneity explores variations in data across different regions or areas. It helps identify areas with unique characteristics or outliers in the data.

Spatial data analysis can be performed using a variety of techniques, including spatial statistics, spatial interpolation, and spatial clustering. These techniques enable us to uncover patterns, trends, and anomalies in spatial data, facilitating better decision-making.

Spatial Statistics: Spatial statistics is a specialized branch of statistics that focuses on analyzing data with spatial dependencies. It includes methods such as spatial autocorrelation analysis, spatial regression analysis, and point pattern analysis. These techniques help quantify the degree of spatial association between data points, identify clusters or spatial outliers, and model relationships between variables while accounting for spatial effects.

Spatial Interpolation: Spatial interpolation is the process of estimating values at unobserved locations based on the values observed at nearby locations. Common interpolation methods include kriging, inverse distance weighting, and spline interpolation. Spatial interpolation is widely used in environmental modeling, weather forecasting, and geostatistics.

Spatial Clustering: Spatial clustering aims to group similar data points that are close to each other in geographical space. Techniques like DBSCAN (Density-Based Spatial Clustering of Applications with Noise) and K-means clustering can reveal spatial patterns and help identify regions with similar characteristics. Clustering is essential in market segmentation, identifying disease hotspots, and natural resource management.

Mapping is a fundamental aspect of spatial data analysis, as it allows us to visualize and communicate spatial patterns effectively. Geographic Information Systems (GIS) play a crucial role in mapping, enabling the creation of maps that incorporate various data layers, such as roads, land use, population density, and environmental factors.

GIS Mapping: GIS software, such as ArcGIS, QGIS, and MapInfo, provides the tools and capabilities to create, analyze, and visualize spatial data. Users can import spatial datasets, overlay them, perform spatial analyses, and generate maps for decision-making.

These maps can range from simple visualizations to complex thematic maps, heatmaps, and 3D maps.

Geospatial Data Visualization: Effective geospatial data visualization enhances the understanding of spatial patterns and relationships. It involves using various types of maps, charts, and graphs to represent spatial data. Examples include choropleth maps (color-coded maps), bubble maps, and cartograms. Choosing the right visualization technique depends on the specific data and the message you want to convey.

Web Mapping and Interactive Maps: Web mapping technologies, such as Leaflet, Google Maps API, and Mapbox, enable the creation of interactive maps for web applications. These maps allow users to explore and interact with spatial data dynamically. Incorporating interactive maps into web applications can enhance user engagement and deliver location-based services.

Deploying spatial data analysis and mapping techniques often involves utilizing specialized software and libraries tailored for geospatial data. For instance, in Python, the **geopandas** library is a popular choice for working with geospatial data, while R offers packages like **sf** for spatial analysis.

Here's a brief overview of how to perform spatial data analysis using Python and **geopandas**:

Installation: To get started with **geopandas**, you need to install it using pip:

Copy code

```
pip install geopandas
```

Loading Spatial Data: Use **geopandas** to read spatial data in various formats, such as shapefiles or GeoJSON files. You can load data into a GeoDataFrame, which is a pandas DataFrame with geospatial capabilities.

pythonCopy code

```
import geopandas as gpd gdf = gpd.read_file('path_to_shapefile.shp')
```

Exploratory Data Analysis (EDA): Conduct exploratory data analysis to understand the distribution, spatial patterns, and relationships within the dataset. You can create basic visualizations and perform spatial queries.

Spatial Analysis: Apply spatial statistics, interpolation, clustering, or other spatial analysis techniques based on your research goals.

Visualization: Visualize your results using **geopandas** and other visualization libraries like **matplotlib** or **seaborn**. Customize the appearance of maps to convey your findings effectively.

In summary, spatial data analysis and mapping techniques provide valuable insights into spatial relationships, patterns, and trends within geospatial data. These techniques are essential across various domains, including urban planning, environmental monitoring, retail, logistics, and healthcare. By leveraging specialized software and libraries, you can harness the power of spatial data to support data-driven decision-making and enhance your understanding of the world around you.

Chapter 8: Integrating R and Python for Advanced Analytics

In the realm of data analytics and business intelligence, the integration of R and Python offers advanced analytical solutions that empower organizations to derive deeper insights and make data-driven decisions. These two open-source programming languages have gained immense popularity among data professionals due to their extensive libraries, robust statistical capabilities, and flexibility in data analysis.

Introduction to R and Python Integration: Combining the strengths of R and Python within the Power BI environment extends the possibilities for advanced data analysis, predictive modeling, and visualization. This integration is made possible through the use of custom R and Python scripts, allowing data analysts and data scientists to leverage the full potential of both languages seamlessly.

Installing R and Python in Power BI: To begin harnessing the power of R and Python in Power BI, users need to ensure that both languages are properly configured and integrated with the Power BI Desktop. This can be accomplished by following a few straightforward steps, including installing R and Python on the local machine and configuring the Power BI settings to recognize these installations.

Executing R Scripts in Power BI: Once R is set up, users can create and execute R scripts directly within Power BI. This opens up opportunities for complex data transformations, statistical analysis, and custom visualizations. R scripts can be embedded in Power Query, where they can transform and manipulate data as needed.

Python Integration in Power BI: Python integration is another powerful feature in Power BI, enabling data professionals to write Python scripts for data analysis and transformation. By incorporating Python visuals or running Python scripts in Power Query, users can perform tasks such as data cleansing, feature engineering, and predictive modeling with ease.

Utilizing Machine Learning Libraries: Both R and Python provide access to a wealth of machine learning libraries, making advanced analytics and predictive modeling accessible to Power BI users. These libraries include scikit-learn, TensorFlow, Keras, and caret in Python, and libraries like caret, xgboost, and randomForest in R. These libraries empower users to build and deploy machine learning models for tasks such as classification, regression, clustering, and anomaly detection.

Creating Custom Visualizations: R and Python scripts can be employed to generate custom visualizations that go beyond the built-in options in Power BI. This flexibility enables users to craft tailored visuals that align precisely with their data analysis goals. Whether it's creating custom charts, heatmaps, or geographic visualizations, R and Python offer limitless possibilities.

Predictive Analytics with R and Python: One of the key advantages of integrating R and Python into Power BI is the ability to perform predictive analytics. By employing machine learning algorithms and techniques available in both languages, users can predict future trends, make forecasts, and identify patterns within their data. This capability is invaluable for businesses looking to gain a competitive edge by leveraging predictive insights.

Scalability and Performance: While the integration of R and Python enriches Power BI with advanced analytical capabilities, it's important to consider scalability and performance aspects. Running resource-intensive scripts can impact the performance of Power BI, particularly when dealing with large datasets. Therefore, it's crucial to optimize scripts, manage resources efficiently, and, if necessary, employ techniques like data sampling to ensure smooth performance.

Deployment and Sharing: Sharing Power BI reports that incorporate R and Python scripts is straightforward. When publishing reports to the Power BI service, the R and Python scripts are automatically executed in the cloud, making the reports fully interactive for end-users. However, it's essential to ensure that the necessary libraries and dependencies are available in the cloud environment.

Security and Governance: Security and governance considerations should not be overlooked when using R and Python in Power BI. Organizations must establish best practices for securing sensitive data, ensuring compliance with regulations, and managing access to scripts and data sources. Power BI's role-based security and data governance features can play a pivotal role in maintaining data integrity and confidentiality.

Continuous Learning and Community Support: Both R and Python have vibrant and active communities that provide a wealth of resources, tutorials, and forums for learning and troubleshooting. Data professionals can tap into these communities to expand their knowledge and address challenges encountered while working with R and Python in Power BI.

In summary, the integration of R and Python in Power BI represents a significant leap in the realm of advanced data analytics and business intelligence. These languages provide the tools and capabilities needed to tackle complex data analysis tasks, predictive modeling, and custom visualizations. By mastering the art of combining R, Python, and Power BI, organizations can unlock new dimensions of insight, enabling them to make data-driven decisions that drive success in today's data-centric world.

Chapter 9: Machine Learning Integration in Power BI

Building machine learning models within the Power BI ecosystem represents a significant step forward in harnessing the full potential of data-driven decision-making. By seamlessly integrating machine learning capabilities, Power BI empowers users to create predictive models, uncover valuable insights, and drive informed business strategies.

To embark on the journey of building machine learning models in Power BI, users must first ensure they have the necessary components in place. This includes installing the required R or Python libraries for machine learning, which can be achieved by executing specific CLI commands within the respective environments.

For those utilizing R, installing packages such as "caret" and "randomForest" can enhance the machine learning capabilities available within Power BI. Similarly, Python users may need to install libraries like "scikit-learn," "TensorFlow," or "XGBoost" to leverage powerful machine learning algorithms.

Once these libraries are installed, users can begin the process of data preparation. High-quality data is the foundation of any successful machine learning model, and Power BI's data transformation capabilities can help clean, shape, and aggregate data for analysis.

The Power Query editor is a valuable tool for data preparation, allowing users to filter, sort, and manipulate data before feeding it into machine learning algorithms. CLI commands may be utilized to perform specific data transformations or calculations, ensuring that the dataset is primed for model training.

Selecting the appropriate machine learning algorithm is a crucial step in building predictive models. Power BI provides a range of machine learning algorithms that can be applied through user-friendly interfaces, eliminating the need for extensive coding or scripting.

Regression, classification, clustering, and time series forecasting are some of the common machine learning tasks that Power BI supports. Users can leverage these tasks to address various business challenges, such as predicting sales, classifying customer behavior, segmenting markets, or forecasting future trends.

When selecting a machine learning algorithm, it's essential to consider the nature of the problem and the characteristics of the dataset. For example, linear regression may be suitable for predicting continuous values, while decision trees or random forests could be more appropriate for classification tasks.

After selecting an algorithm, users can train and evaluate their machine learning model directly within Power BI. The tool provides a user-friendly interface that simplifies the process of splitting data into training and testing sets, configuring model parameters, and assessing model performance.

CLI commands can also come into play when fine-tuning model parameters or conducting more advanced model evaluation techniques. For example, users may employ cross-validation techniques to assess model generalization or hyperparameter tuning to optimize model performance.

Once a machine learning model is trained and evaluated, it can be deployed within Power BI to make predictions on new data. The model's predictive capabilities can be integrated into reports and dashboards, allowing users to gain real-time insights and make data-driven decisions.

CLI commands are typically not required for model deployment within Power BI, as the tool provides an intuitive interface for incorporating machine learning predictions into existing reports. Users can create visuals that showcase model predictions, confidence intervals, or classification results.

Monitoring and maintaining machine learning models are essential aspects of the process. Power BI offers features that allow users to track model performance, detect anomalies, and retrain models as needed. These capabilities ensure that machine learning models remain accurate and relevant over time.

Furthermore, Power BI enables users to take advantage of automated machine learning (AutoML) capabilities. AutoML simplifies the model-building process by automatically selecting the best-performing algorithms and hyperparameters, making it an ideal option for users who may not have extensive machine learning expertise.

To enhance the interpretability of machine learning models, Power BI provides features for model explainability. Users can access insights into model decisions, variable importance, and feature contributions, helping them understand why the model makes specific predictions.

In addition to the built-in machine learning capabilities, Power BI offers the flexibility to integrate custom R or Python scripts directly into reports. This advanced feature allows users to leverage their coding skills and incorporate custom machine learning models, scripts, or visualizations.

CLI commands may be necessary when incorporating custom machine learning scripts or deploying external models. Users can execute these commands to install required packages or libraries, manage dependencies, and ensure seamless integration.

Machine learning in Power BI is not limited to standalone models. Users can also employ machine learning algorithms within Power Query to perform data transformations, enrich datasets, or generate new features. This approach extends the scope of machine learning within the data preparation phase.

To facilitate collaboration and sharing of machine learning insights, Power BI supports publishing reports and dashboards to the Power BI service. Once published, reports can be accessed and interacted with by stakeholders, ensuring that the benefits of machine learning are distributed throughout the organization.

When working with sensitive data or compliance requirements, it's crucial to implement security and governance measures. Power BI provides robust security features, role-based access control, and data protection options to safeguard data and ensure regulatory compliance.

In summary, building machine learning models in Power BI opens up a world of opportunities for data-driven decision-making. With a user-friendly interface, support for various machine learning tasks, and the flexibility to incorporate custom scripts, Power BI empowers users to harness the full potential of machine learning. Whether predicting future trends, classifying data, or clustering segments, Power BI's machine learning capabilities offer a powerful toolkit for data professionals to unlock insights and drive business success.

Real-time machine learning integration represents a significant leap forward in the world of data analytics, enabling organizations to make immediate, data-driven decisions that can have a profound impact on their operations. In the context of Power BI, real-time machine learning integration refers to the ability to deploy and execute machine learning models that provide predictions and insights in real time, as data streams into the system.

To harness the power of real-time machine learning in Power BI, users must first ensure they have the necessary infrastructure and tools in place. This typically involves setting up a dedicated environment for deploying and running machine learning models, such as Azure Machine Learning or a custom server with the required libraries and resources.

CLI commands may come into play during the setup process, as users may need to install specific libraries, frameworks, or dependencies to support their machine learning models. These commands ensure that the environment is properly configured to handle real-time model execution.

Once the environment is prepared, the next step is to develop and train machine learning models. Power BI offers integration with various machine learning frameworks and services, including Azure Machine Learning, TensorFlow, and ONNX, allowing users to build and train models using their preferred tools.

The choice of machine learning framework depends on the specific requirements of the task at hand. For example, Azure Machine Learning is an excellent choice for organizations that prioritize scalability and cloud-based solutions, while TensorFlow provides extensive support for deep learning tasks.

After developing and training a machine learning model, it can be deployed to the real-time environment. Deployment options may vary depending on the chosen framework, but typically, models can be deployed as REST APIs, web services, or containerized applications.

CLI commands can be useful for packaging and deploying machine learning models to the real-time environment. Users may need to create containers, define API endpoints, and configure authentication and authorization settings to ensure secure access to the models.

Once the machine learning model is deployed and exposed as a service, it becomes accessible to Power BI. Users can leverage Power BI's real-time data streaming capabilities to feed data to the model and receive predictions or insights in real time.

Real-time data streaming in Power BI can be achieved through various means, including Power Automate, Azure Stream Analytics, or custom connectors. These tools enable users to ingest, transform, and transmit data from various sources to the deployed machine learning model.

CLI commands may also be utilized to set up and configure data streaming pipelines, ensuring that data flows seamlessly from source systems to the machine learning model for real-time analysis.

When data is streamed to the machine learning model, the model processes the incoming data, makes predictions, and sends the results back to Power BI. Users can then incorporate these real-time insights into their reports and dashboards, providing up-to-the-minute information for decision-makers.

Power BI offers a range of visualization options for displaying real-time machine learning results, including tables, charts, and custom visuals. Users can design interactive reports that update in real time as new data arrives and predictions are generated.

Advanced users may choose to integrate custom visuals or scripts to enhance the presentation of real-time machine learning insights. This can be accomplished by embedding JavaScript or Python code directly into Power BI reports.

Monitoring and performance optimization are critical aspects of real-time machine learning integration. Users must continuously monitor the performance of deployed models to ensure they are delivering accurate and timely predictions. CLI commands can be employed to schedule regular model evaluations and automate performance monitoring tasks.

In cases where model performance degrades over time or data distributions change, retraining the model becomes necessary. Users can automate the retraining process by setting up scheduled tasks or triggers based on predefined conditions. CLI commands can facilitate the automation of model retraining procedures.

Real-time machine learning integration extends beyond traditional predictive modeling. Users can also implement anomaly detection, sentiment analysis, fraud detection, and recommendation systems in real time, depending on their business needs. The flexibility of Power BI and its integration capabilities make it a versatile platform for a wide range of real-time analytics applications.

Security and access control are paramount when dealing with real-time machine learning integration. Organizations must implement robust authentication mechanisms and role-based access control to ensure that only authorized users can interact with the real-time models and access sensitive data.

Furthermore, data privacy and compliance considerations must be addressed, particularly when dealing with real-time data streaming. Organizations should adhere to regulatory requirements and implement data anonymization or encryption measures to protect sensitive information.

In summary, real-time machine learning integration in Power BI represents a cutting-edge approach to data analytics. By leveraging CLI commands and the capabilities of machine learning frameworks and services, organizations can deploy, execute, and monitor machine learning models in real time. This enables them to make data-driven decisions with speed and precision, ultimately driving better business outcomes and competitive advantage.

Chapter 10: Real-world Case Studies in Advanced Power BI Applications

Advanced Power BI solutions have found applications across a multitude of industries, revolutionizing the way organizations analyze data and make informed decisions. In the financial sector, for instance, Power BI has become an indispensable tool for banks, investment firms, and insurance companies. These organizations use Power BI to gain real-time insights into market trends, portfolio performance, and risk assessment.

Advanced Power BI solutions in the financial industry often involve complex data modeling to handle vast amounts of financial data. CLI commands play a role in automating data extraction and transformation processes, enabling organizations to streamline data integration.

Moreover, financial institutions leverage advanced DAX functions to calculate key performance indicators (KPIs) such as return on investment (ROI) and risk-adjusted returns. These calculations enable analysts and portfolio managers to make data-driven investment decisions.

The healthcare sector has also witnessed the transformative power of Power BI. Hospitals and healthcare providers utilize Power BI to analyze patient data, monitor healthcare trends, and optimize resource allocation. For instance, CLI commands can be used to automate the extraction of patient records from electronic health record (EHR) systems.

Machine learning integration with Power BI enables predictive analytics in healthcare, helping organizations forecast patient admission rates, identify disease outbreaks, and allocate medical resources efficiently. Furthermore, the visualization capabilities of Power BI enable healthcare professionals to create interactive dashboards for tracking patient outcomes and clinical performance.

Manufacturing companies have embraced Power BI to enhance production efficiency and quality control. They deploy Power BI to collect data from sensors, machines, and production lines, which is crucial for monitoring equipment performance and detecting anomalies. Custom visualizations and drill-through actions allow engineers and plant managers to dive deep into the data for root cause analysis.

CLI commands are used to automate data collection and integration processes, ensuring that real-time data from the factory floor is readily available for analysis. Aggregations and summarization techniques help organizations identify trends in production metrics and make timely adjustments to optimize output.

The retail industry leverages Power BI to gain a competitive edge in a highly dynamic market. Advanced data modeling techniques enable retailers to create comprehensive customer profiles, segment their customer base, and tailor marketing strategies accordingly. Retailers can use CLI commands to extract data from point-of-sale systems, e-commerce platforms, and customer relationship management (CRM) software.

Real-time analytics in retail involves monitoring inventory levels, tracking sales performance, and making pricing decisions on the fly. Power BI's ability to connect to various data sources ensures that retailers have access to up-to-the-minute sales data. Furthermore, machine learning algorithms can be integrated into Power BI to implement demand forecasting and inventory optimization models.

In the energy sector, Power BI helps organizations manage and visualize large volumes of data from sensors and monitoring devices across oil fields, power plants, and renewable energy installations. CLI commands are used to automate data collection and preprocessing tasks, ensuring that data is readily available for analysis.

Power BI's advanced geospatial capabilities are valuable in the energy industry for visualizing geographic data, such as the locations of oil wells or wind farms. These visualizations aid in resource allocation, maintenance scheduling, and risk assessment. Power BI can also integrate with energy trading systems to provide real-time market data and trading insights.

Government agencies and public sector organizations are increasingly adopting Power BI to improve data-driven decision-making. CLI commands are employed to extract data from diverse government systems and databases, enabling agencies to consolidate and analyze data related to public health, education, transportation, and more.

Power BI's data visualization capabilities assist government entities in presenting data to the public in a clear and transparent manner. Interactive dashboards are often used to communicate key performance indicators, budget allocations, and progress on public initiatives.

The telecommunications industry relies on Power BI for network monitoring, customer analysis, and revenue forecasting. CLI commands enable telecom providers to collect and process vast amounts of data from network equipment, call records, and customer interactions.

Advanced analytics in telecom involve the application of machine learning models to predict customer churn, optimize network performance, and detect fraudulent activities. Power BI allows telecom operators to create dynamic dashboards that provide real-time insights into network health and customer behavior.

In the education sector, institutions use Power BI to assess student performance, track enrollment trends, and improve educational outcomes. CLI commands assist in automating data extraction and integration from student information systems, learning management platforms, and assessment tools.

Time intelligence functions in Power BI help educational institutions analyze academic progress over time, identifying areas where interventions are needed to support students. Custom visualizations enable educators to create personalized dashboards for student performance tracking.

The transportation and logistics industry harnesses Power BI to optimize supply chain operations, monitor vehicle fleets, and enhance route planning. CLI commands are employed to extract data from logistics software, GPS devices, and warehouse management systems.

Power BI's mapping and geospatial capabilities enable logistics companies to visualize the movement of goods, track delivery routes, and optimize transportation costs. Predictive analytics models can be integrated to forecast demand and optimize inventory levels.

In summary, advanced Power BI solutions have permeated various industries, offering organizations the ability to unlock insights from their data and make data-driven decisions. Whether it's in finance, healthcare, manufacturing, retail, energy, government, telecommunications, education, or transportation, the versatility and power of Power BI, combined with CLI automation, have become essential tools for driving innovation, efficiency, and competitiveness across diverse sectors.

Complex business problems often require advanced solutions, and Power BI has proven to be a game-changer in addressing these challenges. Whether it's optimizing supply chains, predicting customer behavior, or analyzing vast datasets, Power BI offers a versatile toolkit to tackle intricate issues.

One of the complex problems that Power BI can address is demand forecasting. By harnessing historical sales data and integrating it with external factors like economic indicators or seasonality patterns, businesses can use Power BI to build robust forecasting models. These models can help companies anticipate customer demand more accurately, leading to better inventory management and cost savings.

To implement demand forecasting using Power BI, businesses can utilize advanced statistical models and time intelligence functions. CLI commands can automate the data extraction process from various sources, ensuring that the forecasting model is continuously updated with the latest data.

Another challenge that organizations face is customer churn prediction. Identifying customers at risk of leaving is crucial for retention efforts and maintaining revenue streams. Power BI can be employed to create predictive models that analyze customer behavior, engagement metrics, and historical churn data.

These models often involve machine learning algorithms, such as logistic regression or decision trees, to predict the likelihood of customer churn. Advanced DAX functions within Power BI enable businesses to calculate churn probabilities and visualize these insights on interactive dashboards.

CLI commands can facilitate the integration of customer data from different sources, such as CRM systems or marketing platforms, into Power BI for real-time monitoring of customer churn indicators.

For companies operating in highly competitive markets, pricing optimization is a complex challenge. Determining the optimal pricing strategy requires analyzing market conditions, competitor pricing, and customer preferences. Power BI can help organizations build dynamic pricing models that consider these factors.

Power BI's data modeling capabilities enable the creation of pricing algorithms that adjust prices based on real-time market data. These algorithms can be integrated into pricing tools, providing sales teams with pricing recommendations for individual customers or products.

Additionally, CLI commands can automate the data retrieval process, ensuring that pricing models are continuously fed with up-to-date market and competitor information.

Supply chain optimization is a critical concern for manufacturing and logistics companies. Complex supply chains involve numerous variables, including production schedules, inventory levels, transportation routes, and supplier performance. Power BI can provide end-to-end visibility into the supply chain and enable predictive analytics to enhance efficiency.

By integrating data from various supply chain systems, Power BI can create comprehensive dashboards that monitor key performance indicators (KPIs) such as lead times, order fill rates, and on-time deliveries. CLI commands can automate data extraction from enterprise resource planning (ERP) systems, warehouse management systems (WMS), and transportation management systems (TMS).

Predictive analytics models can leverage this data to optimize inventory levels, reduce transportation costs, and identify potential disruptions in the supply chain. Machine learning algorithms can also be deployed to forecast demand accurately and adjust production schedules accordingly.

For financial institutions, managing risk is a complex but essential task. Credit risk assessment, in particular, involves evaluating the creditworthiness of borrowers and managing the risk associated with lending. Power BI can be used to build sophisticated credit risk models that analyze financial data, credit scores, and economic indicators.

These models employ machine learning techniques to predict the probability of default and assess the risk level of individual loans or portfolios. Power BI's visualization capabilities enable risk managers to monitor credit risk in real-time and make informed decisions.

CLI commands play a crucial role in automating data integration processes, ensuring that financial data is continuously updated for risk assessment models.

Another complex business problem solved with Power BI is fraud detection. Detecting fraudulent activities in financial transactions or online activities requires the analysis of large datasets and the identification of anomalous patterns.

Power BI's data transformation and modeling capabilities can prepare the data for fraud detection algorithms, which can range from rule-based systems to more advanced machine learning models. CLI commands can streamline the data extraction process from transaction logs, databases, or online sources.

Once integrated into Power BI, these models can generate alerts or visualizations that highlight suspicious activities. Interactive dashboards enable fraud analysts to investigate anomalies further and take appropriate action.

In healthcare, predictive analytics can address the complex challenge of patient readmissions. Hospitals and healthcare providers can use Power BI to build readmission prediction models based on patient history, clinical data, and demographic information.

These models can identify patients at high risk of readmission, allowing healthcare professionals to implement preventive measures, such as post-discharge follow-up or care plan adjustments. CLI commands can automate the extraction of patient data from electronic health records (EHR) and other healthcare systems.

Advanced analytics in Power BI can also assist in optimizing healthcare resource allocation, such as the scheduling of medical staff or the allocation of hospital beds during peak periods.

In summary, Power BI's versatility and advanced capabilities make it a powerful tool for solving complex business problems across various industries. From demand forecasting to customer churn prediction, pricing optimization, supply chain management, credit risk assessment, fraud detection, and patient readmission prediction, Power BI empowers organizations to make data-driven decisions and achieve better outcomes. CLI commands further enhance its utility by automating data processes, ensuring data accuracy, and enabling real-time monitoring of complex challenges.

Conclusion

In the world of data analytics and business intelligence, the Power BI bundle, consisting of four comprehensive books, serves as an indispensable resource for individuals and organizations striving to harness the full potential of their data. Across these four volumes, we have embarked on a journey from the foundational aspects of Power BI to its most advanced capabilities, equipping both beginners and experienced analysts with the knowledge and skills required to become true masters of data.

In "POWER BI ESSENTIALS: A BEGINNER'S GUIDE TO DATA VISUALIZATION MASTERY," readers have been introduced to the fundamental concepts of Power BI. They've learned how to import, transform, and visualize data, create compelling reports and dashboards, and gained insights into best practices for effective data storytelling. This book has laid the groundwork for a strong foundation in data visualization and analysis.

"MASTERING POWER BI: ADVANCED TECHNIQUES AND BEST PRACTICES FOR ANALYSTS," the second book in this bundle, takes readers on a deep dive into the advanced capabilities of Power BI. From mastering the intricacies of DAX formulas to leveraging custom visuals and optimizing data models, this volume equips users with the expertise needed to tackle complex analytical challenges. It's a vital resource for those seeking to elevate their data analysis skills.

The third book, "POWER BI DATA MODELING: BUILDING ROBUST DATASETS FOR EFFECTIVE ANALYSIS," has delved into the heart of Power BI's data modeling capabilities. Readers have learned how to design efficient and flexible data models, create relationships between tables, and optimize data for enhanced performance. Building robust datasets is essential for unlocking the true potential of Power BI, and this book has provided the knowledge and techniques needed to excel in this critical aspect.

Finally, "EXPERT POWER BI: ADVANCED ANALYTICS AND CUSTOM VISUALIZATIONS MASTERY," the fourth book in the bundle, has explored the realm of advanced analytics and custom visualizations. Readers have discovered how to integrate R and Python for advanced analytics, implement machine learning models, and create custom visuals using D3.js and the Custom Visual SDK. This book has showcased the limitless possibilities of Power BI, allowing users to push the boundaries of data analysis and visualization.

As we conclude this Power BI bundle, we want to emphasize the transformative power of data mastery. In an era where data is ubiquitous and essential for decision-making, the skills and knowledge acquired through these four books are invaluable. Whether you are just beginning your journey into the world of data analytics or are already an experienced analyst, this bundle provides a comprehensive guide to harnessing the full potential of Power BI.

We hope that the insights, techniques, and best practices shared in these books empower you to unlock new opportunities, make data-driven decisions, and drive positive changes in your organization. The journey to data mastery may be challenging, but it is also immensely rewarding. With the right tools and knowledge, you can turn data into a powerful asset, gaining a competitive edge and contributing to the success of your business. Thank you for embarking on this journey with us, and we wish you continued success in your endeavors with Power BI and data analytics. Remember, data mastery is not an endpoint but a continuous pursuit, and these books are your trusted companions on that journey.